Philosophical Profiles

Philosophical Profiles

Essays in a Pragmatic Mode

RICHARD J. BERNSTEIN

upp

University of Pennsylvania Press
Philadelphia

First published in the United States 1986 by the
University of Pennsylvania Press, Philadelphia

First published in Great Britain 1986 by Polity Press,
Cambridge

Library of Congress Cataloging-in-Publication Data
Bernstein, Richard J.
   Philosophical profiles.

   Includes index.
   1. Philosophy, Modern—19th century—Addresses,
essays, lectures.   2. Philosophy, Modern—20th century—
Addresses, essays, lectures.   I. Title.
B803.B43   1986   190   85-16431
ISBN 0-8122-7955-6
ISBN 0-8122-1216-9 (pbk.)

Typeset by DMB (Typesetting), Oxford
Printed in Great Britain by Billing & Sons, Ltd., Worcester

To the Memory of my Mother and Father
for their Loving Encouragement

Contents

Preface		ix
Introduction		1
1	Philosophy in the Conversation of Mankind	21
2	What is the Difference that Makes a Difference? Gadamer, Habermas, and Rorty	58
3	From Hermeneutics to *Praxis*	94
4	Nietzsche or Aristotle?: Reflections on Alasdair MacIntyre's *After Virtue*	115
5	Why Hegel Now?	141
6	Negativity: Theme and Variations	176
7	Heidegger on Humanism	197
8	Judging – the Actor and the Spectator	221
9	Rethinking the Social and the Political	238
10	John Dewey on Democracy: The Task Before Us	260
	Notes	273
	Index	305

Preface

I have entitled this collection of essays – all of which have been written during the past decade – *Philosophical Profiles: Essays in a Pragmatic Mode*. A profile is a partial view that highlights the features of a figure, typically a face. We know from the history of art that there are not only many different styles of drawing a profile, but that a profile can draw out what is visible and invisible, what is revealed and concealed. More recently, "profile" has taken on the meaning of an essay, which although presenting a selective view of its subject, nevertheless focuses on essential characteristics. A profile is always drawn or written from a particular perspective. In studying profiles we frequently learn as much about what is being portrayed as we do about the perspective from which it is seen. This point is closely related to a theme that has been central for the pragmatic tradition and which is prominent in recent hermeneutics. Peirce tells us, "We cannot begin with complete doubt. We must begin with all the prejudices which we actually have when we enter upon the study of philosophy. These prejudices are not to be dispelled by a maxim, for they are things which it does not occur to us *can* be questioned." And Gadamer claims that all understanding involves prejudgments and prejudices. They are indeed what enable us to understand anything. But for both Peirce and Gadamer, it is precisely by encountering what is other than us that we risk, test, modify, and refine our prejudgments. The essays in this volume begin with sympathetic portrayals of challenging thinkers. Each of these thinkers – in very different ways – has attempted to come to grips with some of the most troubling and perplexing issues in modern life. I have sought to present a fair and judicious account of what they are saying in order to risk and test my own prejudgments. These essays can be considered critical conversations in a sense so aptly described by Gadamer when he tells us that "it is characteristic of every true conversation that each opens himself to the other person, truly accepts his point of view as worthy of consideration and gets inside the other to the extent that he understands not a particular individual, but what he says." The expression "critical" and its cognates "critic" and "critique" have been sadly abused in recent times. There is a vulgar sense of "critical" where it means little more than "scoring negative points." But this abuse of the term should not blind us to the tradition of critique which was initiated by Kant and has undergone subtle transformations throughout the nineteenth and twentieth centuries. There is always a moment of negativity or distancing in critique, but a critique demands that one seeks to understand what is being criticized. Hegel was the most brilliant practitioner of what has come to be called "immanent critique" – the type of critique that seeks to identify the inner movement and dynamics of a "shape of consciousness" in order to bring out the "truth" implicit in it, to reject what is limited, and to pass beyond what is being criticized. Although my aims are far more modest than Hegel's, it is this practice of immanent critique that I have attempted to emulate. In the Introduction, I explain my subtitle, "Essays in a Pragmatic Mode." Pragmatism, until recently, has been thought of by many as passé – a movement in American philosophy that flourished at the turn of the century but has now been surpassed. My own view, which I attempt to support in these essays, is that the pragmatic tradition is neither passé nor dead – that the pragmatic thinkers were indeed ahead of their time, and that there are now signs of a "return" to this tradition, especially if we think of a tradition in the manner of Alasdair MacIntyre when he declares that "a living tradition is an historically extended, socially embodied argument, and an argument precisely in part about the goods which constitute that tradition."

In preparing these essays for publication, my thoughts frequently returned to my graduate student days at Yale during the 1950s, and especially to the influence of four teachers: Carl G. Hempel, Charles W. Hendel, John E. Smith, Paul Weiss, as well as to the remarkable group of graduate students who attended Yale. At a time when analytic philosophy was sweeping American graduate departments, Yale steadfastly maintained a tradition of pluralism. No school or orientation dominated our philosophic discussions, and we daily experienced how one can respect and learn from diverse philosophic points of view. Although I have explored a variety of thinkers and movements in my philosophic journey since then, I have never forgotten the lessons of intellectual civility that I learned at Yale.

Each of the essays included in this volume was written for a special occasion, and I have added a note explaining their context when this is not evident. At first I thought I would modify some of the essays, especially when there is some repetition. But I have decided to leave the essays as they originally appeared because even the repetitions may help the reader to discern more clearly the threads that run through these essays and the ways in which they are intertwined. Some of the material from these essays has been modified and incorporated into my book, *Beyond Objectivism and Relativism: Science, Hermeneutics, and Praxis*, but each was written as an independent essay.

"Philosophy in the Conversation of Mankind" is a critical study of Richard Rorty, *Philosophy and the Mirror of Nature* which appeared in *The Review of Metaphysics*, 33 (June, 1980). "What Is the Difference That Makes a Difference? Gadamer, Habermas, and Rorty" was published in *PSA 1982*, vol. 2, edited by P. D. Asquith and T. Nickles (East Lansing, Michigan, 1983). "From Hermeneutics to Praxis" was published in *The Review of Metaphysics*, 35 (June, 1982), "Nietzsche or Aristotle?: Reflections on Alasdair MacIntrye's *After Virtue*" appeared in *Soundings*, 67 (Spring, 1984). "Why Hegel Now?" is a critical study of Charles Taylor, *Hegel* which appeared in *The Review of Metaphysics*, 31 (September, 1977). "Negativity: Theme and

Variations" was published in *Praxis International*, 1 (April, 1981). "Heidegger on Humanism" was published in *Praxis International*, 5 (July, 1985). It will also appear in the proceedings of the Conference on American Pragmatism and Phenomenology sponsored by Pennsylvania State University. "Judging – the Actor and the Spectator" was published in *Proceedings of History, Ethics, Politics: A Conference Based on the Work of Hannah Arendt*. Robert Boyers edited the *Proceedings*. "Rethinking the Social and the Political" will appear in the *Graduate Faculty Philosophy Journal* of the New School for Social Research. "John Dewey on Democracy: The Task Before Us" appeared in *Post-Analytic Philosophy*, edited by John Rajchman and Cornel West (New York: Columbia University Press, 1985).

I am grateful to the editors and publishers concerned for permission to reprint this material.

Introduction

I

It is difficult not to notice a curious unrest in the philosophic atmosphere of the time, a loosening of old landmarks, a softening of oppositions, a mutual borrowing from one another on the part of systems anciently closed, and an interest in new suggestions, however vague, as if the one thing sure was the inadequacy of the extant school-solutions. The dissatisfaction with these seems due for the most part to a feeling that they are too abstract and academic. Life is confused and superabundant, and what the younger generation appears to crave is more of the temperament of life in its philosophy, even though it were at some cost of logical rigor and formal purity.[1]

William James wrote this in 1904 in an article that appeared in the first volume of the new professional journal, *The Journal of Philosophy, Psychology, and Scientific Methods* (the title was later changed to the *Journal of Philosophy*). Except for the grace of James's style, this passage has a contemporary ring, for it might have been written to describe the present philosophic situation. James, and later John Dewey, warned us about what might happen to philosophy in America with the growth of academic professionalism. In "The Need for a Recovery of Philosophy" (1917), Dewey declared "I believe that philosophy in America will be lost between chewing a historic cud long since reduced to woody fiber, or an apologetics for lost causes (lost to natural science) or a scholastic formalism, unless it can

somehow bring to consciousness America's own needs. . . ."[2]
Dewey continued to emphasize this theme. When he wrote a
new introduction for the republication of *Reconstruction in Philosophy* in 1948 (twenty-five years after its original publication), he
said:[3]

> Today Reconstruction *of* Philosophy is a more suitable title than
> Reconstruction *in* Philosophy. For the intervening events have
> sharply defined, have brought to a head the basic postulate of
> the text: namely, that the distinctive office, problems and subject matter of philosophy grow out of the stresses and strains in
> the community life in which a given form of philosophy arises,
> and that, accordingly, its specific problems vary with the
> changes in human life that are always going on and that at times
> constitute a crisis and a turning point in human history.

But by 1948, Dewey's voice was barely heard by professional
philosophers in America; the brutal truth is that despite
Dewey's enormous influence in the first quarter of the twentieth century, he was no longer taken seriously as a philosopher. He was viewed as a fuzzy-minded thinker who might
have had his heart in the right place, but not his head. Academic professionalism in philosophy had triumphed, and with
this triumph not only Dewey but the philosophers associated
with the "golden age" of philosophy in America including
Peirce, James, Mead, Santayana, Royce, and Whitehead were
marginalized.[4]

Philosophy in America was already in the process of being
transformed during the late 1930s, due to the growing influence
of the emigré philosophers forced to leave Europe. Reichenbach,
Carnap, Tarski, Feigl, Hempel (and many others associated
with logical positivism and the "new" logic) were setting the
agenda for philosophy. Logical positivism in the militant form
of the Vienna Circle or in the more polemical form advocated
by A. J. Ayer did not take deep root in America. But a positivistic temper, and the legacy of logical empiricism in the disciplines of the philosophy of the natural sciences and logic, did
flourish. In the period following the Second World War, when
there was an enormous growth of academic institutions, there

was almost a scurrying to refashion graduate schools in America so that they would become respectable analytic departments. This was a time of great confidence among professional philosophers. It was felt that philosophy had to give up its pretensions to grand systems and syntheses; it must be much more modest in its scope and claims. But there was a collective sense among the analytic community that philosophers had "finally" discovered the techniques and conceptual tools to achieve high standards of clarity and logical rigor – and consequently were able to make genuine progress in solving and dissolving problems. This was also a time when the Anglo–American/Continental split in philosophy became an almost unbridgeable chasm. What was going on in European "philosophy" was taken to be pretentious, obscure, and muddled. By the new standards of what constituted "doing philosophy," Continental "philosophy" no longer counted as *serious* philosophy. Of course, there were pockets of resistance to the new analytic style of doing philosophy. There were those who still defended and practiced speculative philosophy in the style of Whitehead; there were those who saw greater promise in phenomenology and existentialism; there were those who sought to carry on philosophy in the pragmatic tradition. But philosophers who had not taken "the linguistic turn" were clearly on the defensive. Richard Rorty captures the mood of this time when he writes:[5]

In 1951, a graduate student who (like myself) was in the process of learning about, or being converted to, analytic philosophy, could still believe that there were a finite number of distinct specifiable problems to be resolved – problems which any serious analytic philosopher would agree to be *the* outstanding problems. For example, there was the problem of the counterfactual conditional, the problem of whether an "emotive" analysis of ethical terms was satisfactory, Quine's problem about the nature of analyticity, and a few more. These were problems which fitted nicely into the vocabularly of the positivists. They could easily be seen as the final, proper formulation of problems which had been seen, as in a glass darkly, by Leibniz, Hume and Kant. Further there was agreement on what a

solution to a philosophical problem looked like, – e.g., Russell on
definite descriptions, Frege on meaning and reference, Tarski
on truth. In those days, when my generation was young, all of
the conditions for a Kuhnian "normal," problem-solving discipline were fulfilled.

There were other influences shaping the character of analytic
philosophy at the time. In the post-war period, there was also a
receptivity to the type of "ordinary language philosophy" or
"conceptual analysis" that was so fashionable at Oxford. Ryle,
Austin, and the later Wittgenstein (as filtered and domesticated
through Anglo-American spectacles) rivaled the more formal-
istic methods favored by logical empiricists. But whether one's
allegiances were to the more formal or informal methods of
analysis, there was a shared conviction that philosophers could
now make genuine progress in solving and dissolving well-
formulated problems. Soon, a new generation of philosophers
was trained in America who not only mastered analytic techniques, but whose contributions surpassed the work of their
teachers. Quine was a new hero, for he represented a transi-
tional figure who had assimilated what was taken to be most
enduring in the pragmatic tradition but whose style of argumentation and logical finesse owed more to Carnap and Tarski
than to Peirce, James, or Dewey. Davidson, Kripke, and Putnam soon became the philosophers to be taken seriously. With
the increased sophistication of analytic philosophy, there was
also a growing complexity. Whereas, with an earlier generation
of logical positivists and empiricists, the ramifications of their
claims for other fields of inquiry could be clearly discerned –
even if they were controversial and provocative – it was difficult for many outsiders (or even insiders to philosophy who
were not tuned into the latest controversies in the professional
journals) to figure out the significance of the problems that
analytic philosophers took to be so central. It looked as if philosophers were perfecting a jargon that was barely intelligible to
others. But for insiders this is what was to be properly expected
as philosophy became more sophisticated – just as in any other
specialized discipline. Looking back at the development of

analytic philosophy a generation after its triumph, Rorty continues his sketch by telling us:[6]

> To recite this list of problems and paradigms is to evoke memories of a simple, brighter, vanished world. In the interlocking "central" areas of analytic philosophy – epistemology, philosophy of language, and metaphysics – there are now as many paradigms as there are major philosophy departments. . . . Any problem that enjoys a simultaneous vogue in ten of the hundred or so "analytic" philosophy departments in America is doing exceptionally well. The field these days is a jungle of competing research programs, programs which seem to have a shorter and shorter half-life as the years go by. The fifteen years after Reichenbach wrote witnessed the rise and fall of "Oxford philosophy." In the fifteen years since "West Coast Semantics" swept eastward and effected a *translatio imperii* from Oxford to the UCLA–Princeton–Harvard axis, we have had several brief shining moments in which the future of philosophy, or at least the philosophy of language seemed clearly marked out. But each of these illuminations has suffered eclipse. There is no more consensus about the problems and methods of philosophy in America today than there was in Germany in 1920. . . . Most philosophers are more or less "analytic" but there is no agreed-upon inter-university paradigm of philosophical work, nor any agreed-upon list of "central problems." The best hope for an American philosopher is Andy Warhol's promise that we shall *all* be superstars, for approximately fifteen minutes apiece.

Rorty's portrait may seem to be a caricature of what has happened in analytic philosophy, but it is nevertheless a revealing one. It does not do justice to what has been achieved by the analytic style of philosophizing, nor does it mention what has always been characteristic of philosophy in America – its sheer variety and plurality. For despite the hegemony of analytic philosophy, no school, orientation, or paradigm – for all its prestige – has ever completely dominated the American scene. What now does seem to be passing however, is the arrogant ideology that was characteristic of the first wave of analytic philosophy. There are advocates who still claim that the "scandal" of philosophy has finally been resolved, that we now know what are *the* genuine problems of philosophy and how to tackle them, but their voices are becoming shriller and less persuasive. Even a claim made by Michael Dummett a few years ago now seems to have an archaic quaintness:[7]

> Only with Frege was the proper object of philosophy finally established: namely first, that the goal of philosophy is the analysis of *thought*; secondly, that the study of thought is to be sharply distinguished from the study of the psychological process of *thinking*; and finally, that the only proper method of analysing thought consists in the analysis of *language*. . . . the acceptance of these three tenets is common to the entire analytical school . . . [but] it has taken nearly a half-century since his death for us to apprehend clearly what the real task of philosophy, as conceived by him, involves.

For what is now being called into question – even among analytic philosophers – is the very idea of achieving any rational consensus about "the real task of philosophy." And most recently there has been a skeptical questioning of the foundations, presuppositions, and metaphors that have tied together the analytic style of philosophizing. We can see the evidence of this discontent in the stir caused by two recent controversial books: Richard Rorty, *Philosophy and the Mirror of Nature* and Alasdair MacIntyre, *After Virtue*. (Each of these works is critically examined in subsequent essays in this volume.) Both Rorty and MacIntyre are philosophers who exemplify the skills and techniques of argumentation that have been cultivated and prized by Anglo–American analytic philosophers. Prior to the publication of their provocative books, each had established his professional credentials by contributing to the discussion of problems that have been in the foreground of contemporary analytic controversies. Rorty, for example, wrote a number of important papers on such topics as the mind-body problem, incorrigibility, and transcendental arguments. He also wrote a classic introduction to a collection of readings on "the linguistic turn" in which he sorted out the various tendencies and tensions in this turn.[8] MacIntyre has been a leading contributor to analyses of the nature of rationality, the character of the social disciplines, and moral philosophy. A close reading of their earlier works does reveal – even when they seemed to be at the center of analytic debates – a certain marginality. For neither ever completely accepted prevailing orthodoxies. But the rhetoric, scope, and substantive claims of their recent books take a very different turn. Each begins by discussing problems familiar to analytic philosophers, but the subversive character of their projects soon becomes evident. MacIntyre claims that in the modern age nothing less than a "catastrophe" has occurred, that the Enlightenment project of seeking to justify moral claims (which still shapes analytic discussions of moral philosophy) is a failure. He boldly defends an understanding of moral philosophy that is grounded in "the tradition of the virtues" – the tradition of practical philosophy whose canonical texts are the ethical and political writings of Aristotle. As his dramatic narrative unfolds, it becomes clear that MacIntyre is questioning the ahistorical character of so much of modern and analytic philosophy, and even the notions of rationality that have been prominent in philosophy since Descartes. Rorty seeks to undermine what he calls the "Cartesian–Lockean–Kantian tradition" which he takes to be the dominant tradition of modern philosophy, and whose legacy is contemporary analytic philosophy. He wants to expose the self-deceptive illusions of foundationalism, epistemology, and such successor disciplines as the philosophy of language and the philosophy of mind. He views his endeavor as a therapeutic one in the spirit of Wittgenstein – one which may cure philosophers of the misguided belief that philosophy is or can be a *Fach*, a well-defined discipline with a set of problems to be solved. Both Rorty and MacIntyre – who sharply disagree with each other on many issues – deliberately transgress the boundaries of the discourse of contemporary analytic philosophy. Each tries to show how contemporary analytic philosophy which has sought to marginalize so much of philosophy by its exclusionary tactics, has itself become marginal to what Rorty calls – appropriating the phrase from Michael Oakeshott – "the conversation of mankind." Each in different ways is telling a story of the rise and decline of modern philosophy. Each seeks to bring a critical historical perspective to what is now going on in philosophy, a historical perspective that shares in the spirit of Nietzsche's genealogical unmasking.

In this context, I want to focus on the reaction to their books, for it is symptomatic of the current state of philosophizing. Among many hard-core professional philosophers there has been a sense of scandal and even moral outrage. Rorty and MacIntyre have been accused of being intellectually irresponsible. They misrepresent what they are presumably criticizing; they are cavalier in their dismissals and careless in their argumentation. They try to gain their points with rhetorical flourishes rather than by careful analysis. Professional philosophers are frequently impervious to the criticism of outsiders. But the depth of feeling against Rorty and MacIntyre indicates a sense that they ought to know better because they both have been "insiders."

A second typical reaction comes from younger philosophers who have not yet been socialized into accepted styles of philosophizing, and those who have felt that they have been excluded by the "analytic establishment." They welcome what Rorty and MacIntyre are doing as a breath of fresh air. Even if one disagrees with their substantive claims, their books have been enthusiastically welcomed for exposing and indeed mocking the unquestioned presuppositions, "rules of the game," and smug self-understanding of many analytic philosophers about what is the legitimate way of "doing philosophy." Their portraits of modernity and its discontents, their daring in taking up many themes and thinkers who are normally not treated seriously by analytic philosophers, their ironic skepticism and playful debunking, have touched a sensitive intellectual nerve.

Perhaps the most interesting reaction to Rorty and MacIntyre has come from those outside the discipline of professional philosophy. Their works have been widely discussed by scholars in the range of the humanistic and social disciplines. To many outsiders it now appears as if philosophers, who have perfected the art of talking only among themselves are rejoining a larger community of letters. At the very least their books have been taken as evidence that we are witnessing the breakup of the hegemony of analytic philosophy – a breakup that allows for other voices to be heard.

II

When Kuhn in *The Structure of Scientific Revolutions* describes the response to crisis which precedes a revolution in the pattern of scientific development, he tells us: "The proliferation of competing articulations, the willingness to try anything, the expression of explicit discontent, the . . . debate over fundamentals, all of these are symptoms of a transition from normal to extraordinary research. It is upon their existence more than upon revolutions that the notion of normal science depends."[9] There have been those who have questioned the applicability of this description to scientific activity, but it does have relevance for the current state of philosophy. This is a time of turmoil – some might say, chaos – in philosophy where almost "anything goes." Of course, this is not the first time that philosophers have experienced a growing sense of "crisis" (a term that has become a cliché) but there appear to be striking differences between what we are now experiencing and what has happened in the past. Typically when philosophers have perceived a crisis in the foundations of philosophy, they have called for a new paradigm, a new way in which philosophy might become a normal problem-solving discipline. This stance was typical of Descartes, Hume, Kant, Husserl – indeed it has been the typical stance of most modern philosophers. It was once again reiterated when analytic philosophers sought to transform the discipline of philosophy.

But now there is even a questioning of whether it makes sense to speak in this manner. We seem to be living in the era of "posts" – "post-empiricist," "post-analytic," "post-structuralist," "post-modern," and even "post-philosophic." There is enormous confusion about what characterizes this "post-era," an inability and anxiety about even naming it. There is an uneasy sense of fragmentation, jaggedness, a deep suspicion about all fixed distinctions, dichotomies, and hierarchies, a

skepticism about totalizing schemes and "metanarratives." In
some ways the present mood resembles what Hegel called
"skeptical consciousness," where there is a giddy whirl of endless overturning and deconstruction. But whereas Hegel took
this to be only a passing stage in the progressive development
of a restless *Spirit*, we are now being told that this is our permanent condition with no possibility of overcoming it. There
is an endless play of differences with no promise of synthesis; the very idea of synthesis or *Aufhebung* is a self-deceptive
illusion.

Responses to the current mood have also been diverse.
There are those who see it as a symptom of a dangerous rising
wave of irrationalism and nihilism, and who think that now
more than ever philosophers need to articulate and defend
standards of rationality, argumentation, clarity, and rigor.
There are those who delight in the present disorder, who see it
as liberating us from oppressive constraints, exclusionary
power tactics and those unquestioned hierarchies that deeply
mark inherited patterns of thought and language. And there
are those (I include myself in this group) who perceive the present condition as a challenge and opportunity for discriminating between rhetorical excesses and penetrating critiques, for
seeking new ways to make sense of, and gain an overview of,
what appears to be so chaotic. For the arrogance that typified
the positivistic temper and the post-Second World War generation of analytic philosophers is matched by a new sort of arrogance (and there are curious parallels). A generation ago, we
were being told that most of what had been called philosophy
could be relegated to the dustbin of history because philosophers had lacked the conceptual and logical tools to make
serious headway in solving philosophic problems. Now we are
being told that the whole enterprise of philosophic reflection is
based upon unstable and unwarranted foundations, that the
whole history of philosophy has been entrapped in the "metaphysics of presence" and "logocentrism," that philosophy itself
is over. We still seem to be haunted with what I have called the
Cartesian Anxiety. "*Either* there is some support for our being,
a fixed foundation for our knowledge, *or* we cannot escape the

forces of darkness that envelop us with madness, with intellectual and moral chaos."[10]

During the past fifteen years, I have been arguing that one can read our contemporary situation in a very different way, that despite apparent wild fluctuations there are many signs that we are in the process of exorcizing the Cartesian Anxiety. When we penetrate the different philosophic vocabularies which seem to be "incommensurable," we can detect more coherence and commonness than initially seems apparent. It is not that I believe that any grand synthesis is about to appear on the horizon, but that there are subtle criss-crossings and interweavings.[11]

There is "a loosening of old landmarks, a softening of oppositions, a mutual borrowing from one another on the part of systems anciently closed."[12] We can even see this in the cracks and crevices that are beginning to appear in the solid walls that have divided Anglo–American and Continental philosophy. I do not think that this has come about primarily because philosophers working in different traditions are finally learning how to talk with and to listen to each other, but rather because the internal dialectic of the problems that concern them has led to a recognition of affinities and family resemblances. Let me give a few illustrations of the type of interweaving and criss-crossing that has taken place.

The philosophy of the natural sciences has been a central subdiscipline in analytic philosophy. If we look at its development from the early days of the Vienna circle to its flourishing in the 1950s, one can read this development in the light of Kuhn's model of a normal problem-solving discipline. One can follow the successive attempts to state logically rigorous criteria of verifiability or falsifiability, to give a precise characterization of the differences and relations between observational and theoretical languages, to state the requirements for hypothetical-deductive explanation, and to specify the role of correspondence rules. These not only seemed to be well-defined problems; one could also mark the stages in the "solving" of these problems. But by the 1950s, there were not only internal criticisms of what has been called the "Received View" of scientific theory and explanation, but the beginnings of a more radical critique of the basic framework in which logical positivists and empiricists conceived of the nature of science. Hanson, Kuhn, Feyerabend, Toulmin, and Quine – with different emphases – questioned the "image of science" that had been taken for granted by logical empiricists. Familiar distinctions such as the distinction between analytic and synthetic sentences, the distinction between observation and theory, the context of discovery and the context of justification, were subjected to sustained critique.[13] New themes emerged as central, such as the importance of conflicting research programs and traditions, the character of scientific communities, the role of non-algorithmic reasoning in theory choice. The program to demarcate sharply natural science from other forms of inquiry gave way to a much more pluralistic attempt to specify differences and similarities. Logical empiricists had been motivated by a search for *the* criteria by which one could distinguish science from non-science and pseudo-science. They rejected interpretive and hermeneutical accounts of the *Geisteswissenschaften*. But as Mary Hesse has shown, in the development of a postempiricist philosophy and history of science, many of the points that were being made about the character of the natural sciences parallel the points that Continental philosophers were making about the hermeneutical disciplines.[14] The "loosening of old landmarks" has even led some practitioners of the postempiricist philosophy and history of science to recognize the relevance and affinities of what had been taken as alien. Thus, in *The Essential Tension* Thomas Kuhn tells us:[15]

> What I as a physicist had to discover for myself, most historians learn by example in the course of professional training. Consciously or not, they are all practitioners of the hermeneutic method. In my case, however, the discovery of hermeneutics did more than make history seem consequential. Its most immediate and decisive effect was instead on my view of science.

And Kuhn adds:

> The early models of the sort of history that has so influenced me and my *historical* colleagues is the product of a post-Kantian

European tradition which I and my philosophical colleagues continue to find opaque. In my own case, for example, even the term "hermeneutic" . . . was no part of my vocabulary as recently as five years ago; increasingly, I suspect that anyone who believes that history may have deep philosophical import will have to learn to bridge the longstanding divide between Continental and English-language philosophical traditions.

The mention of "hermeneutics" suggests another theme which reveals a thread of elaborate interweaving as we begin to pursue it. Traditionally, "hermeneutics" has been the name of a discipline concerned with the interpretation of sacred and literary texts – certainly a field quite remote from the main interests of analytic philosophy. In the nineteenth century, due primarily to the work of Schleiermacher and Dilthey, the scope of hermeneutics was broadened to encompass humanistic and historical inquiry. In the twentieth century hermeneutics has taken an ontological turn. Both Heidegger and Gadamer have claimed that we are "thrown" into the world as beings who are always engaged in the happening of understanding. So, if we are to understand our being-in-the-world, then we need to understand understanding itself. Hermeneutics has been taken by many analytic philosophers to represent just the sort of wooly thinking that should be rejected and eliminated. Logical positivists delighted in citing sentences from Heidegger to illustrate what they meant by metaphysical nonsense. But during the 1960s, the relevance of hermeneutics was seen in a new context. Most positivistically minded philosophers and social scientists viewed the social sciences as underdeveloped natural sciences of human beings. To the extent that they were *sciences*, they shared the same conceptual features that logical empiricists took to be the distinctive features of the hard (i.e., the physical) sciences. Ironically, while most natural scientists ignored what logical empiricists declared to be the conceptual structure of scientific theory and explanation, many social scientists enthusiastically embraced variations of the "Received View." But the more they insisted on methodological purity, the more evident it became that there was a gross disparity between their self-understanding of their discipline and their actual practice. The heart of the logical empiricist conception of scientific explanation is the hypothetical-deductive model of explanation based upon the appeal to scientific laws. It became something of an intellectual embarrassment among social scientists that there was no rational consensus about what, if anything, could serve in the social disciplines as nomological sentences or scientific laws which would be comparable to laws in the natural sciences.

Increasingly, the very idea of the social disciplines as immature natural sciences was criticized. Here we find a convergence between Anglo–American and Continental critiques. Peter Winch in the *Idea of a Social Science*, drawing upon his interpretation of the later Wittgenstein, argued that it was a conceptual confusion to think that an understanding of social life could be modeled on the logical empiricist understanding of natural science. And such thinkers as Jürgen Habermas were developing an analogous critique of an "objectivist" understanding of the social disciplines. What was becoming evident is that social explanation involves an interpretative or hermeneutical component – a thesis which was forcefully argued by Charles Taylor.[16] There was the question of whether and how one might demarcate the natural and social disciplines – an issue which is still being debated – but it became clear that the old positivist attempt to reduce all legitimate scientific explanation to a single conceptual model of explanation was no longer satisfactory. The shift in the understanding of the character and relation of the natural and social disciplines is indicated by the following passage from Anthony Giddens:[17]

> The theory-laden character of observation-statements in natural sciences entails that the meaning of scientific concepts is tied-in to the meaning of other terms in a theoretical network; moving between theories or paradigms involves hermeneutic tasks. The social sciences, however, imply not only this single level of hermeneutic problems, involved in the theoretical metalanguage, but a "double hermeneutic," because social-scientific theories concern a "preinterpreted" world of lay meanings. There is a two-way connection between the language of social science and ordinary language. The former cannot ignore the categories

used by laymen in the practical organization of social life; but on the other hand, the concepts of social science may also be taken over and applied by laymen as elements of their conduct. Rather than treating the latter as something to be avoided or minimized as far as possible, as inimical to the interests of "prediction," we should understand it as integral to the subject-subject relation involved in the social sciences.

The debate about the status of the social disciplines, their relation to the natural sciences, and the growing dissatisfaction with the logical empiricist understanding of both natural and social science was not a purely methodological question. There was also a hidden practical agenda. We can see here evidence of another theme of interweaving. Part of the legacy of logical empiricism was a dismissal of any serious philosophic concern with substantive questions of moral or political philosophy. Once the noncognitive character of all value claims had been "exposed," there was little more to be said about "value judgments." While many analytic philosophers rejected a stark emotivist theory of value judgments, they shared the non-cognitive bias of the positivists. At best, ethics (as a "legitimate" branch of philosophy) was to be thought of as "metaethics" – the conceptual analysis of ethical terms and sentences. There was nothing that philosophers *qua* philosophers could contribute to the substantive discussion of normative ethical and political issues. But during the 1960s when there was so much international unrest, protest, and student radical activity, there was a growing dissatisfaction with the thinness of "metaethics" and the ideology of value-neutrality. This was a time when such figures as Herbert Marcuse, Hannah Arendt, and Jürgen Habermas – all of whom were schooled in Continental traditions of philosophy – appeared to have much greater relevance for understanding the practical issues of everyday life than those who were engaged in rarefied metaethical disputes. They all shared the conviction of John Dewey that "philosophy recovers itself when it ceases to be a device for dealing with the problems of philosophers and becomes a method, cultivated by philosophers, for dealing with the problems of men"[18]– the problems of human beings in their everyday lives. While

Arendt and Marcuse had little sympathy (or knowledge) of the pragmatic thinkers, Habermas himself has drawn heavily upon Peirce, Dewey, and Mead in his own elaboration of a critical theory of society and a theory of communicative action. He has also appropriated and developed in a novel fashion many of the insights of "Anglo–American" speech act theory into his own theory of communicative action.

In citing examples of the ways in which the philosophy of the natural sciences under the pressures of its own internal development has shifted so that we can now see its affinities with the Continental tradition of hermeneutics, in showing how the entire discussion of the status of the social and human disciplines has been transformed, and in noting some of the affinities between Habermas's project and American pragmatism as well as his own distinctive appropriation of speech act theory in his theory of communicative action, my intention has been to illustrate the criss-crossing and interweaving that are now taking place in philosophic discussions. One can also mention the more recent interest in poststructuralist and deconstructionist currents by Anglo–American intellectuals. Foucault and Derrida are now more widely read and discussed by Anglo–American intellectuals in a great variety of fields than is any professional Anglo–American analytic philosopher. There are many analytic philosophers who are scandalized by the popularity of such thinkers as Nietzsche and Heidegger in the fields of comparative literature and literary theory, and who see this as little more than an ephemeral cult of popularity which has nothing to do with "serious" philosophy. But it is hard to resist the conclusion that the tangled field of philosophy (and even the limits and boundaries of what constitutes philosophy) is now in a state of ferment.

But one can also detect common concerns (if not common problems) in the diverse philosophic currents – concerns which are shared and are at the center of the thinkers discussed in this volume. Each in his or her own way has been seeking to come to a deeper understanding of modernity, its discontents, pathologies, and prospects. Each is concerned to gain a critical perspective on what is even meant by "modernity." MacIntrye tells us that a catastrophe has occurred in our moral lives and moral philosophy, and claims that "a new dark age" is already upon us. Rorty thinks that we are coming to the end of the "Cartesian–Lockean–Kantian tradition," and speaks oxomoronically of a "postphilosophical philosophy" which is no longer based on seeking for "metaphysical comfort." Marcuse and Habermas, while exposing what they take to be the dark side of the Enlightenment legacy, nevertheless seek to redeem the human aspiration for freedom, autonomy, and happiness. Arendt interprets modernity as a triumph of *animal laborans* and the triumph of the social over the political. Heidegger locates our ills in the rise of modern subjectivism and humanism – a humanism that is rooted in the metaphysical tradition and whose essence is revealed in the threat of calculative thinking and what he calls "*Gestell.*" Gadamer speaks of the deformation of *praxis* that has taken place in the modern age and tells us that the point of philosophical hermeneutics is to correct the peculiar falsehood of modern consciousness, the idolatry of scientific method and the anonymous authority of science. He argues that hermeneutic philosophy, which is the heir to the tradition of practical philosophy, vindicates "the noblest task of the citizen – decision-making according to one's own responsibility." And although Dewey would sharply disagree with Gadamer about the character and role of "scientific method" in our practical lives, he shares a great deal in common concerning the contemporary threats to community life. In the following essays, I have sought to enter into conversation with each of the thinkers discussed, to penetrate to the heart of their projects, and to criticize their differing understandings of modernity. I have called these essays "essays in a pragmatic mode" because my own thinking has been informed and shaped by what I take to be most enduring in the pragmatic tradition. As I interpret the current philosophic scene there is a "return" to what was a point of departure for the pragmatic thinkers. There is now a prospect that the type of reconstruction of philosophy that Dewey advocated is beginning to take place. I see this in the giving up of the multifarious varieties of foundational projects. The pragmatists did not think that philosophy can or should be some sort of superscience or even a distinctive discipline with its own well-defined set of problems. They were skeptical of the tendency to reify changing fluid distinctions into epistemological and metaphysical dichotomies. They rejected all forms of totalizing schemes or totalizing critiques. They defended a robust pluralism that does justice to the tangled quality of our experience. But they did not think of pluralism as a type of relativism where we are emprisoned in our self-contained paradigms, frameworks, or forms of life. It is the openness of our limited horizons that they defended, not their closure. They were well aware of the danger of a type of fragmentation and hermetic isolation where only brute manipulative power rules. And they highlighted the ways in which all human life is shaped by social practices – practices which always present us with the challenge of practical reconstruction.

A theme that keeps surfacing in many contemporary philosophic discussions stands at the center of the pragmatic vision – the theme of community and communication. We discover variations on this theme in MacIntyre's plea for "the construction of local forms of community within which civility and intellectual and moral life can be sustained"[19] and in Rorty's call for "a renewed sense of community." "Our identification with our community – our society, our political tradition, our intellectual heritage – is heightened when we see this community as *ours* rather than *nature's, shaped* rather than *found*, one among many which men have made. In the end the pragmatists tell us, what matters is our loyalty to other human beings clinging together against the dark, not our hope of getting things right."[20] For Gadamer and Habermas too – for all their differences – the same theme emerges as dominant. It is reflected in Gadamer's scanning the horizon for the vestiges of human solidarity and in his perceptive analyses of the type of dialogue and conversation that constitutes our being-in-the-world. Habermas's elaborate theory of communicative action is intended to show how communicative rationality is itself built into the very structures of human intersubjectivity, and how "communicative reason operates in history as an avenging force."[21] In still a different register we can detect this theme in Arendt's own incisive analysis of those public spaces in which individuals in their plurality can appear to each other as equals, mutually make public freedom into a tangible worldly reality, and rationally seek to persuade each other about their conduct. The differences among these thinkers are as deep and significant as anything that they share in common. It is disingenuous to gloss over the serious conflicts and dissonances that are characteristic of contemporary philosophic, cultural, and everyday life. We *are* threatened today by a grotesque wild pluralism in which we no longer even know how to communicate with each other.

This is not just a theoretical problem limited to intellectuals, but a practical problem experienced in our everyday lives. But I also think that there is evidence that we are overcoming another fluctuation between extremes that has been characteristic of modern life – the fluctuation between apocalyptic hopes with its fantasies of a "total" break with history and the paralyzing despair that results when these hopes are dashed. Dewey and the pragmatists told us that what matters is how we concretely respond and cope with the crises and perplexities that we confront. The confusion and skepticism about the prospects for philosophy is not a new phenomenon. In 1930, in his essay, "What I Believe," Dewey wrote:[22]

> The chief intellectual characteristic of the present age is its despair of any constructive philosophy – not just in its technical meaning, but in the sense of any integrated outlook and attitude. The developments of the last century have gone so far that we are now aware of the shock and overturn in older beliefs. But the formation of a now coherent view of nature and man based upon facts consonant with science and actual social conditions is still to be had. . . . Skepticism becomes the mark and even the pose of the educated mind. It is more influential because it is no longer directed against this and that article of the older creeds but is rather a bias against any kind of far-reaching ideas, and a denial of systematic participation on the part of such ideas in the intelligent direction of affairs.

But skepticism about firm foundations and totalizing schemes is not incompatible with cultivation of "reflective intelligence" and imagination – an intelligence which is not the "faculty of intellect honored in textbooks and neglected elsewhere, but which is the sum-total of impulses, habits, emotions, records, and discoveries which forecast what is desirable and undesirable in future possibilities, and which contrive ingeniously on behalf of imagined good." [23]

Dewey was well aware that he was advocating a faith in intelligence – a faith that is at once precarious and requires passionate commitment. It is this practical commitment that I take to be the primary legacy of the pragmatic tradition – one which can still serve to orient our lives.

1

Philosophy in the Conversation of Mankind

I

Richard Rorty has written one of the most important and challenging books to be published by an American philosopher in the past few decades.[1] Some will find it a deeply disturbing book while others will find it liberating and exhilirating – both, as we shall see, may be right and wrong. Not since James and Dewey have we had such a devastating critique of professional philosophy. But unlike James and Dewey (two of Rorty's heroes), who thought that once the sterility and artificiality of professional – and indeed much of modern philosophy since Descartes – had been exposed, there was an important job for philosophers to do; Rorty leaves us in a much more ambiguous and unsettled state. I will examine Rorty's book from a variety of perspectives, beginning with a general overview and then moving to more finely meshed descriptions. My aim is not only to illuminate the power and subtlety of Rorty's analysis and to show its inner unity, but to locate basic issues that are left unresolved.

In a book that is filled with all sorts of "jolts" and apparently outrageous claims, one of the first is Rorty's declaration that the three most important philosophers of the twentieth century are Wittgenstein, Heidegger, and Dewey. Grouping these three together may appear to be something of a "category mistake" because according to the common wisdom, it would be hard to imagine three thinkers who are as far apart in philosophical temperament, style, and concern. What they share in common, according to Rorty, is that "each tried, in his early years, to find a new way of making philosophy 'foundational' – a new way of formulating an ultimate context for thought." But eventually,

> Each of the three came to see his earlier effort as self-deceptive, as an attempt to retain a certain conception of philosophy after the notions needed to flesh out that conception (the seventeenth-century notions of knowledge and mind) had been discarded. Each of the three, in his later work, broke free of the Kantian conception of philosophy as foundational, and spent his time warning us against those very temptations to which he himself had once succumbed. Thus their later work is therapeutic rather than constructive, edifying rather than systematic, designed to make the reader question his own motives for philosophizing rather than to supply him with a new philosophical program. (p. 5)

This passage indicates Rorty's intellectual affinities and what he wants to stress in these "three most important philosophers of our century." But he is not primarily concerned with the thought of Wittgenstein, Heidegger, and Dewey, except in the sense that he sees himself as doing, in a far more modest and concentrated way, the type of "philosophical therapy," "deconstruction," and "overcoming of tradition" that typifies the essential thrust of their later work. Rorty's primary focus is contemporary analytic philosophy – especially the philosophy of mind and epistemology – its historical origins, the ways in which it emerged out of the womb of seventeenth-century notions of mind and knowledge, the ways in which analytic philosophy has become increasingly sterile and remote from the "conversation of mankind," and its (possible) demise. He seeks to show that the self-image or self-conception that many analytic philosophers share – that we have finally discovered the right methods and the correct way of stating philosophical problems so that they can be solved – is a self-deception, a grand illusion. On the contrary, sophisticated analytic philosophers are themselves caught in metaphors such as "our glassy essence" and "mirroring" nature or reality that have gone stale. The very issues that seem so vital in analytic philosophy – problems of mind-body identity, whether knowledge can or cannot be characterized as justified true belief, the theory of reference and meaning – are themselves bound up with historical assumptions that can be exposed and questioned. These are "problems" not to be solved but to be dissolved or deconstructed. The way to perform this type of therapy is to dig deep into the language games in which they are embedded and to see how these language games are themselves the result of a series of historical accidents, options, and confusions. Roughly speaking, Rorty uses a two-stage strategy in carrying out his critique. The first stage is a "softening up" technique where he addresses the problems and positions that are currently being debated and shows that as we sharpen the issues and points of difference, the various controversies fall apart (and do not lead to significant new foundational philosophical truths). These are the sections that will probably capture the imagination of analytic philosophers. They will recognize types of arguments with which they are familiar and will pounce upon – as they rightfully should – what is sound and unsound, convincing and unconvincing in Rorty's arguments. But although the book is filled with arguments, many of which are brilliant and ingenious, Rorty at several points warns against the love of argument that has characterized *one* strand in philosophy ever since Plato. What is unsettling and disturbing about Rorty's argumentative style is that he refuses to play the game that can be recognized as "normal" philosophy, i.e., he doesn't seem to be primarily concerned with carefully stating issues in such a manner so that one can proceed to develop the strongest arguments in support of a correct "position." Rather, he wants to show that there is something wrong with the whole approach to philosophy as a discipline that deals with basic problems and advances by clarifying and solving these problems. As one follows the nuances of his arguments, it begins to dawn on the reader that just when he thinks he is getting down to the hard core of these disputes, he discovers that there is no core.

But assuming for the moment that Rorty is successful in this deconstructive technique, the question naturally arises, how did philosophers ever get themselves into a situation of thinking that something extremely important is at issue in advancing a theory of reference or meaning, or stating the necessary and sufficient conditions for what is to count as knowledge, or solving the mind-body problem. This highlights the second stage or aspect of Rorty's strategy. He exposes the *historical* origins of what we now take to be standard philosophic problems and he searches for the historical roots of those philosophical "intuitions" that play such a primary role in philosophical debate. If Rorty is right, then most analytic philosophers are not only wrong, they are self-deceived about what they are doing – at least insofar as they think of "their discipline as one which discusses perennial, eternal problems – problems which arise as soon as one reflects" (p. 3). Indeed, it should be clear that if Rorty is right, then most systematic philosophers – past and present – have misunderstood what they have been doing. We can already see that although Rorty focuses on recent analytic philosophy, there are much broader ramifications to his critique – a critique that finally turns into a meditation on the philosophical enterprise itself.

In order to carry out this critique, Rorty develops a historical reconstruction of modern philosophy which is the context from which analytic philosophy emerges. Rorty is sufficiently impressed by Heidegger to be aware of how we might trace the source of the trouble back to Plato, but for his purposes he begins his "history" with the founders of modern philosophy, Descartes, Locke, and Kant. The "ideal type" of what philosophy as a discipline is supposed to be that Rorty wants to undermine and debunk may be stated as follows:

> Philosophy can be foundational in respect to the rest of culture because culture is the assemblage of claims to knowledge, and philosophy adjudicates such claims. It can do so because it understands the foundations of knowledge and it finds these foundations in the study of man-as-knower, of the "mental processes" or the "activity of representation" which make knowledge possible. To know is to represent accurately what is outside the mind; so to understand the possibility and nature of knowledge is to understand the way in which the mind is able to construct such

representations. Philosophy's central concern is to be a general
theory of representation, a theory which will divide culture up
into areas which represent reality well, those which represent it
less well, and those which do not represent it at all (despite their
pretense to do so). (p. 3)

This conception of philosophy which may appear to be intuitive
and obvious is one that has a long, complicated, and devious history.

We owe the notion of a "theory of knowledge" based on an
understanding of "mental processes" to the seventeenth century,
and especially to Locke. We owe the notion of "the mind" as a
separate entity in which "processes" occur to the same period,
and especially to Descartes. We owe the notion of philosophy as
the tribunal of pure reason, upholding or denying the claims of
the rest of culture to the eighteenth century, and especially to
Kant, but this Kantian notion presupposed general assent to
Lockean notions of mental processes and Cartesian notions of
mental substance. (pp. 3–4)

These notions which we have inherited from the seventeenth and
eighteenth centuries do *not* represent great breakthroughs or discoveries which set philosophy on a secure path. Rather they
were "inventions" – the invention of distinctions and problems
that were blended with potent metaphors which captured the
imagination of philosophers and set the direction for "normal"
philosophizing.

One of the many spinoffs of Rorty's reflections is a distinctive
understanding of how the history of philosophy has developed.
He rejects the view that there are perennial problems of philosophy which arise as soon as we begin to reflect. He is equally
relentless in his criticism of a variant of this which takes the
more "charitable" view that our philosophic ancestors were
dealing with basic problems, but the trouble is that they did so
in an obscure and confused manner. Rorty displaces this self-
congratulatory understanding of the history of philosophy (as
the dialectical unfolding of problems) which he claims has had
a distortive influence on the writing of the history of philosophy

and a mystifying effect on our understanding of philosophy as a discipline.

His alternative, which can be seen as a novel blending of themes suggested by Heidegger, Derrida, Foucault, Kuhn, and Feyerabend, may be stated as follows: there are moments in history when, because of all sorts of historical accidents – like what is going on in some part of culture such as science or religion – a new set of metaphors, distinctions, and problems is invented and captures the imagination of followers. For a time, when a particular philosophical language game gets entrenched, it sets the direction for "normal" philosophizing. After a while, because of some other historical accidents – like the appearance of a new genius or just plain boredom and sterility – another cluster of metaphors, distinctions, and problems usurp the place of what is now seen as a dying tradition. At first the abnormal talk of some new genius may be dismissed as kookiness or as not being "genuine" or "serious" philosophy. But sometimes this abnormal talk will set philosophy off in new directions. It is an illusion to believe that we are always dealing with the same basic problems of philosophy. We must resist the Whiggish temptation to rewrite the history of philosophy in our own image – where we see our predecessors as "really" treating what we now take to be fundamental problems. The crucial point is to realize that a philosophical paradigm does *not* displace a former one because it can better formulate the problems of a prior paradigm. Rather, because of a set of historical contingencies, it "nudges" the former paradigm aside. This is what happened in the seventeenth century when within a relatively short period of time the entire tradition of scholasticism collapsed and no longer seemed to have much point. After such a revolution or upheaval occurs, philosophers have a difficult time figuring out what was the point of the elaborate language game that had evolved. If they do not dismiss it out of hand, they are ineluctably tempted to reinterpret it as an anticipation of their present concerns. While Rorty refuses to make any predictions about what will happen next in philosophy, he certainly suggests that this is likely to happen again with the problematic of modern philosophy and its offspring, analytic philosophy.

To understand a historical movement such as analytic philosophy or even the whole tradition of modern philosophy, one must uncover the set of metaphors, distinctions, confusions, and problems that are characteristic of the language games or the forms of life that established the patterns for normal philosophizing. Briefly stated, the history of modern philosophy is the history of the rise and fall of the "mind" and the prized philosophical discipline – "epistemology."

II

Rorty's book is divided into three parts and consists of eight chapters: part 1, *Our Glassy Essence*, comprises two chapters, "The Inventions of the Mind," and "Persons Without Minds"; part 2, *Mirroring*, which is the central part of the book, contains four chapters, "The Idea of a 'Theory of Knowledge'," "Privileged Representations," "Epistemology and Empirical Psychology," and "Epistemology and Philosophy of Language"; and part 3, *Philosophy*, concludes with two chapters, "From Epistemology to Hermeneutics," and "Philosophy Without Mirrors." In the next three sections I will treat some of the highlights of each of these parts and show how Rorty seeks to get back to (and behind) those "intuitions" and preanalytic distinctions that seem to arise as soon as we begin to reflect. Thus, for example, the mind-body problem is taken to be a basic problem for philosophy because it appears to be intuitively evident that there is some important distinction between what is "mental" and what is "physical," even though we may be perplexed about how to characterize this distinction and what to make of it. But, Rorty tells us, "In my Wittgensteinian view, an intuition is never anything more or less than familiarity with a language-game, so to discover the source of our intuitions is to relive the history of the language-game we find ourselves playing" (p. 34). Now every philosopher who wants to get clear about the mind-body problem is obliged to ask what are the criteria for distinguishing the "mental" and the "physical." In what I called the "softening up" stage of Rorty's strategy he quickly runs through several of the major criteria that philosophers have invoked to characterize the "mental": intentionality, nonspatiality, immateriality, temporality, the presumed "phenomenal quality" of pains and other "raw feels." He concludes his survey with the claim that

> the only way to associate the intentional with the immaterial is to identify it with the phenomenal, and that the only way to identify the phenomenal with the immaterial is to hypostatize universals and think of them as particulars rather than abstractions from particulars – thus giving them a non-spatial-temporal habitation. (p. 31)

Consequently if we refuse to make this hypostatization, and see through the trap of invoking a specious metaphysical distinction, then we would have an easy dissolution of the mind-body problem. As Rorty himself points out, it is a bit too quick and easy. Furthermore, carrying out his therapeutic analogy, he tells us "What the patient needs is not a list of his mistakes and confusions but rather an understanding of how he came to make these mistakes and became involved in these confusions" (p. 33). If we are ever finally to get rid of the mind-body problem we need to be able to give a satisfactory answer to such a question as:

> How did these rather dusty little questions about the possible identity of pains and neurons ever get mixed up with the question of whether man "differed in kind" from the brutes – whether he had dignity rather than merely value? (p. 33)

Posing a question like this should already make us realize that "the mind-body" problem is a misnomer. At best it is a label for a cluster of quite distinct and different problems that have become fused and confused together. We can see this by considering the partial list that Rorty gives "of the features which philosophers have, at one time or another, taken as marks of the mental":

1. ability to know itself incorrigibly ("privileged access")
2. ability to exist separately from the body

3. nonspatiality (having a nonspatial part or "element")
4. ability to grasp universals
5. ability to sustain relations to the inexistent ("intentionality")
6. ability to use language
7. ability to act freely
8. ability to form part of our social group, to be "one of us"
9. inability to be identified with any object "in the world" (p. 35)

Confusion is compounded, because all too frequently when it is argued that a given feature simply will not serve to mark off the "mental," the response has been that the feature in question is not the *really* important or essential feature. For heuristic purposes, Rorty distinguishes three clusters of issues: the problem of consciousness, the problem of reason, and the problem of personhood. Clarifying the differences and the interrelations among these problems is one of Rorty's primary aims. In part 1, *Our Glassy Essence*, Rorty concentrates on the problem of consciousness, focusing on 1, 2, and 3 in his list. One reason for this is that many contemporary analytic philosophers have written as if the problem of consciousness *is* the heart of the mind-body problem. One need only think of Smart's opening statement in his article that set off so much of the contemporary debate:

> There does seem to be, as far as science is concerned, nothing in the world but increasingly complex arrangements of physical constituents. All except for one place; in consciousness. That is, for a full description of what is going on in man you would have to mention not only physical processes in his tissues, glands, nervous system, and so forth, but also his states of consciousness; his visual, auditory and tactual sensations, his aches and pains. . . . So sensations, states of consciousness, do seem to be the one sort of thing left outside the physicalist picture, and for various reasons I just cannot believe that this can be so. That everything should be explicable in terms of physics . . . except the occurrence of sensations seems to me to be frankly unbelievable.[2]

In unraveling the problem of consciousness, Rorty's task is to show how this problem arose and how we became preoccupied with "rather dusty little questions about the possible identity of pains and neurons." The story he unfolds goes back to Plato and Aristotle. But the point of his historical excursion into classical and scholastic philosophy is to make us keenly aware of how different the so-called mind-body problem was before and after Descartes – to show us that what we now (after Descartes) take to be obvious and intuitive distinctions did not exist prior to Descartes's "invention" of the mind. Descartes invented the mind in the sense that it is only after Descartes that the problem of *consciousness* became a central problem for philosophy. What then for Descartes was the essential feature or criterion of the "mental"? According to Rorty's reconstruction, Descartes's effective criterion is an appeal to "indubitability." Despite Descartes's own conviction that he had hit upon a rock bottom metaphysical distinction between the mind and the body, Descartes, by appealing to indubitability, sowed the seeds for transforming (or creating) the mind-body problem into an epistemological issue about the nature and consequences of indubitability – which is itself the origin of the contemporary obsession with incorrigibility and privileged access.

Now one can imagine a critic of Rorty objecting at this point (at the end of his first chapter) as follows: despite the historical learning and imagination that is evidenced in Rorty's history of the origin of the problem of consciousness, and despite the rhetoric about "dusty little questions," the tables can easily be turned on Rorty. For this exercise in historical reconstruction does not dissolve anything. On the contrary, Rorty's narrative can be read as showing just why the problem of consciousness is the nub of the mind-body problem – why it is so important to clarify the relation between pains and neurons. Nothing Rorty has said thus far indicates that the problem is either unimportant or has yet been satisfactorily resolved.

I think that Rorty is perfectly aware that this is the "natural" objection to make at this point. The aim of his second chapter, "Persons Without Minds," is to meet the objection squarely – to show that when we work through all the major twists and turns in contemporary analytic debates about the status of consciousness the entire problematic dissolves. He does this in a most ingenious fashion. He invents a science fiction tale where the general characters are Antipodeans who live on the other side of the galaxy and seem to be just like us in all respects with one great difference. For them neurology and biochemistry had been the first disciplines in which technological breakthroughs were achieved. Unlike us they do not make any first person or third person reports about pains, "raw feels," and minds. Where we use "mentalese" they speak about the stimulation of neurons and C-fibers. In the twenty-first century some of our tough-minded analytic philosophers visit the Antipodeans and confront the problem of trying to figure out whether the Antipodeans have minds, and whether they experience consciousness in the way in which we do. The device is imaginative and playful but the point is deadly serious. For Rorty uses it to work through virtually all the major moves that have been made by philosophers – both substantive and metaphilosophical – in the debate that has gone on from Feigl to Kripke. In what is one of the densest chapters of the book, we have nothing less than a reenactment of the attempts by analytic philosophers to state and solve the problem of consciousness. Rorty argues that all attempts to invent imaginative thought-experiments or resolve the issues by an appeal to the analysis of meanings fail. As the discussion gets more heated and sharper, Rorty focuses on the notion of a "phenomenal property" and smokes out what he takes to be the key principle involved:

> P) Whenever we make an incorrigible report on a state of ourselves, there must be a property we are presented with which induces us to make the report. (p. 84)

As he phrases it, this principle "enshrines the Cartesian notion that 'nothing is closer to the mind' than itself, and involves an entire epistemology and metaphysics, a specifically dualistic one" (p. 84). So the problem becomes what to make of, and what to do with this principle (P). Indeed most of the positions that have been taken on the mind-body problem (as the problem of consciousness) can be characterized in relation to the stand that they take to (P) – including behaviorism, various forms of materialism, and linguistic dualisms. So Rorty runs through the various "positions" in order to show that while they can be interpreted as containing important insights, none of them bring us any closer to a resolution of the outstanding issues.

Despite Rorty's disclaimers, it begins to look as if he himself is doing what he keeps telling us we should not do – that he is in effect advocating a "substantive" position on the mind-body problem – a position that looks like a sophisticated form of materialism. In a way he is and in a way he is not.

What the principle (P) shows is how the contemporary problem of consciousness depends on the status of incorrigibility and privileged access. But at this point, Rorty makes what might seem to be a surprising move. He claims that the proper response is *not* to argue for or against principle (P), but to drop it altogether "and thus be neither dualists, skeptics, behaviorists, nor 'identity theorists'" (p. 97). The denouement comes when Rorty declares:

> The real difficulty we encounter is, once again, that we are trying to set aside the image of man as possessor of a Glassy Essence, suitable for mirroring nature with one hand while holding on to it with the other. If we could ever drop the whole cluster of images which Antipodeans do not share with us, we would not be able to infer that matter had triumphed over spirit, science over privacy, or anything over anything else. These warring opposites are notions which do not make sense outside a cluster of images inherited from the Terran seventeenth century. No one except philosophers, who are professionally obligated to take these images seriously, will be scandalized if people start saying "The machine told me it didn't really hurt – it only, very horribly, seemed to." Philosophers are too involved with notions like "ontological status" to take such developments lightly, but no other part of culture is. . . . Only the notion that philosophy should provide a permanent matrix of categories into which every possible empirical discovery and cultural development should be fitted without strain impels us to ask unanswerable questions like "Would this mean that there were no minds?" "Were the Antipodeans right in saying 'There never were any of these things you call "raw feels"'?"

The above passage sums up the substance of what Rorty has to say about the problem of consciousness. But one might still want to object that this only shows that Rorty is really a materialist (and the passage appears in a section entitled "Materialism without Mind-Body Identity"). Such a claim would not be wrong, but it would certainly miss the point. For the triumphal verdict that Rorty is a materialist *manqué* only gains its rhetorical force because we are infected by a set of images and categories that Rorty is urging us to set aside. If we insist on clinging to talk about materialism (and Rorty might ask, Why bother?), then the point is to realize how innocuous and how unphilosophical "materialism" really is. It amounts to the unphilosophical claim that someday our great-grandchildren may talk and act like Antipodeans and relegate the problem of consciousness to the dustbin of historical curiosities.

III

Part 2, *Mirroring*, deals with the rise, nature, and demise of (and some recent attempts to salvage) epistemology. The moral of this part is a variation of part 1 and deepens Rorty's argument. Just as the modern notion of "mind" has its origins in the seventeenth century, so does epistemology which is so frequently taken to be either identical with philosophy or the heart of philosophy. Just as we can already envision the passing of the obsession with the "mind," so Rorty argues that we already have the grounds for envisioning the collapse of epistemology.

Rorty begins his examination of epistemology by probing its origins and the way in which it has thrived upon a central confusion that has plagued the theory of knowledge ever since – the confusion between the *causal* conditions of the genesis of knowledge and the *justification* of knowledge claims. He also argues that by the end of the nineteenth century, epistemology became so well fixed that it became virtually identical with philosophy as a discipline. For the past hundred years, it has seemed that the first task of philosophers is to resolve epistemological issues before any progress can be made with other problems and areas of philosophy. The historical probing of the origins of epistemology is followed by what Rorty himself considers to be the central chapter of the book, "Privileged Representations" which deals with the work of Sellars and Quine. Once we fully appreciate the force and consequences of Sellar's critique of the "Myth of the Given" and Quine's skeptical arguments about the language-fact distinction, then we have grounds for not only abandoning the major distinctions that have set the context for modern philosophy but also questioning analytical philosophy. But Rorty is not finished. The final two chapters of this part examine what he considers two misguided attempts to "save" epistemology by finding successor disciplines – empirical psychology and the philosophy of language – which might replace traditional epistemology and presumably answer the "real" problems that our epistemological predecessors were trying to answer.

Since Rorty considers his discussion of Sellars and Quine as the centerpiece of his book, I want to concentrate on the novel interpretation that he offers of their work. According to Rorty's historical reconstruction of epistemology, it is basically the "Kantian picture of concepts and intuitions getting together to produce knowledge" (p. 168) that makes sense of the idea of a "theory of knowledge" as a specifically philosophical discipline distinct from psychology.

> This is equivalent to saying that if we do not have the distinction between what is "given" and what is "added by the mind" or that between the contingent (because influenced by what is given) and the "necessary" (because entirely "within" the mind and under its control), then we will not know what would count as a "rational reconstruction" of our knowledge. (p. 169)

Although these two related distinctions were attacked throughout the history of the analytic movement, it is only with the arguments of Sellars and Quine that they have been fully discredited. Sellars and Quine invoke the same argument in their critiques, "one which bears equally against the given-versus-nongiven and the necessary-versus-contingent distinctions. The crucial premise of this argument is that we understand knowledge when we understand the social justification of belief, and thus have no need to view it as accuracy of representation" (p. 170). Unlike many critics of Sellars and Quine who think they have gone too far with their holistic tendencies, Rorty claims that they have not gone far enough. The consequence of their arguments is *not* to advocate a better way of doing epistemology, or even to see that epistemology can now be replaced by a "legitimate" scientific inquiry, but simply to put an end to epistemology *tout court*.

> It is as if Quine, having renounced the conceptual-empirical, analytic-synthetic, and language-fact distinctions, were still not quite able to renounce that between the given and the postulated. Conversely Sellars having triumphed over the later distinction, cannot quite renounce the former cluster. Despite courteous acknowledgement of Quine's triumph over analyticity, Sellars's writing is still permeated with the notion of "giving the analysis" of various terms or sentences, and with a tacit use of the distinction between the necessary and the contingent, the structural and the empirical, the philosophical and the scientific. Each of these two men tends to make continual, unofficial, tacit, heuristic use of the distinction which the other has transcended. It is as if analytic philosophy could not be written without at least *one* of the two great Kantian distinctions, and as if neither Quine nor Sellars were willing to cut the last links which bind them to Russell, Carnap, and "logic as the essence of philosophy." (pp. 171–2)

I cannot go into the details of Rorty's interpretation, defense, and critique of Sellars and Quine. Rorty develops an extremely perceptive analysis of their work, a strong defense of their claims against many of the objections that have been raised by others, and at the same time a penetrating critique. For example, many critics have argued that Quine's later work, especially his reflections on the indeterminacy of translation, reveals a blatant contradiction – or at least a deep tension – with his own pragmatic and holistic arguments. Rorty locates and specifies this tension better than anyone else (see p. 202). I am primarily interested in how Rorty "uses" Sellars and Quine – the role that they play in the dramatic narrative he is unfolding. Sellars

and Quine complete the critique of the Kantian legacy of epistemology and lead us to a "holistic" view of knowledge, to
what Rorty labels "epistemological behaviorism." (The choice
of these terms "holism" and "epistemological behaviorism"
are unfortunate because they suggest that we are dealing with a
new and better epistemological position. Every time we are
tempted to make this move, i.e., to replace one position by what
now seems to be a better philosophical position, Rorty pulls the
rug from under our feet.) How then are we to understand what
Rorty means by "epistemological behaviorism" and "holism"?

> Explaining rationality and epistemic authority by reference to
> what society lets us say, rather than the latter by the former, is the
> essence of what I shall call "epistemological behaviorism," an
> attitude common to Dewey and Wittgenstein. This sort of
> behaviorism can best be seen as a species of holism – but one
> which requires no idealist metaphysical underpinnings. It
> claims that if we understand the rules of a language-game, we
> understand all that there is to understand about why the moves
> in that language-game are made. . . . If we are behaviorist in
> this sense, then it will not occur to us to invoke either of the
> traditional Kantian distinctions. (p. 174)

In short, to advocate "epistemological behaviorism" is not to
advocate a new subtle epistemological position; rather it is to
see through and to abandon epistemology, to see that the whole
project only makes sense if we accept some form of the Kantian
distinctions which have now been rejected. As for "holism,"
Rorty warns us that "A holistic approach to knowledge is not a
matter of antifoundationalist polemic, but a distrust of the whole
epistemological enterprise" (p. 181). Consequently "to be a
behaviorist in epistemology . . . is to look at the normal scientific discourse of our day bifocally, both as patterns adopted for
various historical reasons, and as the achievement of objective
truth, where "objective truth" is no more and no less than the
best idea we currently have about how to explain what is going
on" (p. 385).

Anticipating the charge that epistemological behaviorism
and holism require abandoning objectivity, truth, and the
growth of knowledge, Rorty insists:

For the Quine-Sellars approach to epistemology, to say that
truth and knowledge can only be judged by the standards of the
inquirers of our own day is not to say that human knowledge is
less noble or important, or more "cut off from the world" than
we have thought. It is merely to say that nothing counts as
justification unless by reference to what we already accept, and
that there is no way to get outside our beliefs and our language
so as to find some test other than coherence.

To say that the True and the Right are matters of social practice may seem to condemn us to a relativism which, all by itself,
is a *reductio* of a behaviorist approach to either knowledge or
morals. . . . Here I shall simply remark that only the image of a
discipline – philosophy – which will pick out a given set of scientific or moral views as more "rational" than the alternatives by
appeal to something which forms a permanent neutral matrix
for all inquiry and all history, makes it possible to think that
such relativism must automatically rule out coherence theories
of intellectual and practical justification. One reason why professional philosophers recoil from the claim that knowledge may
not have foundations, or rights and duties an ontological
ground, is that the kind of behaviorism which dispenses with
foundations is in a fair way toward dispensing with philosophy.
(pp. 178–9)

There are many analytic philosophers who share Rorty's
skepticism about traditional epistemology. But for them the
basic trouble is that genuine philosophic issues have been
obscured by epistemological formulations. We need to reformulate the relevant issues in a "purified" philosophy of
language or a scientific empirical psychology. But Rorty is
relentless in his critique of those who think epistemology can be
salvaged in this way. In the last two chapters of *Mirroring*, he
exposes two attempts to found successor disciplines to epistemology. Neither "empirical psychology" nor the "new
philosophy of language" help to solve epistemological problems. Once again there are striking inversions. (Rorty's use of
this technique, where he shows how things turn out to be the
very opposite of what they purport to be, is a variant of Hegel's
own use of this dialectical strategy.) From Rorty's perspective,
the new concern with the issue of "realism" and the belief that

the way to deal with the foundations of philosophy is through "formal semantics" do *not* represent advances in philosophy. On the contrary, Putnam insofar as he temporarily misled us into thinking that the issue of metaphysical realism is an important one for philosophy, and Dummett insofar as he thinks that Frege has shown us the way to get at the foundations of philosophy turn out to be arch reactionaries. It would be hard to imagine a more antithetical understanding of modern philosophy and analytic philosophy than that presented by Dummett and Rorty. Dummett, acknowledging that philosophers have mistakenly claimed that they have discovered the "real" foundations of philosophy, is nevertheless convinced that there are real foundations and that we have now discovered how to go about finding them.[3] From Rorty's point of view this is a despairing attempt to save analytic philosophy – one that cannot quite give up holding on to the "problem of representation" and the belief that there is something to be preserved from the metaphor of mirroring reality.

IV

There will be some readers who when they reach this point in Rorty's book (after 311 densely argued pages) will breathe a sigh of relief. They may not be acquainted with the latest subtleties in the analytic controversies about the mind-body problem, or the pros and cons of a causal theory of reference, or why so many professionals are excited by the work of Davidson, Putnam, Kripke, Dummett, and their colleagues. But they may have felt that somehow philosophy took a wrong turn with the analytic movement. They may feel some satisfaction that Rorty has written the type of critique that could only be written by an "insider," and that he has shown that the emperor has no clothes – or at least is scantily clad. If only Anglo–American philosophers had taken a different turn; if only, for example, they had followed the lead of Husserl who opened up the field of phenomenology, then we might have avoided the tangled mess which has consumed so much technical competence. But if this is the way they have read Rorty, they have *misread* him and they have missed the real sting of his critique. Rorty is not denigrating the contribution of analytic philosophers, despite the severity of his critique. The first two parts of the book employ (with novel twists) the insights and arguments of analytic philosophers to show how they lead to surprising and unexpected conclusions. But even more important, Rorty has dropped enough hints along the way to show how his critique can be generalized. "Professional philosophy" is not to be identified with any school in philosophy but cuts across schools. Many of Rorty's most incisive criticisms are just as relevant to those Continental philosophers who think of themselves as having taken the "transcendental turn." From Rorty's perspective, the differences between Russell and Husserl are insignificant when compared with what they share in common. Each in his distinctive way played a crucial role in reinforcing the image of philosophy as a foundational discipline. Furthermore, it should now be clear that Rorty's primary object of attack is any form of systematic philosophy which shares the conviction that there are real foundations that philosophy must discover and that philosophy as a discipline can transcend history and adumbrate a permanent neutral matrix for assessing all forms of inquiry and all types of knowledge.

Nevertheless, for those who think in terms of Anglo–American philosophy and Continental philosophy, it will be noticeable that in the final part, *Philosophy*, a new set of characters and a new set of problems enter the stage. Heidegger, Gadamer, Sartre, Habermas, Apel, Foucault, and Derrida are discussed along with Kuhn and Feyerabend. Rorty now takes up such familiar "Continental" distinctions as that between Spirit and Nature, *Geisteswissenschaften* and *Naturwissenschaften*. But there is no change of theme. In this carefully orchestrated work all this material is integrated into a reflection on philosophy itself – a reflection that emerges from the first two parts of the book. Rorty is provocative and refreshing because he cuts across the stale polemic and the irritable defensiveness that characterize much of the nondialogue between Anglo–American and

Continental philosophy. He is equally devasting and equally illuminating about both sides of this great divide.

In order to get this last part into clear focus, it may be helpful to raise a number of doubts and suspicions that will surely have occurred to many readers. Is Rorty simply engaging in a destructive critique or does he have anything constructive to say? It certainly looks as if he is leading us to historicism, skepticism, relativism, and nihilism. At times, Rorty even uses these labels to characterize his project. Presumably we all know that these are philosophical dead ends and can be refuted by carefully constructed self-referential arguments. How then does Rorty get out of this bind? How does he meet the objection that any critique must take a stand someplace on what is True and Right – and this stance itself demands some sort of philosophic justification? One of the main purposes of the final·part of his book is to answer these doubts and to adumbrate an alternative understanding of philosophy as a voice in the conversation of mankind. But before turning to Rorty's own self-understanding of the philosophical enterprise, I want to clarify the sense in which the above "labels" do and do not apply to Rorty.

If by historicism we mean that history itself is a foundational discipline, that the explanations that philosophers seek can only be found in the study of history, or even if we understand by historicism the curious variant that Popper attacked where a historicist is supposed to be someone who believes that there are laws of history which enable us to predict the future, then Rorty is certainly *not* a historicist. On the contrary, he has presented some of the strongest arguments against such a position. For he has been arguing and trying to show us that there is *no* foundational discipline – neither history, nor philosophy, nor science, nor poetry. There is no part of culture that is more privileged than any other part – and the illusion that there *must* be such a dicipline is one that needs to be exorcized. Further, given Rorty's insistence on historical accidents, contingencies, and options, it does not make any sense to think that history could ever aspire to be a predictive discipline. But if by historicism we mean that a healthy historical sense of how philosophic language games arise, get entrenched, and pass away may cure us of the belief that there are perennial philosophical problems, then Rorty is certainly a historicist and tells us that this is the moral of his book.

If by skepticism we mean the type of epistemological doctrine that insists that we can never really know what is beyond the "veil of ideas" and that our claims to knowledge can never "really" be justified, then it is difficult to imagine a more forceful attack on such skepticism. Such an epistemological skepticism gains its force from accepting the very metaphors that Rorty urges us to abandon. If Rorty's therapy were successful, if we could rid ourselves of the desire for constraint and compulsion and the fear that, unless we discover the (nonexistent) foundations of knowledge, we are faced with intellectual and moral chaos, then epistemological skepticism would no longer be a position to be "refuted" – it would simply wither away. If by skepticism we mean that we have grounds for being suspicious of all attempts to escape history, to discover the foundations of knowledge, language, or philosophy, and to delineate a permanent neutral framework for evaluating all claims to knowledge, then this is what Rorty has been advocating.

If by relativism we mean that there is no truth, objectivity, and standards for judging better and worse arguments or moral positions, then Rorty is certainly *not* a relativist, and suggests that such a relativism has become something of a straw man for philosophers to attack. Rorty's aim is not to deny or denigrate "truth" and "objectivity" but to demystify these "honorific" labels. If by relativism we mean epistemological behaviorism, that there is no other way to justify knowledge claims or claims to truth than by appealing to those social practices which have been hammered out in the course of human history and are the forms of inquiry *within* which we distinguish what is true and false, what is objective and idiosyncratic, then Rorty advocates such a relativism. But this does not mean that "anything goes."

If by nihilism we mean that whether we are dealing with knowledge or morals, anything is just as good or as true as anything else, then again Rorty is *not* a nihilist. On the contrary, such a position is frequently adopted by those who think this is the only alternative to the claim that knowledge and morals have foundations. But if nihilism means being liberated from the illusion that there is something to which we can appeal which will or ought to command universal assent, that there is no way of escaping from human freedom and responsibility in making moral decisions, and no ultimate support to which we can appeal in making such decisions, then Rorty happily thinks of himself as a nihilist.

The point I am emphasizing can be stated in a slightly different way. "Historicism," "Skepticism," "Relativism," and "Nihilism," are typically thought to be so objectionable because they are taken to be positions to which we are driven when we give up the claim that there are "real" foundations for truth, objectivity, knowledge, and morals. They are all shaped in the image of what might be called the Cartesian Anxiety – the grand Either/Or – either there is some basic foundational constraint or we are confronted with intellectual and moral chaos. Rorty is *not* advocating that we take sides on this fundamental dichotomy that has shaped the Cartesian–Lockean–Kantian tradition. Rorty's main therapeutic point is to liberate us from this Either/Or, to help us to see through it, and to set it aside.

But still we want to know what function, if any, philosophers can perform and what type of self-understanding of philosophy emerges if we give up these various "self-deceptions" that Rorty exposes. In the final part of the book where Rorty seeks to answer this question, he "works through" what initially seems to be a bewildering array of distinctions: Spirit and Nature, *Geisteswissenschaften* and *Naturwissenschaften*, commensurability and incommensurability, normal and abnormal discourse, familiarity and unfamiliarity, epistemology and hermeneutics, systematic and edifying philosophy, and philosophy as inquiry and philosophy as conversation. Rorty's "asides" are frequently as illuminating and incisive as his main points. But I want to touch on the significance of some of these distinctions only insofar as they enable us to grasp Rorty's own understanding of philosophy.

By "commensurable" Rorty means "able to be brought under a set of rules which will tell us how rational agreement can be reached on what would settle the issue on every point where statements seem to conflict. These rules tell us how to construct an ideal situation, in which all residual disagreements will be seen to be 'noncognitive' or merely verbal, or else merely temporary – capable of being resolved by doing something further" (p. 316). Modern philosophy shaped by the Cartesian–Lockean–Kantian tradition in *both* its analytic and Continental forms has been obsessed with the search for commensuration. This is the quest that is characteristic of epistemology. Hermeneutics, as Rorty understands it, is not the name of a new method or discipline, an alternative way to achieve commensuration, but rather largely a struggle against the assumption that all contributions to culture are commensurable. Hermeneutics "is an expression of hope that the cultural space left by the demise of epistemology will not be filled – that our culture should become one in which the demand for constraint is no longer felt" (p. 315). The distinction between the "commensurable," and the "incommensurable," which Rorty takes over from recent debates in the philosophy of science, is one that he generalizes. It is applicable to all domains of discourse, whether they be science, philosophy, poetry, or literary criticism.

Earlier, when characterizing Rorty's understanding of the history of philosophy, I indicated that he sees it as consisting of periods of "normal discourse" where there is agreement about problems, procedures, and the "correct" way of finding solutions followed by periods of abnormal discourse when strange and new ways of speaking and writing appear. He radicalizes Kuhn's distinction of "normal" and "abnormal" discourse because Rorty sees this as a feature of all discourse and culture (as Kuhn himself sometimes suggests). It is during periods of "normal" discourse that epistemology thrives, because these are the times when there is agreement, when it does appear as if *all* discourse might be commensurable and philosophy might be able to clarify the rules of commensuration. But there is always a danger of confusing what is historically stable with the permanent and eternal, or in thinking that the domain in which such stability has been achieved is the measure for all other domains. (Rorty even envisions the possibility that other parts of culture such as morals or poetry might be taken as our paradigms of normality rather than science, just as there was a time in the West when theological discourse played this role.) By introducing such bland distinctions as the "normal" and the "abnormal" or the "familiar" and the "unfamiliar," Rorty deliberately wants to make us aware of how "relative" these distinctions are to the changing scene of culture.

Throughout his book Rorty has been attacking the "Cartesian–Lockean–Kantian tradition" of modern philosophy, but implicitly and explicitly he has been contrasting this tradition with another attitude toward philosophy. He speaks of

> figures who, without forming a "tradition," resemble each other in their distrust of the notion that man's essence is to be a knower of essences. Goethe, Kierkegaard, Santayana, William James, Dewey, the later Wittgenstein, the later Heidegger are figures of this sort. . . . These writers have kept alive the suggestion that, even when we have justified true belief about everything we want to know, we may have no more than conformity to the norms of the day. They have kept alive the historicist sense that this century's "superstition" was last century's triumph of reason, as well as the relativist sense that the latest vocabulary, borrowed from the latest scientific achievement, may not express privileged representations of essences, but be just another of the potential infinity of vocabularies in which the world can be described. (p. 367)

The mainstream of philosophers Rorty calls "systematic philosophers," and the peripheral ones – following Kierkegaard – he calls "edifying philosophers." What is common to edifying philosophers is that they use every means they can to voice their skepticism about the "whole project of commensuration."

> In our time, Dewey, Wittgenstein, and Heidegger are the great edifying, peripheral thinkers. All three make it as difficult as possible to take their thought as expressing views on traditional philosophical problems, or as making constructive proposals for

philosophy as a cooperative and progressive discipline. They make fun of the classic picture of man, the picture which contains systematic philosophy, the search for universal commensuration in a final vocabulary. They hammer away at the holistic point that words take their meaning from other words rather than by virtue of their representative character, and the corollary that vocabularies acquire their privileges from the men who use them rather than from their transparency to the real. . . .

Edifying philosophers want to keep space open for the sense of wonder which poets sometimes cause – wonder that there is something new under the sun, something which is *not* an accurate representation of what was already there, something which (at least for the moment) cannot be explained and can barely be described. (pp. 368–70)

Now it might seem as if Rorty is casting his lot with edifying philosophy (although he realizes that there is something paradoxical about the very notion of an edifying philosopher). Edifying philosophy is always reactive and parasitic upon the pretentions of systematic philosophy. Edifying philosophers are frequently Rorty's heroes, and he himself admires and emulates their use of satire, ridicule, and paradox. But this is not quite where Rorty leaves us. He suggests a new metaphor for understanding philosophy and the role that it can play in culture – philosophy as *conversation* rather than philosophy as *inquiry*. Rorty is alluding to Oakeshott's conception of conversation in "The Voice of Poetry in the Conversation of Mankind." Philosophy like poetry is best understood as one of the many voices in the conversation of mankind. A conversation can be civilized, illuminating, intelligent, revealing, exciting. Truth may be relevant to a conversation, but so can many other things, and a conversation is not to be thought of as a disguised inquiry into truth or the discovery of foundations. To view philosophy as a form of conversation which is itself part of the larger conversation of mankind is to begin "to get the visual, and in particular the mirroring, metaphors out of speech altogether" (p. 371). It also means recognizing that as culture changes one or another voice may play a more significant role in the conversation. From this perspective we can view edifying philosophers as conversational partners rather than "seeing them as holding views on subjects of common concern" (p. 372). "One way of thinking of wisdom as something of which the love is not the same as that of argument, and of which the achievement does not consist in finding the correct vocabularly for representing essence, is to think of it as the practical wisdom necessary to participate in a conversation" (p. 372). Rorty concludes his book with an eloquent plea for dropping the notion of "philosophers as knowing something about knowing which nobody else knows so well" and dropping the notion that their voice "always has an overriding claim on the attention of the other participants in the conversation" (p. 392). Instead we should be frank about the "useful kibitzing" that philosophers sometimes provide. Rorty's entire book can be read as an ironic variation on the Peircian theme of not blocking the road to inquiry. For it is not open inquiry that needs defense today, but open civilized conversation. Rorty thinks it is idle to speculate about what will happen next in philosophy, but in his final sentence he tells us, "The only point on which I would insist is that philosophers' moral concern should be with continuing the conversation of the West, rather than with insisting upon a place for the traditional problems of modern philosophy within that conversation" (p. 394).

V

Rorty never becomes shrill or strident in his critique of "professional philosophy," "modern philosophy," and "analytic philosophy." With the possible exception of Quine, there has not been an American philosopher since William James who has written with as much wit, humor, playfulness, and seductive eloquence. All this is combined with a moral seriousness and passion that seeks to unmask pretentions, illusions, and self-deceptions, that seeks to make us aware of our historical limitations or, to use a classical turn of phrase, to make us aware of our human finitude. Although I am sympathetic with his powerful and challenging critique, there is something fundamentally wrong with where Rorty leaves us. In this final section I want to argue that the moral of the tale he tells is not quite the one that he suggests. In a manner similar to the way in which Rorty uses Sellars and Quine (against themselves) I want to show that Rorty himself does not quite see where his best insights and arguments are leading him. Much of this book is about the obsessions of philosophers and the pictures that hold them captive. But there is a sense in which Rorty himself is obsessed. It is almost as if he cannot quite "let go" and accept the force of his own critique. It is as if Rorty himself has been more deeply touched by what he is attacking than he realizes. Rorty keeps pointing to and hinting at an alternative to the foundationalism that has preoccupied modern philosophy without ever fully exploring this alternative. Earlier I suggested that one way of reading Rorty is to interpret him as trying to help us to set aside the Cartesian Anxiety – the Cartesian Either/Or – that underlies so much of modern philosophy. But there is a variation of this Either/Or that haunts this book – *either* we are *ineluctably* tempted by foundational metaphors and the desperate attempt to escape from history *or* we must frankly recognize that philosophy itself is at best a form of "kibitzing." Suppose, however, that Rorty's therapy were really successful; suppose we were no longer held captive by metaphors of "our glassy essence" and "mirroring," suppose we accepted that knowledge claims can never be justified in any other way than by an appeal to social practices, suppose we were purged of the desire for constraint and compulsion, then what? The scene of culture and the voice of philosophy in the conversation of mankind look very different from the one that Rorty proposes. To flesh out what I mean, I will begin with what might seem to be external and peripheral matters and then move closer to the heart of Rorty's vision.

I can isolate Rorty's obsession by comparing him with one of his heroes, John Dewey. Rorty thinks that Dewey is one of the three most important philosophers of our century because, while in his early work he tried to provide a new foundation for philosophy, he – like Heidegger and Wittgenstein – came to see this earlier effort as self-deceptive. Dewey in his later work "spent his time warning us against these very temptations to which he had succumbed." From what Rorty says here and in other places, the story is a bit more complicated, for according to Rorty, Dewey himself was briefly tempted – or bullied – into thinking he had to supply a new metaphysical foundation for his own naturalistic vision.[4] But as might be suspected, this is the "bad" Dewey, and his lasting contribution is "therapeutic rather than constructive, edifying rather than systematic, designed to make the reader question his own motives for philosophizing rather than supply him with a philosophical program." But this interpretation of Dewey is a gross distortion, one that is more revealing about Rorty than it is about Dewey. It is true as far as it goes, but Dewey was not nearly as obsessed with attacking epistemology and the "spectator theory of knowledge" as is Rorty. What Rorty leaves out – or fails to give its just due – is that Dewey was primarily concerned with the role that philosophy might play *after* one had been liberated from the obsessions and tyrannies of the "problems of philosophy." Dewey would certainly agree with Rorty that all justification involves reference to existing social practices and that philosophy is not a discipline that has any special knowledge of knowing or access to more fundamental foundations. But for Dewey this is where the real problems begin. What are the social practices to which we should appeal? How do we discriminate the better from the worse? Which ones need to be discarded, criticized, and reconstructed? Dewey sought to deal with these problems without any appeal to "our glassy essence," "mirroring," or foundational metaphors. According to Rorty's own analysis, these are genuine problems, but Rorty never quite gets around to asking these and related questions. He tells us, of course, that there is no special philosophical method for dealing with such issues and no ahistorical matrix to which we can appeal. But accepting this claim does not make these issues disappear. Whatever our final judgment of Dewey's success or failure in dealing with what he called the "problems of men," Dewey constantly struggled with questions which Rorty never quite faces – although his whole reading of modern philosophy is one that points to the need for reflective intellectuals to examine them. Sometimes Rorty writes as if any philosophic attempt to sort out the better from the worse, the rational from the irrational (even assuming that this is historically relative) must lead us back to foundationalism and the search for an ahistorical perspective. But Rorty has also shown us that there is nothing inevitable about such a move. Following Rorty, we do not have to see this enterprise as finding a successor foundational discipline to epistemology, but rather as changing the direction of philosophy, of giving the conversation a different turn. Ironically, for all his critique of the desire of philosophers to escape from history and to see the world *sub specie aeternitatis*, there is a curious way in which Rorty himself slides into this stance. He keeps telling us that the history of philosophy, like the history of all culture, is a series of contingencies, accidents, a history of the rise and demise of various language games and forms of life. But suppose we place ourselves *back* into our historical situation. Then a primary task is one of trying to deal with present conflicts and confusions, of trying to sort out the better from the worse, of focusing on which social practices ought to endure and which demand reconstruction, of which types of justification are acceptable and which are not. Rorty might reply that there is no reason to think that the professional philosopher is more suited for such a task than representatives of other aspects of culture. But even this need not be disputed. We can nevertheless recognize the importance and the legitimacy of the task of "understanding how things in the broadest possible sense of the term hang together in the broadest possible sense of the term."[5]

In saying this, I do not think that I am saying anything that Rorty himself does not suggest, but he does not grapple with the issues. In part, I think this is due to his own unwarranted anxiety that philosophers cannot quite help getting caught in the snares of the type of foundationalism which he has so devastatingly criticized. This is why Rorty himself is still not liberated from the types of obsessions which he claims have plagued most modern philosophers. The point can be approached from a slightly different perspective by examining a central example that Rorty gives to support his type of historicism.

In his discussion of Kuhn's work and in sorting out what he takes to be right and wrong in the controversies between Kuhn and his critics, Rorty takes up what might be considered the hard case – the controversy between Galileo and Bellarmine.

> But can we then find a way of saying that the considerations advanced against the Copernican theory by Cardinal Bellarmine – the scriptural descriptions of the fabric of the heavens – *were* "illogical or unscientific"? This, perhaps, is the point at which the battle lines betwen Kuhn and his critics can be drawn most sharply. Much of the seventeenth century's notion of what it was to be a "philosopher" and much of the Enlightenment's notion of what it was to be "rational" turns on Galileo's being absolutely right and the church absolutely wrong. To suggest that there is room for rational disagreement here – not simply for a black-and-white struggle with reason and superstition – is to endanger the very notion of "philosophy." (p. 328)

Rorty points out that Kuhn does not give an explicit answer to the question. However, Kuhn's writings provide an "arsenal of argument for a negative answer." "In any case, a negative answer is implied by the argument of the present book" (p. 328). It is important to clarify just what Rorty is and is not claiming. He is certainly not suggesting that the issues raised in the dispute between Galileo and Bellarmine are unimportant. On the contrary, the fate of European culture was affected by the resolution of issues raised in this debate. But Rorty argues that there are no permanent standards, criteria, or decision procedures to which one could univocally appeal which would declare Galileo on the side of truth, objectivity, and rationality, or sharply distinguish Galileo's arguments from Bellarmine's "irrationality."

> The conclusion I wish to draw is that the "grid" [to use Foucault's term] which emerged in the later seventeenth century and eighteenth century was not there to be appealed to in the early seventeenth century, at the time that Galileo was on trial. No conceivable epistemology, no study of the nature of human knowledge, could have "discovered" it before it was

hammered out. The notion of what it was to be "scientific" was in the process of being formed. If one endorses the values – or perhaps the ranking of competing values – common to Galileo and Kant, then indeed Bellarmine was being "unscientific." We are heirs of three hundred years of rhetoric about the importance of distinguishing sharply between science and religion, science and politics, science and art, science and philosophy, and so on. This rhetoric has formed the culture of Europe. It made us what we are today. We are fortunate that no little perplexity within epistemology, or within the historiography of science, is enough to defeat it. But to proclaim our loyalty to these distinctions is not to say that there are "objective" and "rational" standards for adopting them. (pp. 330–1)

Rorty insists that it is an illusion to think that philosophers stand as neutral third parties to this significant debate, and that they are able to score points for one side or the other by appealing to ahistorical standards of rationality and objectivity. But it is instructive to see what Rorty passes over all too rapidly. Suppose we try the thought experiment of imagining ourselves back into the context of this debate, and suppose too that we are liberated from thinking that the issues can be resolved by an appeal to permanent epistemological standards. What then? Certainly the issues do not disappear. Our task is precisely to "hammer out" the relevant issues involved, to clarify them and to try to sort out what are the better and worse arguments. This is not a matter of arbitrarily endorsing one set of values over competing values, but rather trying to give the strongest "historical reasons" to support one side or the other. The issues *cannot* be resolved simply by appealing to existing social practices, for the heart of the controversy is the genuine and serious conflict of competing social practices. How are we to understand what are the relevant "historical reasons" – or even what we mean by "historical reasons"? Rorty's language itself reflects what he is presumably opposing. When he places "objective" and "rational" in scare quotes and contrasts this with "three hundred years of rhetoric" he is implicitly aping those who think that either there are rock bottom permanent standards of objectivity and rationality or there is only "mere" rhetoric. But Rorty himself has deconstructed this sense of objectivity and rationality. He distinguishes two senses of "objective" and "subjective."

> "Objectivity" in the first sense was a property of theories, which, having been thoroughly discussed, are chosen by a consensus of rational discussants. By contrast, a "subjective" consideration is one which has been, or would be, or should be, set aside by rational discussants – one which is seen to be, or should be seen to be, irrelevant to the subject matter of the theory. . . . For a consideration to be subjective, in this sense, is simply for it to be unfamiliar. So judging subjectivity is as hazardous as judging relevance.
>
> In a more traditional sense of "subjective," on the other hand, "subjective" contrasts with "corresponding to what is out there" and thus means something like "a product only of what is in here" (in the heart, or in the "confused" portion of the mind which does not contain privileged representations and thus does not accurately reflect what is out there). In this sense "subjective" is associated with "emotional" or "fantastical," for our hearts and our imaginations are idiosyncratic, while our intellects are, at their best, identical mirrors of the self-same external objects. (pp. 338–9)

Throughout the history of philosophy these two different senses of "objective" and "subjective" have been confused and tangled together. "In this way, the tradition since Plato has run together the 'algorithm versus no algorithm' distinction with the 'reason versus passion' distinction" (p. 339). While there is an innocuous sense in which we employ the second distinction, Rorty has argued that we are on the very brink of misunderstanding when philosophers try to blow this up into something like the issue of realism versus idealism. It is the first distinction that is the effective distinction for sorting out what is "objective" and "subjective." This is a variable and changeable distinction both with respect to different historical epochs and with respect to different fields of inquiry. But the key reference here is to a consensus achieved by *rational discussants*. How are we to decide who are the rational discussants and in what sense they are "rational"? This is not "merely" a rhetorical question, but frequently the most vital question to be confronted. What we learn from Rorty is that philosophers do not have any special knowledge or any special access to permanent standards to answer this question. Sorting out rational discussants from those who are judged to be irrational is precisely the type of issue that needs to be "hammered out." But nothing that Rorty says lessens the importance of the question. Indeed everything he says and shows indicates that this is the sort of question that philosophers or, if one prefers, "reflective intellectuals" ought to be addressing.

There is something askew in Rorty's emphasis. Throughout he argues as if we are confronted with two alternatives: *either* all justification, whether in matters of knowledge or morals, appeals to social practices *or* to illusory foundations. He has been primarily concerned with criticizing the second alternative because he rightly thinks that this is the one to which most modern philosophers have been drawn – disputing only what are the foundations and how they are to be known. But suppose we reject this second alternative and concentrate on the one that Rorty advocates. As Rorty well knows, any defense of a consensus view is open to the criticism of how are we to distinguish a rational from an irrational consensus. His constant references to the "best" social practices and to what "rational" discussants would accept indicates his awareness of this problem. But he has very little to say about it. For to deny that there is some absolute or definitive way of making this distinction is not to deny that there is a vital distinction to be made. Sometimes it seems as if Rorty himself is guilty of a version of the "Myth of the Given" – as if social practices are the sort of thing that are *given*, and that all we need to do is to look and see what they are. But surely this is an illusion. To tell us, as Rorty does over and over again, that "to say the True and Right are matters of social practice" (p. 179) or that "justification is a matter of social practice" (p. 186) or that "objectivity should be seen as conformity to norms of justification we find about us" (p. 361), will not do. We want to know how we are to understand "social practices," how they are generated, sustained, and pass away.

But even more important we want to know how they are to be
criticized. For in any historical period we are confronted not
only with a tangle of social practices, but with practices that
make competing and conflicting demands upon us. There is
danger here of reifying the very idea of a social practice and
failing to appreciate that our very criticisms and arguments
about what is rational and irrational are constitutive of traditions and social practices.

Rorty seems to be deeply ambivalent about the prospects for
philosophy. The moral of his work is to suggest and to advocate
a need for a turn in the role that philosophy plays in the conversation of mankind. Even his "historicism" points to a way in
which philosophy can play a much more vital and central role
when we accept our historical limitations but nevertheless try
to make sense of the conflicts and confusions that confront us
and to gain a critical perspective. At the same time he draws
back from taking this seriously, from entering the very area of
problems that he has opened up for us.

There is the same lack of balance in the moral decisionism
that runs through the book. For all his criticism of Kant, Rorty
praises Kant for helping us to see that the

> attempt to answer the question of justification by discovering new
> objective truths, to answer the moral agent's request for justifi-
> cations by descriptions of a privileged domain, is the
> philosopher's form of bad faith – his special way of substituting
> pseudo-cognition for moral choice. Kant's greatness was to
> have seen through the "metaphysical" form of this attempt, and
> to have destroyed the traditional conception of reason to make
> room for moral faith. Kant gave us a way of seeing scientific
> truth as something which can never supply an answer to our
> demand for a point, a justification, a way of claiming that our
> moral decision about what to do is based on *knowledge* of the
> nature of the world. (p. 383)

Unfortunately, according to Rorty, Kant misled us into thinking
that there is nevertheless a decision procedure for moral choice.
But here too Rorty seems to be presupposing what he has so effectively criticized, viz., that "justifying" moral (and social and

political choices) is *either* a matter of deceiving ourselves into thinking there is some ultimate ground to which we can appeal or a matter of personal (arbitrary?) decision. One would have thought that this is just the type of misleading either/or that he wants to expose. For sometimes we can and do try to justify or warrant our moral decisions by giving the best reasons we can give to support them even when we recognize that there can be disagreements about what constitutes good reasons. And sometimes we are forced to reflect on what does and ought to count as good reasons even when we recognize that there is no algorithm or eternal standards to which we can appeal to settle the relevant issues. If we accept Rorty's claim that all justification, whether of knowledge or moral choices, cannot hope to escape from history and only makes sense with reference to social practices, we are still faced with the critical task of determining which social practices are relevant, which ones ought to prevail, be modified, or abandoned. "Hammering this out" is not a matter of "mere" rhetoric or "arbitrary" decision, but requires argumentation.

One perspective for understanding the moral of Rorty's book is to see his work as an attempt to recover the notion of *phronesis* – the type of practical reasoning that Aristotle sketched for us which does not make any appeal to ultimate foundations, eternal standards, or algorithms. But Aristotle also sowed the seeds for the distrust that philosophers have of *phronesis* by contrasting it in the strongest possible way with the contemplative understanding of *noesis*. Rorty not only questions this contrast, but more significantly, he shows us that the more we understand what goes on in theoretical and scientific reasoning, the more we realize how closely it resembles the forms of reasoning and decision making exemplified by the person who exhibits *phronesis*. This is a major reversal or an inversion. For typically philosophers have taken *theoria* – or more accurately their images of what *theoria* is supposed to be like – to be the standard by which practical wisdom is to be judged. Once we make the turn Rorty advocates, once we realize that we are dealing with forms of discourse which differ from each other in degree and not in kind, once we realize that effective rationality is always a form

of *rational* persuasion which can never attain a definitive ahistorical closure, then the reflective task would seem to be to
clarify the different forms of *phronesis* and *rational* persuasion.

One might imagine Rorty replying that it is not his intention
to deny that there are genuine conflicts, problems created by
competing social practices, and uncertainties that demand
reflective understanding. These are all involved in the image of
philosophy as conversation that he wants to substitute for phil-
osphy as the inquiry into foundations. Rather his main point is
to challenge the presumption that philosophers have some
special knowledge or method which enables them to do this
better than anyone else. He also claims that a healthy historical
sense reveals that there have been times when theologians,
poets, scientists, and literary critics have performed this function better than professional philosophers. But I do not want to
dispute these claims or even Rorty's skepticism about the way
in which professional philosophy has become a marginal voice
in the conversation of mankind. I do want to argue that we can
give a very different twist to Rorty's critique of philosophy. We
can see it as a type of therapy that can liberate us from stale
metaphors and fundamental misconceptions about what philosophy can achieve. Despite many rearguard actions and misguided attempts to salvage traditional problems or to reformulate
them in new and sophisticated ways, we can see that there are
many signs of playing out the legacy of notions inherited from
the seventeenth century. Underneath the polemic between
various advocates of "objectivism" and "relativism," one can
detect that philosophers themselves are increasingly coming to
realize that there is something wrong with the entire framework
and the categorical distinctions that keep these debates alive.

The choice that confronts us is not one of opting for
philosophy as "kibitzing" or playing out a few more variations
on the same old tired themes. Rorty worries about and warns
against the temptation of philosophers to think that they must
come up with "constructive programs" which turn out to be
new self-deceptive apologies for foundational disciplines. He
himself is obsessed with the obsessions of philosophers. But he
has shown us that we can set aside these obsessions and need

not be tempted to answer unanswerable questions. But there are plenty of questions concerning justification, objectivity, the scope of disciplines, the proper way of distinguishing rational from irrational discussants, and *praxis* that are answerable and demand our attention – even when we concede that any answers are themselves subject to historical limitations. Rorty's book can be read as helping to bring about a turning in philosophy and in seeing how ideas which were once liberating have become intellectual strait-jackets. But once we make this turning, once we are liberated from the metaphors and pictures that have held us captive, once we set aside the anxieties about constraint and compulsion that have been so powerful in philosophy, then the scene of culture and the potential contribution of the voice of philosophy in the conversation of mankind becomes far more alive and dramatic.

2

What is the Difference that Makes a Difference? Gadamer, Habermas, and Rorty[1]

If we take the whole history of philosophy, the systems reduce themselves to a few main types which under all the technical verbiage in which the ingenious intellect of man envelopes them, are just so many visions, modes of feeling the whole push, and seeing the whole drift of life, forced on one by one's total character and experience, and on the whole *preferred* – there is no other truthful word – as one's best working attitude.[2]

There are many ways to characterize what we are talking about when we speak of modernity and postmodernity. But one description – as it pertains to philosophy – might go something like this. The "core problem" for philosophy in the modern world has been to resolve what Michael Dummett has called the "scandal" of philosophy – "the scandal caused by philosophy's lack of a systematic methodology." Characterizing this scandal, Dummett tells us that:[3]

it has been a constant preoccupation of philosophers to remedy that lack, and a repeated illusion that they had succeeded in doing so. Husserl believed passionately that he had at last held the key which would unlock every philosophical door, the disciples of Kant ascribed to him the achievement of devising a correct philosophical methodology: Spinoza believed that he was doing for philosophy what Euclid had done for geometry; and before him, Descartes supposed that he had uncovered the one and only proper philosophical method. I have mentioned only a few of the many examples of this illusion; for any outsider to philosophy far the safest bet would be that I am suffering from a similar illusion by making the same claim for Frege. To this I can offer only the banal reply which any prophet has to make to any skeptic: time will tell. HA HA HA

Dummett expresses a primary concern of modern philosophy that has persisted from Descartes until the present – to turn philosophy into a "rigorous science," to discover its proper object, its systematic methodology, to overcome the situation where philosophy appears to be the endless battleground among competing opinions (*doxai*) and finally becomes a legitimate form of knowledge (*episteme*). This search to discover some basic constraints is not only characteristic of philosophy but pervades the entire range of the cultural disciplines. But recently there has been another analysis of the "scandal" of philosophy – that the real scandal is that we are still taken in and mesmerized by the very conception of philosophy that Dummett embraces: where we presuppose that there is a "proper object" of philosophy; that there are philosophic problems which are to be solved once and for all; and that there is a "systematic methodology" for doing this. If we really want to overcome the scandal of philosophy, then what is needed is a form of philosophical therapy which will rid us of the illusion and the self-deception that philosophy is or can be such a foundational discipline. What characterizes so much of what is sometimes called post-modernity is a new playful spirit of negativity, deconstruction, suspicion, unmasking. Satire, ridicule, jokes and punning become the rhetorical devices for undermining "puritanical seriousness." This *esprit* pervades the writings of Rorty, Feyerabend, and Derrida. Where an earlier generation of philosophers like Sartre was telling us that the human predicament is one of unhappy consciousness with no possibility of overcoming it, it almost seems as if we are now being told that our condition is one of "absolute dialectical unrest" – which Hegel took to be the essence of skeptical self-consciousness.

Using an older positivist and emotivist terminology, we might say that those who take a "pro-attitude" toward this new phenomenon (one which bears a strong affinity with a domesticated Nietzsche) think of it as a liberating spirit which releases us from the tyranny of Western metaphysics – what Heidegger called "the onto-theo-logical constitution of metaphysics." And for those who have an "anti-attitude" toward this destruction and deconstruction, they think of it as opening the flood-gates to nihilism, irrationalism, subjectivism, and rampant relativism.

Frequently the opposing poles that I am sketching have been characterized by traditional binary oppositions: rationalism/irrationalism, objectivism/subjectivism; absolutism/relativism. But we are increasingly coming to realize that these traditional dichotomies obscure more than they illuminate, and that they gain their seductive power from an entire mode of thinking, acting, and feeling which itself is being called into question. There is an almost desperate attempt to break out of, and move beyond, the dichotomies that have characterized modern thought together with an enormous amount of confusion and uncertainty about what this even means.

It is against this background that I want to take a close look at *some* of the characteristic themes and emphases in the work of Gadamer, Habermas, and Rorty. What initially strikes us are the crucial and consequential differences among them – the hard and fast barriers that seem to separate them. At one extreme there is Habermas, who some may think of as the "last" great rationalist. Habermas has attempted to resolve the scandal of philosophy by showing us that the legacy of the philosophic tradition is redeemed in a new reconstructive science – a comprehensive theory of rationality that focuses on the centrality of communicative action and discourse, and which can serve as a ground for a critical theory of society. At the other extreme is Rorty, who mocks the very idea of such a "theory" and thinks that it is just another misguided variation of the discredited foundational project of modern philosophy.

Although Rorty appropriates the term "hermeneutics," he tells us "it is not the name for a discipline, nor for a method of achieving the sorts of results which epistemology failed to achieve, nor for a program of research. On the contrary, hermeneutics is an expression of the hope that the cultural space left by the demise of epistemology will not be filled – that our culture should become one in which the demand for constraint and confrontation is no longer felt."[4] From Gadamer's perspective this is a very strange sort of hermeneutics. For what Gadamer takes to be basic for philosophical hermeneutics is that it points the way to an "entirely different notion of knowledge and truth"[5] that is revealed and realized through *understanding*. So from Gadamer's perspective, Rorty's hermeneutics is mutilated or castrated, for it is a hermeneutics without the claim to knowledge and truth.

The thesis that I want to play out is that a closer look at what is going on here reveals that what at first appear to be dramatic and consequential differences begin to look more like differences of emphasis. I am not saying that the three of them are really saying the same thing, or that the differences that divide them are unimportant, but I will try to show how different these differences look once we start probing. I want to show this by focusing on the themes of *praxis*, practice, practical truth, and discourse as they appear in their thinking. Let me begin with Gadamer and then move on to Habermas and Rorty in order to show the interplay – the *Spiel* that takes place here.

The most intriguing and most central theme in Gadamer's understanding of philosophical hermeneutics is the fusion of hermeneutics and *praxis*. In the context of *Wahrheit und Methode* this becomes evident when Gadamer takes up the issue of "application" and argues for the relevance of Aristotle's *Ethics* in order to clarify "the rediscovery of the fundamental hermeneutic problem." Against an older tradition of hermeneutics that sought to divide it into three distinct subdisciplines: *subtilitas intelligendi* (understanding); *subtilitas explicandi* (interpretation); and *subtilitas applicandi* (application); Gadamer argues that these are three moments of the *single* process of understanding.[6] They are internally related so that all genuine understanding involves not only interpretation but also application. What Gadamer means is revealed through his own interpretation and appropriation of *phronesis*, which he carefully distinguishes from theoretical knowledge or *episteme* on the one hand, and technical skill or *techne*, on the other hand. *Phronesis* is a form of reasoning and practical knowledge where there is a distinctive type of mediation between the universal and the particular. It is not the application of Method or the subsumption of particulars under fixed determinate rules or universals. Furthermore, the distinctive feature of such practical knowledge is that it involves "the peculiar interlacing of being and knowledge, determination through one's own becoming, *Hexis*, recognition of the situational Good, and *Logos*."[7]

Gadamer claims that Aristotle's analysis of *phronesis* and the ethical phenomenon is a "kind of model of the problems of hermeneutics."[8] For as he tells us:[9]

> We, too, determined that application is neither subsequent nor a merely occasional part of the phenomenon of understanding, but codetermines it as a whole from the beginning. Here too application was not the relating of some pre-given universal to the particular situation. The interpreter dealing with a traditional text seeks to apply it to himself. But this does not mean that the text is given to him as something universal, that he understands it as such and only afterwards uses it for particular applications. Rather, the interpreter seeks no more than to understand this universal thing, the text, i.e. to understand what this piece of tradition says, what constitutes the meaning and importance of the text. In order to understand that, he must not seek to disregard himself and his particular hermeneutical situation. He must relate the text to his situation, if he wants to understand at all.

Most of the fundamental themes in philosophical hermeneutics are implicit in this passage, or can be related to it. Gadamer's major critique of nineteenth-century hermeneutics is that it neglected the *positive* role that forestructures, prejudgments, and prejudices play in *all* understanding. He claims that it was only with Heidegger that the positive enabling role of forestructures was fully appreciated, and this ontological insight requires a new understanding of the famous hermeneutical circle. This is the basis of Gadamer's *apologia* for prejudice against the

"Enlightenment's prejudice against prejudices." Prejudices which are constitutive of our being and our historicity are not only unfounded, negative, and blind. They can also be "justified" and *enabling*, they open us to experience (*Erfahrung*). We are always being shaped by effective history (*Wirkungsgeschichte*); consequently to understand is always to understand differently. Because all understanding involves a dialogical encounter between the text or the tradition that we seek to understand and our hermeneutical situation, we will always understand the "same thing" differently. We always understand from our situation and horizon, but what we seek to accomplish is to enlarge our horizon, to achieve a fusion of horizons (*Horizontverschmelzung*). Gadamer stresses that horizons – whose medium is language – are *not* self-enclosed; they are essentially open and fluid. Against subjectivist, relativist, and historicist misinterpretations of our hermeneutical situation, Gadamer stresses the need to situate our horizon within a larger horizon; to open ourselves to the claim to truth that works of art, texts, and tradition make upon us; to allow them to "speak to us." Gadamer tells us, "The best definition for hermeneutics is: to let what is alienated by the character of the written word or by the character of being distantiated by cultural or historical distances speak again."[10] All of this can be taken as a commentary on the meaning of our finitude and historicity. For there is no Archimedean point, no transcendental position, no theoretical perspective that lies outside our historicity. Consequently there can never be absolute knowledge, finality in understanding, or complete self-transparency of the knower. We always find ourselves in an open dialogical or conversational situation with the very tradition and history that is effectively shaping us.

If we closely examine Gadamer's writings since the publication of *Wahrheit und Methode*, we can discern a subtle but important shift that has taken place – a change of emphasis that marks a return to concerns of his earliest writings. For in *Wahrheit und Methode* Gadamer introduces *phronesis* and *praxis* in order to elucidate the character of philosophical hermeneutics. Ethics and politics are not thematic in the book. The interpretation of works of art, texts, and history is thematic. But since the publication of *Wahrheit und Methode* Gadamer has been increasingly concerned with moving in the other direction, with exploring the consequences of hermeneutics for *praxis*. He claims that "hermeneutic philosophy is the heir to the older tradition of practical philosophy," that the "chief task of philosophy is to justify this way of reason and to defend practical and political reason against the domination of technology based on science. That is the point of philosophical hermeneutics. It corrects the peculiar falsehood of modern consciousness; the idolatry of scientific method and the anonymous authority of the sciences and it vindicates again the noblest task of the citizen – decision-making according to one's own responsibility – instead of conceding that task to the expert."[11]

Gadamer, in the spirit of dialogical encounter that is so central to his thinking, has sought to learn from, and appropriate the "truth" from his critics and dialogical partners. Indeed, in his writings during the past twenty years, Gadamer begins to sound more and more like Habermas. Fundamental to both of them has been the categorical distinction between the technical and the practical (Habermas even acknowledges that in part it was Gadamer's work that made him sensitive to the importance and centrality of this distinction). Gadamer, like Habermas, has been critical of the deformation of *praxis*, where *praxis* is taken to be exclusively the application of science to technical tasks. Gadamer too tells us that "in modern technological society public opinion itself has in a new and really decisive way become the object of very complicated techniques – and this, I think, is the main problem facing our civilization."[12] The theme which is so central for Habermas – that there is a categorial distinction between purposive-rational action and communicative action, and that there are different types of rationalization processes corresponding to the different levels of action and rationality is echoed in Gadamer. There is in fact a latent *radical* strain – a supplement –in Gadamer's thinking which at times he fails to realize. This becomes evident when he tells us that "genuine solidarity, authentic community, should be realized,"[13] or when in answering the question "What is Practice?" he declares "practice is conducting oneself and acting in solidarity. Solidarity, however, is the decisive condition and basis of all social reason."[14] There are even passages in Gadamer that sound like the echoes of the older Frankfurt School. For example, he describes Hegel's legacy as follows:[15]

> The principle of freedom is unimpugnable and irrevocable. It is no longer possible for anyone still to affirm the unfreedom of humanity. The principle that all are free never again can be shaken. But does this mean that on account of this, history has come to an end? Are all human beings actually free? Has not history since then been a matter of just this, that the historical conduct of man has to translate the principle of freedom into reality? Obviously this points to the unending march of world history into the openness of its future tasks and gives no becalming assurance that everything is already in order.

I am fully aware of the nuances that separate Gadamer and Habermas even when they use the same expressions – "dialogue," "solidarity," and "freedom." But that is just the point that I want to make – that what at first appears to be so extreme and confrontational begins to look more like differences of emphasis. The fundamental thesis that I want to advance is that despite Gadamer's manifest (and real) conservative strain, his fear of the "dogmatism" and the potential "terror" of what he calls "planning reason," there is a powerful latent radical strain in his thinking that is constantly pulling us in a different direction. Gadamer's entire project of philosophical hermeneutics can be read as an attempt to recover what he takes to be the deepest and most pervasive theme in Western philosophy and culture – that the quintessence of our being is to *be dialogical*. This is not just the "mode of being" of the "few," but is a real potential of every person – a potential that ought to be actualized. It is this dialogical character of what we truly are that is deformed and threatened by modern technological society. A cardinal principle of Gadamer's hermeneutics is that when we seek to understand a text, the vital question is what the text *says*, its meaning. This meaning is not to be confused or identified with the psychological intentions of the author. If we apply this principle to Gadamer's own texts, then we detect a tension or conflict between what the texts "mean" and what he has "intended." This tension is even exhibited in Gadamer's self-conscious integration of Aristotelian, Platonic, and Hegelian motifs. The appeal to *phronesis* as a model of practical wisdom has traditionally had elitist connotations from the time of Aristotle through Burke right up to the contemporary vogue of neo-Aristotelianism. Aristotle himself never thought of *phronesis* as an "intellectual virtue" that could be ascribed to *all* human beings; but only to the few, only to those rare and gifted individuals (men) who had been properly educated. Gadamer softens this elitist aura of *phronesis* by blending it with his understanding of dialogue and conversation which he appropriates from Plato. When this is integrated with the Hegelian "truth" – "the principle that *all* are free never again can be shaken" – then the implicit "radicalization" of *phronesis* becomes evident. It is Gadamer who tells us that "the point of philosophical hermeneutics" is to vindicate "the noblest task of the citizen – decision-making according to one's own responsibility."[16]

There is an implicit *telos* here, not in the sense of what *will* work itself out in the course of history, but rather in the sense of what *ought* to be realized. So if we take the theme of application or appropriation to our historical situation concretely, then this sets a task for us which can guide our practical lives, i.e., to attempt to realize that type of society in which the *idea* of open authentic dialogue and conversation becomes a concrete reality in which *all* have the *real* opportunity to participate. Considering the fragility of the conditions required for such dialogue, it would be a gross perversion of Gadamer's phenomenological insight to think that such an idea can serve as an *organizational* principle of society. Nevertheless, the very idea of such a dialogical rationality is a regulative ideal that can and ought to orient our *praxis*.

This is why I think that if we want to get at the important differences that still separate Gadamer and Habermas, it is more important to focus on the meaning and role of *truth* and *criticism* for each of them, rather than on the slogan: "hermeneutics versus critique of ideology." But even here the differences turn out to be different from what at first seems so apparent. Consider the concept of truth which is not only the most central theme in Gadamer's work, but also the most elusive. At first it looks as if what Gadamer means by "truth" is a blending of motifs that he has appropriated from Hegel and Heidegger. Like them, Gadamer rejects and criticizes the dominant conception of truth as *adequatio intellectus et rei* – at least when it comes to understanding the type of truth that pertains to hermeneutical understanding. But Gadamer also carefully distances himself from both Hegel and Heidegger. He categorically rejects what Hegel took to be the ground of his own understanding of truth, that the "true is the whole," which is realized in *Wissenschaft*. The following passage is typical of Gadamer's distancing himself from Hegel.[17]

> For Hegel it is necessary, of course, that the movement of consciousness, experience, should lead to a self-knowledge that no longer has anything different or alien to itself. For him the perfection of experience is "science," the certainty of itself in knowledge. Hence his criterion of experience is that of self-knowledge. That is why the dialectic of experience must end with the overcoming of all experience, i.e., in the complete identity of consciousness and object. We can now understand why Hegel's application to history, insofar as he saw it as part of the absolute self-consciousness of philosophy, does not do justice to the hermeneutical consciousness. The nature of experience is conceived in terms of that which goes beyond it; for experience itself can never be science. It is in absolute antithesis to knowledge and to that kind of instruction that follows from general theoretical or technical knowledge. The truth of experience always contains an orientation towards new experience. . . . The dialectic of experience has its own fulfillment not in definitive knowledge, but in that openness to experience that is encouraged by experience itself.

It is also evident that Gadamer draws back from Heidegger's "radical" thinking about the meaning of *aletheia*. In his published work, Gadamer is usually respectful and cautious in his comments on Heidegger. But occasionally he indicates his strong disagreements with Heidegger. See the Foreword to the second

edition of *Truth and Method*.[18] But what is even more important
and revealing is that when Gadamer appeals to the concept
of truth to justify what he has to say about the relevance of
Aristotle, *phronesis*, and the tradition of practical philosophy to
our hermeneutical situation, he is implicitly appealing to a concept of truth which (pragmatically speaking) comes down to
what can be *argumentatively validated by a community of interpreters
who open themselves to tradition.*

If we focus on the meaning of "criticism" for Gadamer, he
tells us "it is a grave misunderstanding to assume that the emphasis on tradition which enters all understanding implies an
uncritical acceptance of tradition and sociopolitical conser-
vatism. . . . In truth the confrontation of our historic tradition
is always a critical challenge to this tradition. . . . Every experience is such a confrontation."[19] But however sympathetic one
may be with Gadamer's critique of objectivism, foundationalism, and the search for an Archimedean point that lies outside our historicity, there is a question that he never adequately
answers for us. All criticism presupposes some principles,
standards, or criteria of criticism, no matter how open, tentative, and historical these may be. Tradition itself is not a
seamless whole, and what is most characteristic of *our* hermeneutical situation is that there are *conflicting* traditions making
conflicting claims upon us. We need to gain some clarity about
what are and what ought to be the standards for "a critical
challenge" to tradition. It may be true, but it certainly is not
sufficient to tell us that there are no fixed rules or determinate
universals that can serve as standards for criticism. If reason is
"social reason" – or is genuinely intersubjective – then we need
to elucidate the intersubjective principles that can guide our individual criticisms and decisions. Furthermore, to insist, as
Gadamer himself does, that the principles, laws, *nomoi* are
themselves "handed down" to us from tradition and require
concrete application does not help us to resolve questions concerning the *conflict* of these *nomoi*, or questions that arise when
traditional *nomoi* no longer seem to "bind" us.[20]

The perspective that I think is more illuminating for understanding the differences that make a difference between

Gadamer and Habermas is one which emphasizes how much they share in common in the "application" theme. Already, in Habermas's initial review of *Wahrheit und Methode*, he declared, "I find Gadamer's real achievement in the demonstration that hermeneutic understanding is linked with transcendental necessity to the articulation of an action orienting self-understanding." [21] It is instructive to see how this is worked out and transformed in Habermas's own attempt to develop a comprehensive theory of communicative action and rationality. For Habermas, no less than Gadamer, we cannot escape from our own horizon in seeking to understand what appears to be alien to us. This has crucial significance for the entire theory of rationality, for Habermas too argues that it is an illusion to think that we can assume the position of disinterested observers and theoreticians when it comes to understanding other forms of life and what purport to be other standards of rationality. One never escapes the situation of taking an *evaluative* stance toward the validity claims made by others. If we want to "describe" other forms of life, or earlier stages of our social development, then one can only do this by adopting a "performative" attitude of one who *participates* in a process of mutual understanding.

It is important to distinguish different roles or types of evaluation in this context. Habermas's main point is that "classifying" or "describing" speech acts (whether such speech acts are made in our own or an alien language) *presuppose* that we understand the types of validity claim that they make. An interpreter must have the ability to make clear to himself or herself the implicit reasons that move participants to take the positions that they do take. In order to *understand* an expression, the interpreter must bring to mind the reasons with which the actor would under suitable circumstances defend its validity. Consequently the interpreter is drawn into the process of assessing validity claims. But this process of determining that a validity claim has been made is not *yet* to make an evaluative judgment about the soundness of the validity claim. Habermas's point can be illustrated by appealing to the now famous example of Zande witchcraft. We could not even begin to understand

Zande witchcraft unless we had the ability to discriminate what the Azande consider to be reasons for acting in one way or another. To do this requires a *preunderstanding* on our part of what it means to make a validity claim. This is the sense in which describing or understanding the *meaning* of what the Azande are doing requires *assessing* validity claims. But it is a different (although related question) to evaluate whether the reasons given by the Azande are good or bad reasons, and even here we need to make an important distinction. For understanding the practice of Zande witchcraft requires that we can discriminate what the Azande *themselves* consider good or bad reasons for acting. (Presumably the Azande themselves can make *mistakes*.) This judgment can also be distinguished from a judgment whether (and in what sense) the *types* of reasons that the Azande give are adequate. Habermas is, of course, aware of the ever present danger of ethnocentricism, of unreflectively imposing alien standards of judgment and thereby missing the *point* or *meaning* of a practice. But it is an illusion to think that we can escape from ethnocentricism by thinking that we can *describe* alien linguistic practices without assessing the validity claims that are implicitly made in speech acts.[22]

The theme of our historicity in which we are always applying or appropriating what we seek to understand to our historical situation is no less fundamental for Habermas than it is for Gadamer. But for Habermas, unlike Gadamer, the primary problem becomes how can we reconcile this performative participation with the type of intersubjective understanding that makes the claim to objectivity. When Habermas seeks to develop a comprehensive theory of communicative action, a universal pragmatics, he is *not* claiming that we do this *sub specie aeternitatus*, or that we assume the position of an "infinite intellect." Rather he is claiming that from within the horizon of our hermeneutical situation, we can seek to elucidate the "unavoidable" conditions and principles of communicative action, discourse, and rationality. We aspire to universality recognizing that any such claim is clearly fallible. If one were to translate Habermas's project into Gadamerian terms, it might be put like this: Gadamer, you yourself have argued that all understanding involves application, and furthermore that our hermeneutical horizon is limited but not closed. Indeed you emphasize the very openness of language that is the condition for all understanding. So the question becomes, what is it about the linguistic medium within which we participate that allows for such appropriation and understanding? How are we to account for the fact that we can in principle always understand that which strikes us as alien and strange? What is it about the very character of language and rationality that enables us to grasp the possibility of the type of dialogue, conversation, and questioning that you yourself have so penetratingly elucidated?

Now it might seem as if what I am trying to show is that if we press Gadamer's claims and insights we are led to the very concerns that are central for Habermas. I do think this is true, but it needs to be carefully qualified because it can suggest a misleading asymmetry whereby an "immanent critique" of Gadamer inevitably leads to Habermas's project. But I also think that such a critique can be *reversed*, that we can use Gadamer to highlight some of the latent tensions in Habermas's project. But before turning to what I take to be internal conflicts within Habermas, let me try to pin down the way in which the differences between Habermas and Gadamer now appear. Habermas can be interpreted as highlighting difficulties and lacunae in what Gadamer has accomplished – difficulties concerning the question of truth, especially as it pertains to practical discourse; and difficulties concerning the practice of criticism, whether it be the criticism of the traditions that have formed us or the criticism of present society. Furthermore, Habermas can be used to highlight some of the difficulties in the very appeal to *phronesis*. For Gadamer himself has stressed that *phronesis* involves a mediation and codetermination of the universal and the particular. In the context of ethical and political action, by the "universal" Gadamer means those principles, norms, and laws that are funded in the life of a community and orient our particular decisions and actions. Gadamer stresses how all such principles and laws require judgment and *phronesis* for their concrete application.

This makes good sense when there are shared *nomoi* that inform the life of a community. But what happens when there is a breakdown of such principles, when they no longer seem to have any normative power, when there are deep and apparently irreconcilable conflicts about such principles, or when questions are raised about the very norms and principles that ought to guide our *praxis*? What type of discourse is appropriate when we question the "universal" element – the *nomoi* – that is essential for the practice of *phronesis*? These are the issues that Habermas pursues, and they are not just Habermas's questions but ones which Gadamer raises for us.

But now let me turn directly to Habermas and explore how a hermeneutical perspective can sharpen our perception of the tensions that stand at the heart of his thinking. In this context, I want to discuss the very *idea* of a theory of communicative action. What kind of theory or intellectual endeavor is it, and how is it to be justified or warranted? Habermas speaks with "two voices" which might be called the "pragmatic" and the "transcendental." Alternatively, I can clarify what I mean by employing a distinction that Charles Taylor makes in his book on Hegel between "strict dialectics" and "interpretative dialectics". Taylor distinguishes two ways in which a dialectical argument can command our assent. "There are strict dialectics, whose starting point is or can reasonably claim to be undeniable. And, then there are interpretative or hermeneutical dialectics, which convince us by the overall plausibility of the interpretation they give."[23] This is a most un-Hegelian type of distinction because Hegel's *claim* to truth, system, and *Wissenschaft* depends ultimately on the validity of "strict dialectics." Yet I agree with Taylor that Hegel's most valuable and enduring contribution is what he revealed through interpretative or hermeneutical dialectics. Precisely how is this distinction relevant to Habermas?

At times, especially during the period when Habermas was writing *Erkenntnis und Interesse*, he slips into the language of "strict dialectics" or "strict transcendental argument." This is apparent in the original discrimination of the three "quasi-transcendental" cognitive interests, and is also evident in his earlier attempts to argue that there are four types of validity claim implicit in communicative action. Habermas's constant use of "necessity," what "must be presupposed," what is "unavoidable," easily lead one to think that he is advancing a transcendental argument in the tradition of Kant, even when he stresses his differences with Kant. But in the years since the publication of *Erkenntnis und Interesse*, Habermas has qualified his project to disassociate himself from this *strong* transcendental strain – and with good reason. Not only have there been powerful objections pressed against the possibility of transcendental arguments or strict dialectics, Habermas has seen more clearly that a theory of communicative action is not intended to be a transcendental apriori theory. In stating his reasons for abandoning the expression "transcendental," Habermas tells us that "adopting the expression *transcendental* could conceal the break with the apriorism that has been made in the meantime. Kant had to separate empirical from transcendental analysis sharply."[24] It is just this dichotomy that a reconstructive theory of communicative action is intended to *overcome*. This is why Habermas now prefers to speak about the logic of reconstruction or reconstructive analysis, and to argue that *within* the domain of scientific theories we must distinguish between empirical-analytic theories and reconstructive theories – the latter type illustrated by the work of Chomsky, Piaget, and Kolhberg. A theory of communicative action is intended to be a *scientific* reconstructive theory of this type. There is still a crucial ambiguity here that needs to be resolved. Even if we accept this distinction between empirical-analytic and reconstructive analyses, how are we to understand this distinction? Habermas emphasizes – and this is vital for his entire project – that the distinction is one of alternative research strategies within the domain of scientific knowledge. Questions concerning empirical evidence, confirmation, and falsification (when properly formulated) are just as central for validating reconstructive hypotheses and theories as they are for empirical-analytic disciplines. If we turn to the critical literature concerning those reconstructive disciplines that Habermas takes to be paradigmatic, we find extensive discussion of whether the empirical

and experimental evidence does or does not support the hypotheses advanced by Chomsky, Piaget, and Kohlberg. From a
methodological perspective it is still an open issue whether in
the long run reconstructive strategies or empirical-analytical
strategies will prove scientifically more fruitful. I agree with
Habermas that there are no apriori or conceptual reasons that
are sufficient to rule out the viability of scientific reconstructive
analyses. But there are also no apriori reasons for ruling out the
possibility that such analyses might be replaced or displaced by
new sophisticated empirical-analytic approaches. The important point here is that insofar as we are concerned with advancing scientific knowledge, it is methodologically prudent to be
open to different types of research strategy. Habermas can
draw support from the post-empiricist philosophy of science
–that it is important to keep ourselves open to alternative
research programs or traditions, especially in the early stages of
the development of a new research program. I am stressing
what Habermas himself emphasizes when he defends the claim
that a theory of communicative action, or a universal
pragmatics is a *scientific* theory, one in which "the distinction
drawing on apriori knowledge and a posteriori knowledge
becomes blurred."[25] But, when we turn our attention to the
details of the theory of communicative action, and in particular
to some of the strong claims that Habermas makes, the scientific status of such a theory becomes dubious and questionable.
Consider some of the key claims that Habermas makes about
practical truth and normative validity. The idea of practical
truth is intended to be the analogue to the idea of theoretical
truth; and both sorts of truth can be redeemed and warranted
through appropriate forms of substantive argumentation.
When questions concerning the appropriateness and legitimacy
of claims to universal normative validity are raised, no matter
how these questions and potential conflicts are resolved, the
participants are unavoidably committed to the idea that such
claims can be resolved by argumentative discourse. However
sympathetic one may be to this as a regulative ideal which
ought to be approximated, it is not clear in what sense this is an
"unavoidable" or "necessary" presupposition that is somehow

grounded in the very nature of intersubjectivity. Certainly someone who denies it is not involved in a logical contradiction, nor is it clear in what sense, if any, there is an "existential" or "pragmatic" contradiction.

Sometimes it seems as if what Habermas is doing is surreptitiously defining "practical discourse" in such a manner that while one can always opt out of such discourse, once we commit ourselves to it then we are already committed to the discursive redemption of normative validity claims. But Habermas has not established that such a commitment is "built into" the very nature of practical discourse. It is not helpful to say, that however counterfactual the ideal speech situation may be, it is *anticipated* and *presupposed* in every appropriate speech act. There is, of course, nothing objectionable about the appeal to counterfactuals in scientific theories; establishing them is just as central to empirical-analytic sciences as it is to reconstructive sciences. But there is something very peculiar about Habermas's counterfactual claim; for it is not at all clear what type of scientific evidence is relevant for supporting or refuting such a claim. In this context the Popperian demand for refutability or falsifiability is perfectly appropriate. If we are dealing with a scientific theory, one wants to know what could possibly count as a falsification or a refutation of the theory. What evidence would be relevant to refute the counterfactual claim that despite all signs to the contrary, every speaker who engages in communicative action is committed to the presupposition of the discursive redemption of normative validity claims?

One can also criticize Habermas from the opposite point of view. If a universal pragmatics is intended to be a genuine scientific theory which is hypothetical, fallible, and refutable, then what would be the consequences – especially concerning the redemption of universal claims of normative validity, practical truth, and practical discourse – if it turned out to be the case that such a theory is refuted or falsified? Does this mean that the issue of the type of communicative ethics that Habermas advocates and the decisionism that he opposes is a *scientific* issue to be decided by the success of rival research programs? Habermas gets himself into these and related *aporias* the more he insists on the scientific status of a theory of communicative action. From Rorty's perspective it looks as if Habermas is guilty of the temptation that Rorty so brilliantly exposes in another context – to come up with a "successor discipline" to traditional epistemology which claims to do better what epistemology failed to accomplish.[26]

I have suggested that there is an alternative reading of Habermas when I referred to his pragmatic voice and to interpretative dialectics (which are to be contrasted with his transcendental voice and to strict dialectics). What is fascinating and confusing about Habermas are the ways in which these two voices are superimposed on each other. To explain what I mean about this other voice in Habermas – this other way of reading him – let me cite a passage from Thomas McCarthy's judicious study of Habermas. He opens his study by telling us that:[27]

> his contributions to philosophy and psychology, political science and sociology, the history of ideas and social theory are distinguished not only by their scope but by the unity of perspective that informs them. This unity derives from a vision of mankind, our history and our prospects, that is rooted in the tradition of German thought from Kant to Marx, a vision that draws its power as much from the moral-political intention that animates it as from the systematic form in which it is articulated.

When McCarthy speaks of a vision that draws its power from "the moral-political intention that animates it," he comes very close to what William James means by vision in the passage that I cited at the beginning of this essay. The reading of Habermas that I am suggesting is one that emphasizes this aspect of his thinking, that sees his work *not* as another (failed) attempt of strict dialectics, transcendental argument, or even as proposing a rival scientific theory and research program. Rather, it is a perspective that emphasizes that what he is *really doing* is interpretative dialectics which seeks to command our assent "by the overall plausibility of the interpretation that they give." Whether we focus on Habermas's early reflections on the relation of theory and *praxis*, his delineation of the three primary cognitive interests, his probing of the question of legitimacy, or his most recent attempts to elaborate a reconstruction of historical materialism and a theory of communicative action, these analyses can be viewed as stages in the systematic articulation and defense of "a vision of mankind, our history and our prospects." For the interpretations that Habermas develops in each of these different but interrelated problematics is animated by the same "moral-political intention" – to show us that there is a *telos* immanent in the forms of life that have shaped us and the forms of communication in which we participate. This is not to be understood as a *telos* which represents the march of world history, one which must and will be realized, but rather as a "gentle but obstinate, a never silent although seldom redeemed claim to reason, a claim that must be recognized de facto whenever and wherever there is to be consensual action."[28]

To argue, as I have been doing, for a reading of Habermas that stresses his pragmatic voice and his practice of interpretative dialectics is not *yet* to make a judgment about how plausible his interpretations and narratives really are. I do not think there is any wholesale way of doing this. For this requires that we actually work through the several interrelated problematics and *show* precisely what are the strengths and weaknesses of his interpretations. Here too there is an important lesson to be learnt from Gadamer. It is all too frequently assumed that if we cannot come up with universal fixed criteria to measure the plausibility of competing interpretations, then this means that we have no *rational* basis for distinguishing better and worse, more plausible or less plausible interpretations – whether these be interpretations of texts, actions, or historical epochs. One does not have to neglect the tangled problems that arise when confronted with evaluating conflicting or competing interpretations to appreciate that in concrete cases we can and do make comparative judgments, and seek to support them with *arguments* and the appeal to *good reasons*.[29]

The reading of Habermas that I am advocating can be stated in a slightly different manner. Returning to Gadamer, we can see how he is always pulling us back and reminding us of the inescapability of understanding and interpretation from our historical and hermeneutical horizon. We know, of course, that there are always dangers in doing this; we can be guilty of ethnocentricism, of subtly rewriting history from a Whiggish perspective, of being insufficiently self-critical and reflective about "our standards of rationality." But as Hegel reminds us, sometimes we need to be mistrustful of the very fear of falling into error. For a typical reaction to this fear of falling into error because we are always understanding from the perspective of our hermeneutical horizon is to imagine that we can assume the position of an "infinite intellect"[30] or the type of disinterested transcendental point of view that deceives itself into thinking that it is "outside" of history. Both Gadamer and Habermas see through the speciousness of these flights from our historical situation. Both, although in different ways, have argued that we can take our historical situation and the practices that constitute it seriously, and at the same time we can develop a critical perspective on it that is at once informed by an understanding of our history and is oriented to an open projective future. Both reject the thesis that Popper calls "The Myth of the Framework" – that we are prisoners caught in the framework of "our theories; our expectations; our past experiences; our language" where there is *no* possibility of overcoming these limitations.[31] But this commonness between Gadamer and Habermas points to a double irony. For I am claiming that we can employ Gadamer's analysis of what constitutes hermeneutical understanding, which includes the moments of interpretation and application, to get a clearer grasp of what Habermas is actually *doing* (as distinguished from what he sometimes says he is doing); and I am also suggesting – although I cannot adequately substantiate it here – that Habermas elaborates a more comprehensive, plausible, and powerful interpretation of *our* historical hermeneutical situation than does Gadamer. There is even a further twist here. For in the interpretation of Gadamer that I have developed, we see that there is a latent radical thrust or *telos* in his thinking which points to the demand for the type of society in which every citizen has the opportunity to engage in the open dialogue, conversation, and questioning that he takes to be constitutive of what we are. Gadamer's own analysis and interpretation of modern society, and the main problems confronting it, can be used to *support* the vision of a society in which there is a practical attempt to overcome the forms of systematically distorted communication that block authentic dialogue. Shortly I will try to show how we can also use Rorty to clarify and support the readings of Habermas and Gadamer that I have been adumbrating. But once again, what *initially* strikes us are the sharp differences between Rorty, on the one hand, and Habermas and Gadamer, on the other.

Rorty has dropped enough hints in his published writings to know how he would "go after" both Habermas and Gadamer. There is a dazzling brilliance in Rorty's deconstructions of what he takes to be the misguided pretentions of philosophical discourse. He is certainly sympathetic with Habermas's plea for undistorted communication, but scornful of what happens when "Habermas goes transcendental and offers principles."[32] By constantly leading us to think that what we really need is some sort of *theory* in order to *ground* communication and conversation, Habermas is making the same sorts of mistakes that philosophers have always made in their desperate (and failed) attempts to *discover* real constraints and foundations. Habermas is a victim of the illusion which has haunted modern thinkers – that they must dignify the contingent social practices which have been hammered out in the course of history with something that pretends to be more solid and substantial. I suspect that he might even accuse Habermas of being guilty of the "mistake" that Habermas ascribes to so many other thinkers – of being caught in a "scientistic misunderstanding" of what he is doing. Underlying Habermas's "new" scientific theory of communicative action is nothing more and nothing less than a "moral-political vision." What is perhaps even more misguided from Rorty's perspective is that the constant emphasis in Habermas on *consensus* and the expectation of the redemption of validity claims through argumentation is really retrogressive. When this is unmasked, it turns out to be only another version of what has been the primary bias of modern epistemology, i.e., the assumption that "all contributions to a given discourse are commensurable." "Hermeneutics," as Rorty uses this polemical expression, is "largely a struggle against this assumption."[33] If Rorty is right about what characterizes the Conversation of the West, then we should not fool ourselves into thinking that there are any apriori limitations or any hidden constraints on the invention of new vocabularies and new forms of abnormal discourse. It is the very appeal to something like the idea of a rational consensus that has always been used to block, stifle, or rule out "revolutionary" turns in the conversation. To speak of the argumentative redemption of validity claims through the appropriate level of discourse is either potentially stifling or sheer bluff. It *either* becomes a glorification and reification of what are our *existing* contingent social practices and forms of life *or* a pious and vacuous generality. We do not have the slightest idea – before the fact – of what "rules" of argumentation (if any) will be applicable to new abnormal modes of discourse. Habermas fails to realize that he is just giving expression to the old positivist hope that we can come up with determinate rules which will once and for all tell us (in principle) what will count as legitimate and illegitimate (or meaningless) discourse.

Rorty's major complaint against Habermas can be put in still another way which becomes prominent in Rorty's *apologia* for a neo-pragmatism (shaped more by his reading of James and Dewey than Peirce and Mead). The heart of this neo-pragmatism is a "defense" of the Socratic virtues – "willingness to talk, to listen to the people, to weigh the consequences of our actions upon other people."[34] The point for Rorty is that these "are *simply* moral virtues," and there is no metaphysical or epistemological guarantee of success. "*We do not even know what 'success' would mean except simply continuance*" of the conversation which is "merely *our* project, the European intellectual's form of life."[35] What Nietzsche has helped us to see is that there is no "metaphysical comfort" to be found that *grounds* or secures these moral virtues – and we must resist the temptation to find such comfort. The anti-pragmatist (and in this respect

Habermas would be seen as an anti-pragmatist) thinks that the question of "loyalty to our fellow human beings presupposes that there is something permanent and unhistorical which explains *why* we should continue to converse in the manner of Socrates, something which guarantees convergence to agreement."[36] As Rorty tells us, "For the traditional, Platonic or Kantian, philosopher [and he would include Habermas in this tradition] the possibility of *grounding* the European form of life – of showing it to be more than European, more than a contingent human project – seems to be the central task of philosophy [or a new reconstructive science of communicative action]."[37] And, while Rorty concedes that he has not presented an "argument" for pragmatism or answered the deep criticism that "the Socratic virtues cannot, as a practical matter, be defended save by Platonic means, that without some sort of metaphysical comfort nobody will be able *not* to sin against Socrates,"[38] he leaves little doubt that no one from Plato on has even come close to "succeeding" in *grounding* these virtues. So what has been Habermas's main preoccupation ever since the publication of *Erkenntnis und Interesse* (and seems to be his project from his earliest writings) – to show that we can "ground" critical theory – is only another version of the old Platonic urge to "escape from conversation to something atemporal which lies in the background of all possible conversations."[39]

Rorty is no less devastating in his critique of Gadamer. He would find all the talk of "an entirely different notion of truth and knowledge" that is revealed by hermeneutic understanding a form of mystification. Despite Gadamer's own incisive critiques of epistemology and the Cartesian legacy which he claims has infected and distorted even nineteenth-century hermeneutics, Gadamer himself is unwittingly a victim of the Cartesian persuasion that he is reacting against. For Gadamer is constantly playing on the idea that it is *really* philosophical hermeneutics and not epistemology, Method, or science that can achieve what philosophy has always promised us – some profound access to "truth" that is not available to us by the limited and normal methods of science. Gadamer fits right into the tradition of metaphysical idealism whose principal legacy is "the ability to literary culture to stand apart from science, to assert its spiritual superiority to science, to claim to embody what is most important for human beings."[40] The trouble with Gadamer is that he is only a "half-hearted pragmatist" – what Rorty calls a "weak textualist."[41]

> The weak textualist – the decoder – is just one more victim of realism, of the metaphysics of "presence." He thinks that if he stays within the boundaries of a text, takes it apart, and shows how it works, then we will have "escaped the sovereignty of the signifier," broken with the myth of language as a mirror of reality, and so on. But in fact he is just doing his best to imitate science – he wants a *method* of criticism, and he wants everybody to agree he has cracked the code.

Despite Gadamer's claim that the essential problem of philosophical hermeneutics is not a problem of method at all, and despite Gadamer's claim that to understand and to interpret is always to understand and interpret *differently*, he too wants the "comforts of consensus" – even if it is only the comforts of the consensus of the community of interpreters within the same historical horizon who have the proper *Bildung*.

Rorty, too, would "go after" the central and all important distinction in Gadamer between Method and Truth. For again, despite Gadamer's claims that he never intended to play off Method *against* Truth, and that he wants to acknowledge the legitimacy of science when it is limited to its proper domain, nevertheless the very dichotomy of Method and Truth is suspect. For Rorty would claim that when we take a close look at what goes on in science and what goes on in hermeneutic understanding we discover that the distinction here is only a pragmatic distinction of differences of degree (or a difference in what is contingently taken to be normal and abnormal discourse). Science itself is more like hermeneutical understanding than Gadamer realizes, and disputes about rival hermeneutical interpretations are more like "Method" than Gadamer acknowledges.

I have sought to put Rorty's critique of Gadamer and Habermas in the strongest and most vivid way because here we really *seem* to have some differences that really make a difference. Rorty's "strong" criticisms would no doubt be matched by an equally "strong" rebuttal. Both Gadamer and Habermas would see Rorty as expressing a new sophisticated version of a very old form of relativism – the type of relativism that *each* has sought to expose and defeat. And, if they wanted to get really nasty, they might accuse Rorty of failing to realize the unintended consequences of what he is saying. They might draw on their own respective appropriations of Hegel to accuse Rorty of failing to see how easily a playful relativism which seems so innocent in "civilized" discourse turns into its opposite in the practical realm – how the restless *esprit* of unrestrained dialectical negativity becomes a potent force for unrestrained destruction. Rorty's "techniques" of deconstruction can be turned against himself. For when decoded, his celebration of relativism is perhaps more honestly revealed by Feyerabend when he tells us:[42]

> Reason is no longer an agency that directs other traditions, it is a tradition in its own right with as much (or as little) claim to the centre of the stage as any other tradition. Being a tradition it is neither good nor bad, it simply is. The same applies to all traditions – they are neither good nor bad, they simply are. They become good or bad (rational/irrational; pious/impious; advanced/"primitive"; humanitarian/vicious; etc.) only when looked at from the point of view of some other tradition. "Objectively" there is not much to choose between anti-semitism and humanitarianism. But racism will appear vicious to a humanitarian while humanitarianism will appear vapid to a racist. *Relativism* (in the old simple sense of Protagoras) gives an adequate account of the situation which thus emerges.

In the conflict between Rorty on the one hand, and Gadamer and Habermas on the other, we really seem to have differences that make a difference. There appears to be no way of reducing the gap between what Rorty is telling us and what Gadamer and Habermas are saying. If Rorty is right, then Gadamer and Habermas must both be wrong. One might even be inclined to say that both Gadamer and Habermas are representatives of modernity – at least insofar as they believe that philosophy (when properly reconstructed) still holds out the promise of *knowledge* and *truth*, even when all the necessary concessions are made to the realization of human finitude, fallibility, openness, and historicity; while Rorty is a post-modern thinker who seeks to root out the last buried vestiges of the "metaphysics of presence. " Or using Rorty's terminology, we might say that both Habermas and Gadamer are "weak textualists" while Rorty sides with the "strong textualists" who try to live without "metaphysical comfort." The strong textualist "recognizes what Nietzsche and James recognized, that the idea of *method* presupposes that a *privileged vocabulary*, the vocabulary which gets to the essence of the object, the one which expresses the properties which it has in itself opposed to those which we read into it. Nietzsche and James said that the notion of such a vocabulary was a myth – that even in science, not to mention philosophy, we simply cast around for a vocabulary which lets us get what we want."[43] But, is this yet the "last word"? Are we simply faced with an irreconcilable and incommensurable opposition? I think not, and I now will show that when we probe what Rorty is saying, we will see once again how different the differences begin to look.

In order to decode what Rorty is saying, let me introduce a rough but important distinction between Rorty's metacritique or therapeutic analysis of philosophy and his rhetorical *apologia* for pragmatism. Thus far I have been stressing Rorty's metacritique of the projects of both Gadamer and Habermas. This type of metacritique has become something of an obsession in Rorty. But there is also a subtext, something of what Derrida calls a "supplement" in his work. Rorty has attempted to block any suggestion that he is laying the foundations for a new type of philosophy, a new constructive program. His deliberate use of such vague distinctions as the normal and abnormal, the familiar and unfamiliar, or even systematic and edifying philosophy are rhetorical devices employed to cure us of the expectation or belief that philosophy must be "constructive." Still one keeps asking where does Rorty really stand? What is the basis for his metacritique? Is he an "epistemological behaviorist," a "holist," or a "pragmatist"? Are not these really substantive philosophic positions that need to be defended? Rorty is acutely aware that these are the types of questions that will be raised about his project. Every time we think we can really pin him down, he nimbly dances to another place.

"Epistemological behaviorism" and "holism" are not to be taken as names of new philosophic "positions," but rather as expressions that are intended to call epistemology and the project of modern philosophy into question.[44] He even tells us that "pragmatism is, to speak, oxymoronically post-philosophical philosophy,"[45] One of the deepest aspirations of thinkers since Hegel – including Kierkegaard, Nietzsche, Marx, Freud, Heidegger, Wittgenstein, Foucault, and Derrida has been to "end" philosophy (and the meaning of the end of philosophy has been played out in its multifarious variations). Rorty places himself in this tradition with a further ironical twist about the meaning of the "end of philosophy".[46] This also helps to make sense of what can be called his crypto-positivism which he ironically employs for rhetorical shock value. This becomes manifest when Rorty, for example, tells us "physicalism is probably right in saying that we shall someday be able, 'in principle,' to predict every movement of a person's body (including those of his larynx and his writing hand) by reference to microstructures within his body,"[47] or when he says about Hegel that "under cover of Kant's invention, a new superscience called 'philosophy,' Hegel invented a literary genre which lacked any trace of argumentation. . . ."[48] After all, these are just the claims that positivists have always made. I do not want to suggest that Rorty does not mean what he is saying. He means *precisely* what he is saying, but the irony becomes clear when we realize that whereas the positivists made the sorts of claims against a background where the "tough-minded" natural scientist is taken to be the cultural hero of our time, Rorty is sympathetic with those strong textualists who, without denigrating science, seek to replace the scientist with the poet and the literary critic as the new cultural heroes. In short, Rorty wants to show us how little is said when, to use the positivist turn of phrase, we extract the "cognitive content" of what the positivist is saying. Science is nothing more nor less than a very effective vocabulary for coping, one which is likely to win out over philosophy or any other cultural discipline when it comes to matters of *prediction* or following relatively clear patterns of argumentation. The point is not to get trapped into thinking that it is the *only* vocabulary available to us, or getting seduced into thinking that somehow philosophy or any other cultural discipline ought to be able to beat science at its own "game".

But, let me turn directly to what I have called Rorty's subtext, his rhetorical *apologia* for pragmatism. I speak of it as a rhetorical *apologia* because Rorty does not want to claim that one can argue for it, if we *mean* by argument what goes on in science or what the positivists sought to reify as the standards for all "genuine" argumentation. The content of this pragmatism can be characterized as a defense of the Socratic virtues, "the willingness to talk, to listen to the people, to weigh the consequences of our actions upon other people." It means taking conversation seriously (and playfully) without thinking that the only type of conversation that is important is the type that aspires to put an end to conversation by reaching some sort of "rational consensus," or that all "genuine" conversations are really inquiries about "truth." It means not being fooled into thinking or feeling that there is or must be something more fundamental than the contingent social practices that have been hammered out in the course of history. It means resisting the "urge to substitute *theoria* for *phronesis*," and appreciating that there are no constraints on inquiry save conversational ones and that even these conversational constraints "cannot be anticipated." One of the possible consequences of this type of pragmatism would be a "renewed sense of community."[49] "Our identification with our community – our society, our political tradition, our intellectual heritage – is heightened when we see this community as *ours* rather than nature's, *shaped* rather than *found*, one among many which men have made. In the end, the pragmatists tell us, what matters is our loyalty to other human beings clinging together against the dark, not our hope of getting things right.[50] It would be a mistake and a

slander to think that such a meditation on human finitude entails or leads to an acceptance of the status quo. The critical impulse in Rorty is no less strong than it is in Habermas or even
Gadamer. Rorty is constantly criticizing what he takes to be
the specter of prevailing illusions and self-deceptions, and he
provides "a hint of how our lives might be changed."[51] There
is a profound moral-political vision that informs his work and
suggests what our society and culture may *yet* become. Rorty's
deepest sympathies, as well as his tentativeness, are expressed
when he draws a distinction between two types of "strong
textualists."[52]

> Pragmatism appears in James and Bloom as an identification
> with the struggles of finite men. In Foucault and Nietzsche it
> appears as contempt for one's own finitude, as a search for
> some mighty inhuman force to which one can yield up one's
> identity. . . . I have no wish to defend Foucault's inhumanism,
> and every wish to praise Bloom's sense of our common human
> lot. But I do not know how to back up this preference with argu-
> ment, or even with a precise account of the relevant differences.
> To do so, I think, would involve a full-scale discussion of the
> possibility of combining private fulfillment, self-realization,
> with public morality, a concern for justice.

Now if one brackets Rorty's metacritique and pays close attention to his own "preference" and "vision," there is something
very remarkable about it when we compare what he is saying
with Gadamer and Habermas. For there is a significant over-
lap or family resemblance in these respective visions. This, of
course, does not diminish the significance of the differences
between Rorty on the one hand and Gadamer and Habermas,
on the other. But once again, these differences now begin to
look very different.

We can even find suitable translations for Rorty's key points
in Gadamerian and Habermasian terms. For we can say that
as Rorty interprets the "application" theme to our hermeneutical situation, this means that we accept the radical contingency of the social practices that define what we are. To say
that they are radically contingent does not mean that they are

arbitrary if by this we mean that we can somehow leap out of our historical situation and blithely accept some other set of social practices. Rorty is calling for an honest recognition of what constitutes our finitude and historicity, and for giving up the false "metaphysical comfort" that these practices are grounded in something more fundamental. We can appreciate the extent to which *our* sense of community is threatened and distorted not only by the "material conditions" that characterize our lives but by the faulty epistemological doctrines that fill our heads. The *moral* task of the philosopher or the cultural critic is to defend the openness of human conversation against all those temptations and real threats that seek closure – to keep open the "cultural space left by the demise of epistemology." Even Rorty's neo-pragmatism has undergone a subtle shift in the course of his intellectual development. Rorty's first published article was a defense of Peirce and an attempt to show the family resemblances between Peirce and the post-positivist musings of the later Wittgenstein.[53] In *Philosophy and the Mirror of Nature*, it is Dewey as the critic of foundationalism that replaces Peirce as the hero of pragmatism. And, in some of Rorty's most recent writings, it is James's humanistic pragmatism that he emphasizes. The line of development here is one in which there is "breaking with the Kantian epistemological tradition."[54] There is a certain strain or tension in Rorty's appropriation of the views of the pragmatists. For Peirce, Dewey, and even James, the scientist was still their cultural hero. They sought to imbue philosophy with what they took to be the quintessence of the scientific experimental spirit. But unlike them, Rorty's deepest affinities are with what he calls "literary culture." The narrative that he unfolds is one where representatives of literary culture such as Bloom, Foucault, and Derrida replace professional philosophers as the dominant voice in the present conversation of mankind. Dewey is one of Rorty's heroes but Rorty does not follow Dewey in his socio-political critiques of the "problems of men." But although Rorty himself has not practiced the type of socio-political critique that became so central for Dewey, he expresses deep sympathy with it. Rorty, too, is an apologist for those very democratic virtues that were so central for Dewey and which he sought to make concrete. There is an important difference of emphasis here between Rorty and Habermas – one which also reveals the common ground that they share. For Rorty's descriptions of what characterizes the social-political practices of our time are rather "thin" when compared with the "thick" descriptions of Habermas (or even with the highly illuminating analyses of micro-practices by Foucault). If, as Rorty tells us, the legacy of the pragmatists is to call for a change of orientation on how we can best cope with the world, how we should live our lives so that we can "combine private fulfillment, self-realization, with public morality, a concern with justice," then this demands a critical analysis of the *conflicts* of the social and cultural practices that shape our lives. Further, this change of orientation requires confronting the practical tasks for achieving what Dewey once delineated as the primary task of democracy – "the creation of a freer and more humane experience in which all share and to which all contribute."[55] I suggested earlier that we can use Rorty to get a clearer "fix" on what Habermas is really doing. In Rorty's terms, Habermas's importance is to be found in his "vision of mankind, our history and its prospects." Habermas is a "cultural critic" who has helped to clarify what is *our* human project and who has developed a "moral-political vision" that highlights the demand for the concrete achievement of the very Socratic virtues that Rorty himself defends.

It may be legitimately asked, Where does this *Spiel* of Gadamer, Habermas, and Rorty leave us? Let me first emphasize what I take to be the wrong conclusions to draw. It would be wrong to say that I am suggesting that all three are basically saying the same thing: they are not. It would be a mistake to think that there are no differences among them that make a difference. And, it would be just as faulty and misleading to think that their respective voices can be *aufgehoben* into a grand synthesis. Drawing on the central notion of a conversation that is so vital for all three of them, we can say that we must do as much justice to their differing emphases as to what they share in common. The appeal to the "model" of a conversation can be illuminating. For in any living vital conversation (which is not just the babble of incommensurable opinions), there will always be important differences among the participants; it behooves us to listen carefully to what each is saying, to catch the nuances of their inflections. What I have tried to show is how different these differences appear once we start probing, and listen carefully. But the other side of differences is the common ground that *emerges*. In this final section, it is this common ground that I want to highlight. For I think it tells us something important about our hermeneutical situation and the *agon* between modernity and post-modernity.

Labels in philosophy and cultural discourse have the character that Derrida ascribes to Plato's *pharmakon*:[56] they can poison and kill, and they can remedy and cure. We *need* them to help identify a style, a temperament, a set of common concerns and emphases, or a vision that has a determinate shape. But we must also be wary of the ways in which they can blind us, or can reify what is fluid and changing. The label that I would use to *name* the common project of Rorty, Habermas, and Gadamer is "nonfoundational pragmatic humanism", and I want to comment on each of the expressions in this label. I do not think that much needs to be said about the expression "non-foundational." For here we find a convergence in the major traditions of contemporary philosophy. One line can be drawn that runs from Peirce, James, Dewey, Mead, Wittgenstein, Quine, Sellars, and Rorty. "Non-foundational" is perhaps too weak a term to characterize this movement of thought because it is essentially "*anti*-foundational." Already in his famous papers of 1868, Peirce laid down the main lines of the contemporary attack on the Cartesian legacy. He had the perspicacity to see that carrying out this project would lead us to a revolutionary understanding of human inquiry, signification, and the human condition. This attack on the Cartesian legacy and persuasion is echoed and deepened in the sustained critique of "modern subjectivism" in the *thinking* of Heidegger and Gadamer. Of course, Rorty so presses this anti-foundationalist motif that Habermas (and even Peirce) begin to look like foundationalists from his perspective. But I think that a fairer and more generous interpretation of Habermas would emphasize that he too has been motivated to root out this tendency in the Hegelian–Marxist tradition with which he identifies. Although there are still some rearguard skirmishes, I think we can say, using James's phrase, that the "choice" between foundationalism and non-foundationalism is no longer a "live option;" it is a "dead option."

Both Rorty and Habermas would feel comfortable with the appellation "pragmatic," although I suspect Gadamer would not. It is to Habermas's credit that he has been one of the few German philosophers who (along with Apel) has been able to break out of those blinding prejudices which have been a barrier for Continental philosophers to appreciate the vitality, *esprit*, and relevance of what is best in the American pragmatic tradition. It is not just that Habermas has creatively drawn on the work of Peirce and Mead in developing his own understanding of communicative action, discourse, and rationality, but the American pragmatist with whom Habermas shares the deepest affinity is John Dewey; indeed I think that Habermas is closer in spirit to Dewey than Rorty is. Habermas pursues what Dewey took to be the aim of the reconstruction of philosophy which enables us to cope with the concrete "problems of men" in their socio-political context.

For all Gadamer's erudition, there is no evidence that he has ever grappled with the American pragmatic tradition. He seems to share Heidegger's prejudice about this tradition. But this "blindness" need not get in the way of seeing the affinity between the best of Gadamer and the best of American pragmatism. Of course, the pragmatists have always been more sympathetic with the promise of science in helping us to cope with human problems. But one can find in pragmatism a similar highlighting of what Gadamer calls *phronesis* – practical knowledge and wisdom. Furthermore, there are structural parallels between Gadamer's attack on the Cartesian legacy and that of the pragmatists. But the affinity is more profound than the attack on a common enemy. For just as Gadamer seeks to overcome the misleading epistemological associations of the subject-object distinction that pervade modern thought, this is also true of the pragmatists. Gadamer's suggestion that the "mode of being" of play provides a more penetrating understanding of the way we are in the world corresponds to Dewey's analysis of the dynamic to-and-fro transactional character of "situations." And what Gadamer tells us about the meaning of human finitude, the fallibility of all understanding, and the essential openness of experience to the future are themes which are just as central to the pragmatic tradition.

"Humanism," the third term in the label I am proposing, has become something of a dirty word in recent times. It has been used by its critics to identify everything that they think is wrong in the modern world. The *locus classicus* for the contemporary critique of humanism is Heidegger's "Letter on Humanism," but the attack on humanism has been helped along by the way in which "humanism" has become a "whipping boy" for Lévi-Strauss, Althusser, and Foucault. From Foucault's perspective, "humanism" which the modern world takes to be its greatest contribution to culture turns out to be the *pharmakon* that kills – it names everything that is wrong, stolid, self-deceptive, and bleak in the modern world. When unmasked it seems to be the ideology of the new regime of power/knowledge – the ideology of the "disciplinary society," "the age of bio-power," the "carceral archipelago." In the new post-modern, post-structuralist Manichean theology, "humanism" seems to function as the name for the Kingdom of Darkness. Given the bad press that humanism has received recently from such diverse sources, it might seem best to drop this sign altogether in favor of something that does not evoke such strong emotive reactions. But it is more than a matter of perversity to hold on to this sign and *not* to abandon it in the face of such varied criticisms. One does not have to believe in the deification of human beings to be a humanist, or to be guilty of the *hubris* that neglects the limitations of human finitude, or to be an apologist for the "carceral archipelago" to be a humanist. This is not the place for a scholarly disquisition on the history and vicissitudes of the meaning of "humanism." But one can recognize with Rorty that it is a fitting expression for the "Socratic virtues," or with Gadamer that it signifies the essential dialogical, conversational, questioning character of what we are. One can agree with Habermas that it is a "fiction to believe that Socratic dialogue is possible everywhere and at any time" and be alert to the material conditions that distort and deform such dialogue and prevent its actualization in society. Such a humanism points to the urgency of the practical tasks that confront us in trying to make the world a bit more humane, where our social practices actually become practices whereby we can engage in rational persuasion and *phronesis*, rather than manipulation and strategic maneuvering, and where we seek to root out all hidden forms of domination. It directs us to what Rorty calls a "renewed sense of community" and to working toward a society in which the type of dialogue and *phronesis* that Gadamer celebrates are not mere abstractions. It provides no blue-prints for how to accomplish this (for there are none), and it eschews all forms of false "metaphysical comfort." It means seeking to eliminate the real obstacles that stand in the way of distorted communication – whether these come from the secret police or more subtle and frequently more effective forms of power/knowledge. The common ground that emerges in the play of Rorty, Gadamer, and Habermas – their non-foundational pragmatic humanism – may yet serve as a vision that can move us, "a mode of feeling the whole push, and seeing the whole drift of life" that can enable us to cope with the darkness of our times and orient our *praxis*.

3

From Hermeneutics to *Praxis*

One of the most important and central claims in Hans-Georg Gadamer's philosophical hermeneutics is that all understanding involves not only interpretation, but also application. Against an older tradition that divided up hermeneutics into *subtilitas intelligendi* (understanding), *subtilitas explicandi* (interpretation), and *subtilitas applicandi* (application), a primary thesis of *Truth and Method* is that these are not three independent activities to be relegated to different subdisciplines, but rather they are internally related. They are all moments of the single process of understanding. I want to explore this integration of the moment of application into hermeneutic understanding which Gadamer calls the "rediscovery of the fundamental hermeneutic problem."[1] For it not only takes us to the heart of what is distinctive about philosophical hermeneutics but it reveals some of the deep problems and tensions implicit in hermeneutics. First, I want to note some of the central features of what Gadamer means by philosophical hermeneutics. Then I can specify the problem that he is confronting when dealing with application. This will enable us to see what Gadamer seeks to appropriate from Aristotle, and especially from Aristotle's analysis of *phronesis* in Book VI of the *Nicomachean Ethics*, in elucidating the sense in which all understanding involves application. Gadamer certainly realizes that "Aristotle is not concerned with the hermeneutical problem and certainly not with its historical dimension, but with the right estimation of the role that reason has to play in moral action" (*TM*, p. 278; *WM*,

p. 295),[2] and yet Gadamer claims that "if we relate Aristotle's description of the ethical phenomenon and especially the virtue of moral knowledge to our own investigation, we find Aristotle's analysis is in fact a kind of model of the problems of hermeneutics" (*TM*, p. 299; *WM*, p. 307).[3] But Gadamer's own understanding, interpretation, and appropriation of Aristotle has much richer consequences. It is itself a model of what he means by hermeneutical understanding. It is an exemplar of effective-historical consciousness (*Wirkungsgeschichtliches Bewusstsein*), the fusion of horizons (*Horizontverschmelzung*), the positive role of temporal distance, how understanding is part of the process of the coming into being of meaning, the way in which tradition "speaks to us" and makes a "claim to truth" upon us, and what it means to say that "the interpreter dealing with a traditional text seeks to apply it to himself." Furthermore, when we see how Gadamer appropriates Aristotle's text, we gain a deeper understanding of why the *Geisteswissenschaften* are moral-practical disciplines in the sense in which the *Ethics* and the *Politics* are practical disciplines, and why Gadamer thinks that "hermeneutic philosophy is the heir of the older tradition of practical philosophy" whose chief task is to "justify this way of reason and defend practical and political reason against the domination of technology based on science."[4] Gadamer's own understanding of philosophical hermeneutics can itself be interpreted as a series of footnotes and reflections on his decisive intellectual encounter with Aristotle, an encounter to which he frequently refers and which was initiated by his participation in Heidegger's seminar on the *Nicomachean Ethics*.[5]

In order to orient our discussion, it is important to recall some of the primary characteristics of philosophical hermeneutics. As Gadamer frequently reiterates, "the hermeneutic phenomenon is basically not a problem of method at all. It is not concerned with a method of understanding, by means of which texts are subjected to scientific investigation like all other objects of experience. It is not concerned primarily with amassing ratified knowledge which satisfies the methodological ideal of science – yet it is concerned, here too, with knowledge and

with truth" (*TM*, p. xi; *WM*, p. xxvii). The task is to elucidate
the distinctive type of *knowledge and truth* that is realized whenever we authentically understand.[6] From Gadamer's perspective, it has been the obsession with *Method*, and with thinking
that the primary task of hermeneutics is to specify a distinctive
method of the *Geisteswissenschaften* that can rival the scientific
method of the *Naturwissenschaften* which plagued and distorted
nineteenth-century hermeneutics. This led to a view of understanding as primarily a psychological subjective activity, as
involving some sort of empathy where we can overcome and
leap out of our own historical situation and identify ourselves
with the intentions of the authors of texts or the intentions of
the historical actors that we are studying. There was a "latent
Cartesianism" in this tradition and an acceptance of the basic
dichotomy between what is objective and subjective.[7] But it is
just this dichotomy that Gadamer seeks to question and undermine. According to Gadamer, it is only with Heidegger that
the full dimensions of understanding were fully realized. Implicit in Heidegger and explicit in Gadamer are two central
claims: the ontological primacy of hermeneutics and its universality. We are "thrown" into the world as beings who
understand; and understanding itself is not one type of activity
of a subject, but may properly be said to underlie all activities.

When Gadamer introduces the concept of play and tells us
that play is "the clue to ontological explanation" (*TM*, p. 91;
WM, p. 97), he is seeking to show us that there is a more primordial mode of being for understanding our being in the
world – an alternative to the Cartesian persuasion which rivets
our attention on the subjective attitudes toward what is presumably objective. "Play has its own essence which is independent of the consciousness of those who play." "The players are
not subjects of play; instead play merely reaches presentation
through the players" (*TM*, p. 92; *WM*, p. 98). Play has its own
rhythm, its own buoyancy, its distinctive to-and-fro movement.
This mode of being of play is what Gadamer takes to be
characteristic of our relation with works of art, texts, and indeed anything that is handed down to us. Gadamer introduces
the concept of play in order to highlight the subtle dialectical

and dialogical relation that exists between the interpreter and what he seeks to interpret. We misconceive this relation if we think that we are merely subjects or spectators standing over and against what is objective and what exists *an sich*. We participate in the works of art, texts, and tradition that we encounter, and it is only through understanding that their meaning and truth is realized. The aim of hermeneutical understanding is to open ourselves to what texts and tradition "say to us," to open ourselves to their meaning and the claim to truth that they make upon us.[8] But what Gadamer stresses, building on Heidegger, is that we do *not* do this by forgetting or seeking to bracket our own historicity, our own forestructures, prejudgments, and prejudices. Here we touch upon one of the most controversial features of Gadamer's philosophic hermeneutics, viz., his *apologia* for prejudice against the Enlightenment's "prejudice against prejudice" (*TM*, p. 240; *WM*, p. 255). As Gadamer tells us:[9]

> It is not so much our judgments as it is our prejudices that constitute our being. This is a provocative formulation, for I am using it to restore to its rightful place as a positive concept of prejudice that was driven out of our linguistic usage by the French and English Enlightenment. . . . Prejudices are not necessarily unjustified and erroneous, so that they inevitably distort the truth. In fact, the historicity of our existence entails that prejudices, in the literal sense of the word, constitute the initial directedness of our whole ability to experience. Prejudices are biases of our openness to the world. They are simply the conditions whereby we experience something – whereby what we encounter says something to us.

Gadamer does want to make the all-important distinction between "blind prejudices" which are unjustified and those "justified prejudices that are productive of knowledge" – what we might call "enabling prejudices." This does not diminish the thrust of his claim that *both* sorts of prejudice are constitutive of what we are. But then how do we distinguish between these types of prejudice or prejudgment? One answer is clearly ruled out. We cannot do this by a solitary or monological act of pure self-reflection where we bracket or suspend judgment about *all* of our prejudices. This is what is ontologically impossible – for what we *are*, and what is revelatory of our human finitude is that prejudices are constitutive of our being. Indeed the answer that Gadamer gives to the question of how we make this distinction between blind and enabling prejudices is the very one that Descartes rejected from serious consideration. It is only through the dialogical encounter with what is handed down to us that we can test and *risk* our prejudices. Unlike Descartes (and Hegel), Gadamer sees this as a constant open task, not one that can ever achieve finality or closure. For Gadamer then, there is a threefold temporal character to prejudices. They are themselves inherited from tradition and shape what we are, whether we are aware of this or not. It is because our prejudices themselves have their source in the very tradition that we seek to understand that we can account for our *affinity* with, our belonging to (*Zugehörigkeit*), tradition. While inherited from tradition they are constitutive of what we are *now*. But there is also a projective or anticipatory aspect of our prejudices and prejudgments, a dimension highlighted by Heidegger's own emphasis on fore-structures, i.e., on fore-having, fore-sight, and fore-conceptions.[10] It is through the hermeneutical circle of understanding that we call upon these forestructures which enable us to understand, and at the same time discriminate critically between blind and enabling prejudices.

We can begin to see where Gadamer is leading us and why the problem of application is so important for him. On the one hand, Gadamer tells us that hermeneutic understanding is always tempered to the "thing itself" that we are trying to understand. We seek nothing less than to understand the *same* text or the same piece of tradition. But the *meaning* of what we seek to understand is not self-contained, it does not exist *an sich*. The meaning of a text or of a tradition is only realized through the happening (*pathos*) of understanding. But such understanding is only possible because of the prejudices and prejudgments that are constitutive of what we are – our own historicity. This is why Gadamer tells us that to understand is always to understand *differently*. There is a play, a to-and-fro movement that occurs in all understanding in which both what we seek to understand and our prejudices are dynamically involved with each other. Unlike those who think that such appropriation or application to our hermeneutical situation reveals a distortion or a deficiency which is to be overcome, it is the positive enabling roles of prejudgments and prejudices that become thematic for philosophical hermeneutics.

It is in this context that the problem of application becomes so central for Gadamer. It is here that we can see why Aristotle's analysis of *phronesis* is so important to him. For *phronesis* is a form of reasoning and knowledge that involves a distinctive mediation between the universal and the particular. This mediation is not accomplished by any appeal to technical rules or Method (in the Cartesian sense), or by the subsumption of a pre-given determinate universal to a particular case. Gadamer emphasizes that *phronesis* is a form of reasoning which yields a type of "ethical know-how" in which both what is universal and what is particular are *co-determined*. Furthermore, *phronesis* involves a "peculiar interlacing of being and knowledge, determination through one's own becoming."[11] It is not to be identified with or confused with the type of "objective knowledge" that is detached from one's own being and becoming. Just as *phronesis* determines what the *phronimos* becomes, Gadamer wants to make a similar claim for all authentic understanding, i.e., that it is not detached from the interpreter, but constitutive of his or her *praxis*. Understanding for Gadamer is a form of *phronesis*.

We gain a subtler comprehension of what this means by noting the contrasts that Gadamer highlights when he explores the ways in which Aristotle distinguishes *phronesis* from the other "intellectual virtues," especially from *episteme* and *techne*. *Episteme*, scientific knowledge, is knowledge of what is universal, of what exists "of necessity" and takes the form of the scientific demonstration. The subject matter, the form, the *telos*, the way in which *episteme* is learned and taught, differ from *phronesis*, the form of reasoning appropriate to *praxis*, where there is always a mediation between the universal and the particular which involves deliberation and choice. But it is not primarily the contrast between *episteme* and *phronesis* that Gadamer takes to be instructive for hermeneutics, but rather the careful ways in which Aristotle distinguishes *techne* (technical know-how) from *phronesis* (ethical know-how). And here Gadamer stresses three contrasts.

1   *Techne*, or "a technique is learned and can be forgotten; we can lose a skill. But ethical 'reason' can neither be learned nor forgotten. . . . By contrast, the subject of ethical reason, of *phronesis*, man always finds himself in an 'acting situation' and he is always obliged to use ethical knowledge and apply it according to the exigencies of his concrete situation."[12]

2   There is a different conceptual relation between means and ends in *techne* and *phronesis*. The end of ethical know-how, unlike a technique, is not a "particular thing or product" but rather "*complete* ethical rectitude of a life time."[13] Even more important, while technical activity does not require that the means which allow it to arrive at an end be weighed anew on each occasion, this is what is required in ethical know-how. In ethical know-how there can be no prior knowledge of the right means by which we realize the end. For the end itself is only concretely specified in deliberating about the means appropriate to *this* particular situation.[14]

3   *Phronesis*, unlike *techne*, is a distinctive type of "knowledge-for-the-sake-of-oneself." This is indicated when Aristotle considers the variants of *phronesis*, especially *synesis* (understanding). "It appears in the fact of concern, not about myself, but about the other person. Thus it is a mode of moral judgment. . . . The question here, then, is not of a general kind of knowledge, but of its specification at a particular moment. This knowledge also is not in any sense technical knowledge or the application of such . . . . The person with understanding does not know and judge as one who stands apart and unaffected; but rather, as one united by a specific bond with the other, he thinks with the other and undergoes the situation with him" (*TM*, p. 288; *WM*, p. 306).

What does this analysis of *phronesis* and the ways in which
it differs from both *episteme* and *techne* have to do with the
problems of hermeneutics? The analogy that Gadamer draws,
the reason why he thinks it is a "model of the problems of hermeneutics," is that just as application is not a subsequent or
occasional part of *phronesis* where we relate some pre-given
determinate universal to a particular situation, this is true for
all understanding. And just as with *phronesis* there is always a
mediation between the universal and the particular in which
both are codetermined and become integral to the very being of
the *phronimos*, this is what Gadamer claims is characteristic of
all authentic understanding.

> The interpreter dealing with a traditional text seeks to apply it
> to himself. But this does not mean that the text is given for him
> as something universal, that he understands it as such and only
> afterwards uses it for particular applications. Rather, the inter-
> preter seeks no more than to understand this universal thing,
> the text; i.e., to understand what this piece of tradition says,
> what constitutes the meaning and the importance of the text. In
> order to understand that, he must not seek to disregard himself
> and his particular hermeneutical situation. He must relate the
> text to this situation, if he wants to understand at all. (*TM*,
> p. 289; *WM*, p. 307)

What is striking about this passage is that it applies perfectly
to the way in which Gadamer himself understands, interprets,
and appropriates Aristotle's text. This is what I meant earlier
when I said that Aristotle's analysis of *phronesis* is not only a
model of the problems of hermeneutics but that Gadamer's interpretation of Aristotle is itself a model or exemplar of what is
meant by hermeneutical understanding. In the above passage,
Gadamer tells us that if we are to understand what a text or a
piece of tradition says, then we must not seek to disregard ourselves and our hermeneutical situation. This is characteristic of
the way in which Gadamer approaches Aristotle. For what
Gadamer takes to be basic for *our* hermeneutical situation is
that we are confronted with a world in which there has been a
"domination of technology based on science," that there is a

"false idolatry of the expert," "a scientific mystification of the modern society of specialization," and a dangerous "inner longing in our society to find in science a substitute for lost orientations."[15] It is this problematic that orients Gadamer's questioning of Aristotle's text, for Gadamer's central claim is that there has been a forgetfulness and deformation of what *praxis* really is.

Indeed it is through the dialogical encounter with Aristotle's text that we risk and test our own deeply entrenched prejudices which blind us from grasping the autonomy and integrity of *phronesis*. This does not mean that we approach Aristotle without any prejudices and prejudgments. What enables us to understand Aristotle and appropriate the "truth" of what he says is that we ourselves have been shaped by this effective history. It is not a nostalgic return to Aristotle that Gadamer is advocating, but rather an appropriation of Aristotle's own insights to our concrete situation. Gadamer's interpretation of Aristotle illustrates what he means by the fusion of horizons. We are, of course, questioning Aristotle's text from our own historical horizon. But we distort the very idea of a horizon if we think that it is self-contained, that we are prisoners enclosed within it. "The historical movement of human life consists in the fact that it is never utterly bound to any one standpoint, and hence can never have a truly closed horizon" (*TM*, p. 271; *WM*, p. 288). We come to understand what Aristotle is saying and at the same time come to a deeper understanding of our own situation when we are sensitive to Aristotle's own confrontation with the "professional lawmakers whose function at that time corresponded to the role of the expert in modern scientific society."[16] By appropriating the "truth" of what Aristotle says, especially the way in which he distinguishes practical reason from theoretical and technical reason, we thereby enlarge our own horizon. It is this fusion of horizons that enables us to risk and test our own prejudices. For the dialogical encounter with Aristotle allows us to see how the contemporary understanding of *praxis* has become deformed. We can learn from Aristotle what "practice" really is, why it is not to be identified with the "application of science to technical tasks." Gadamer realizes that in modern society *techne* itself has been transformed, but this only highlights the importance of what we can learn from Aristotle about *praxis* and *phronesis*. He tells us:[17]

> In a scientific culture such as ours the fields of *techne* and art are much more expanded. Thus the fields of mastering means to pre-given ends have been rendered even more monological and controllable. The crucial change is that practical wisdom can no longer be promoted by personal contact and the mutual exchange of views among the citizens. Not only has craftmanship been replaced by industrial work; many forms of our daily life are technologically organized so that they no longer require personal decision. In modern technological society public opinion itself has in a new and really decisive way become the object of very complicated techniques – and this, I think, is the main problem facing our civilization.

The temporal distance between ourselves and Aristotle is not a negative barrier to understanding, but rather positive and productive for understanding. By opening ourselves to what this "piece of tradition" says and to the claim to truth that it makes upon us, we bring to life new meanings of the text. "Understanding must be conceived as part of the process of the coming into being of meaning . . ." (*TM*, p. 147; *WM*, p. 157). And this understanding, like *phronesis*, is a form of moral-practical knowledge which becomes constitutive of what we are in the process of becoming. Gadamer seeks to show us that authentic hermeneutical understanding truly humanizes us; it becomes integrated in our very being just as *phronesis* itself shapes the being of the *phronimos*.

This emphasis on the moment of appropriation in hermeneutical understanding enables us to see why Gadamer thinks that the *Geisteswissenschaften* – when authentically practiced – are moral-practical disciplines. As hermeneutical disciplines, they are not concerned with amassing "theoretical" knowledge of what is strange and alien. Rather they involve the type of appropriation characteristic of *phronesis*. The type of knowledge and truth that they yield is practical knowledge and truth that shapes our *praxis*. This also helps to clarify why the "chief task" of philosophical hermeneutics is to "correct the peculiar false-hood of modern consciousness" and "to defend practical and political reason against the domination of technology based on science." It is in this sense that "hermeneutic philosophy is the heir of the older tradition of practical philosophy."[18]

This fusion of hermeneutics and *praxis* through the appropri-ation of *phronesis* has much broader ramifications. For in a number of different contexts we can discern how a variety of thinkers have been led to a reinterpretation or appreciation of the tradition of practical philosophy in order to come to a critical understanding of modern society. It is an underlying theme in the work of Hannah Arendt and Jürgen Habermas, both of whom share Gadamer's concern sharply to distinguish the technical from the practical. The attempt to clarify and restore the integrity of practical reasoning surfaces in such recent critical appraisals as Richard Rorty's *Philosophy and the Mirror of Nature*, Alasdair MacIntyre's *After Virtue*, and Hilary Putnam's *Meaning and the Moral Sciences*. Differences among these thinkers are as important as the common themes that run through their work. But I do think we are witnessing a new turn in the conver-sation of philosophy and in the understanding of human ration-ality where there is a recovery and appropriation of the type of practical reasoning, knowledge, and wisdom that is character-istic of *phronesis*.

I have indicated that Gadamer's appropriation of this tradi-tion of practical philosophy is not without problems and ten-sions. If we take Gadamer seriously, and press his own claims, then they lead us beyond philosophical hermeneutics. Before I begin my immanent critique, it is important to remember that in *Truth and Method*, Gadamer's primary concern is with the understanding and interpretation of works of art, texts, and tradition, with "what is handed down to us." Ethics and politics are not in the foreground of his investigations. Even his discus-sion of Aristotle is introduced only insofar as it helps to illumin-ate the hermeneutical phenomenon. But it is also clear that if we pay close attention to Gadamer's writings before and after the publication of *Truth and Method*, there has been an under-lying and pervasive concern with ethics and politics – especially with what we can learn from Greek philosophy. In his writings since the publication of *Truth and Method*, Gadamer has returned again and again to the dialectical interplay of hermeneutics and *praxis*. I emphasize this because when we enlarge our horizon and consider the implications of what he is saying for a contemporary understanding of ethics and politics, then a number of difficulties come into sharp relief.

Let me begin with a consideration of the meaning of *truth* for Gadamer, then move to his conception of *criticism.* . This will allow us to take a close look at some of the difficulties with his understanding of *phronesis*. Finally we can turn to the Gadamer's reflection on dialogue and its implications for politics. Truth is not only basic for the entire project of philosophical hermeneutics, but it turns out to be one of the most elusive concepts in Gadamer. After all, the primary intention of *Truth and Method* is to defend and elucidate the legitimacy of speaking of the truth of works of art, texts, and tradition. Gadamer tells us that it was not his intention to play off Method against Truth, but rather to show that there is a "different type of knowledge and truth" which is not exhausted by achievements of scientific method and which is only available to us through hermeneutical understanding.[19] This appeal to truth – a truth that transcends our own historical horizon – is absolutely essential in order to distinguish philosophical hermeneutics from a historicist form of relativism. Gadamer concludes *Truth and Method* with strong claims about this distinctive type of truth.

Thus there is undoubtedly no understanding that is free of all prejudices, however much the will of our knowledge must be directed towards escaping their thrall. It has emerged throughout our investigation that the certainty that is imparted by the use of scientific methods does not suffice to guarantee truth. This is so especially of the human sciences, but this does not mean a diminution of their scientific quality, but on the contrary, a justification of the claim to special humane significance that they have always made. The fact that in the knowing involved in them the knower's own being is involved marks, certainly the limitation of "method," but not that of science. Rather what the tool of method does not achieve must – and effectively can –

be achieved by a discipline of questioning and research, a discipline that guarantees truth [*die Wahrheit verbürgt*]. (*TM*, p. 447;
* *WM*, p. 465)

But what precisely does "truth" mean here? And what does it
mean to say that there is a discipline of questioning and research
that "guarantees truth"? It is much easier to say what "truth"
does not mean than to give a positive account. It might seem
curious (although I do not think it is accidental) that in a work
entitled *Truth and Method*, the topic of truth never becomes fully
thematic and is discussed only briefly toward the very end of
the book.[20] It is clear, however, that like Hegel and Heidegger,
Gadamer criticizes the notion of truth as correspondence, as
adequatio intellectus et rei, at least in regard to the distinctive type
of truth that is achieved through hermeneutical understanding.
What Gadamer means by "truth" is a blending of motifs that
have resonances in Hegel and Heidegger. For like Hegel,
Gadamer seeks to show that there is a truth that is revealed in
the process of experience (*Erfahrung*) and which emerges in the
dialogical encounter with the very tradition that has shaped us.
Even the above passage echoes the typical Hegelian movement
from *Gewissheit* (certainty) to *Wahrheit* (truth). And like Heidegger, Gadamer also seeks to recover the notion of *aletheia* as dis-
closedness (*Erschlossenheit*) and unconcealment (*Unverborgenheit*).
There is even a parallel between Heidegger's claim that *Dasein*
is "equally in truth and in untruth" and Gadamer's claim that
prejudices (both true and untrue prejudices) are constitutive of
being. But Gadamer also distances himself from both Hegel
and Heidegger. He categorically rejects what Hegel himself
took to be the ground for his conception of truth, viz., that
"truth is the whole" which is finally revealed in *Wissenschaft*,
the absolute knowledge that completes and overcomes experience.[21] Gadamer also stands in an uneasy relation with Heidegger, for he knows all too well where Heidegger's meditations
on *aletheia* can lead us. He writes: "When science expands into a
total technocracy and this brings on the 'cosmic night' of the
'forgetfulness of being,' the nihilism that Neitzsche prophesied,
then may one look at the last fading light of the sun that is set in

the evening sky, instead of turning around to look for the first shimmer of its return?" And with explicit reference to Heidegger, he tells us "what man needs is not only a persistent asking of ultimate questions, but the sense of what is feasible, what is possible, what is correct, here and now" (*TM*, p. xxv; *MW*, p. xxv). But even if we play out the similarities and differences with Hegel and Heidegger, the precise meaning of truth for Gadamer still eludes us. What is even more problematic and revealing is that if we closely examine the way in which Gadamer appeals to "truth," he is employing a concept of truth that he never fully makes explicit. His typical phrasing is to speak of the "claim of truth" (*Anspruch auf Wahrheit*) that works of art, texts, and tradition make upon us. Gadamer never says (and it would certainly distort his meaning) that something is true simply because it is handed down to us. What he is always doing is seeking to appropriate critically what is handed down to us. This is just as evident in his claims about the tradition of practical philosophy as it is in his criticism of the "Enlightenment's prejudice against prejudice." When Gadamer, for example, says, "When Aristotle, in the sixth book of the *Nicomachean Ethics*, distinguishes the manner of 'practical' knowledge . . . from theoretical and technical knowledge, he expresses, in my opinion, one of the greatest truths by which the Greeks throw light upon the 'scientific' mystification of modern society of specialization," [22] he is not telling us that this is one of the greatest truths simply because it is what Aristotle's text says. Rather it is true because Gadamer thinks we can now give convincing arguments to show why it is true. The force is not simply on what tradition says to us, or even on the "claim to truth" that it makes upon us, but on the validation of such claims by critical arguments. Gadamer has warned us against reifying tradition and thinking that it is something simply given. [23] Furthermore, tradition is not a seamless whole. There are conflicting traditions making *conflicting* claims of truth upon us. If we take our own historicity seriously, then the challenge that always confronts us is to give the best possible reasons and arguments that are appropriate to our hermeneutical situation in order to validate claims to truth. Gadamer himself makes this point forcefully in his friendly quarrel with Leo Strauss. Commenting on a theme that Gadamer shares with Strauss – the importance of the concept of friendship in Aristotle's ethics for recognizing the limitations of modern ethics – he asks: "Does this insight emerge because we 'read' the classics with an eye that is trained by historical science, reconstructing their meaning, as it were, and then considering it possible, trusting that they are right? Or do we see truth in them, because we are thinking ourselves as we try to understand them, i.e., because what they say seems true to us when we consider the corresponding modern theories that are invoked?" (*TM*, p. 485; *WM*, p. 507). There is no ambiguity in how Gadamer answers his own question. But then this casts the entire question of truth in a very different light. For when it comes to the validation of claims to truth and the correct interpretations of texts, then the essential issue concerns reasons and arguments which are, of course, fallible, and are anticipatory in the sense that they can be challenged and criticized by future argumentation. In effect, I am suggesting that what Gadamer himself is appealing to is a concept of truth which comes down to what can be argumentatively validated by the community of interpreters who open themselves to what tradition says to us. This does not mean that there is some transcendental or ahistorical perspective from which we can evaluate competing claims to truth. We judge and evaluate such claims by the standards and practices that have been hammered out in the course of history. If I am right in pursuing this line of thought which is implicit in Gadamer, then it is extraordinarily misleading – and betrays his own best insights – to say that there is any discipline that "guarantees truth." Rather we can seek only to justify claims to truth by giving the strongest arguments that we can to show why something is true – and this is in fact what Gadamer himself does.

The point that I am making about the concept of truth that is implicit in Gadamer is closely related to the allied concept of criticism. Gadamer tells us, "It is a grave misunderstanding to assume that emphasis on the essential factor of tradition which enters into all understanding implies an uncritical acceptance of tradition and socio-political conservatism. . . . In truth the confrontation of our historic tradition is always a critical challenge of this tradition. . . . Every experience is such a confrontation."[24] But even if we acknowledge what he is saying here and appreciate that this is characteristic of the way in which Gadamer always approaches tradition, there is a problem that Gadamer does not squarely confront. Implicitly or explicitly all criticism appeals to some principles, standards, or criteria. Gadamer is extremely incisive in exposing the fallacy of thinking that such principles, standards, or criteria can be removed from our own historicity, and in showing that there is an essential openness and indeterminacy about them. But even if we grant him everything he wants to say about human finitude rooted in historicity, this does not lessen the burden of the question of what is and what ought to be the basis for the critical evaluation of the problems of modernity. One can be extraordinarily sympathetic with Gadamer's critique of objectivism, foundationalism, the search for some Archimedean point that somehow stands outside of our historical situation. But if we take the theme of application or appropriation seriously, and speak about *our* hermeneutical situation, then we must still address the question of what is the basis for our critical judgments. When Gadamer tells us that "the concept of *'praxis'* which was developed in the last two centuries is an awful deformation of what practice really is" or when he speaks of "the peculiar falsehood of modern consciousness: the idolatry of scientific method and the anonymous authority of the sciences,"[25] he is himself appealing to critical standards and norms of what practice really is, and what is truly a human life – standards and norms that demand rational justification and argumentation. It is not *sufficient* to give a justification that directs us to tradition. What is required is a form of argumentation that seeks to *warrant* what is valid in this tradition.

Characteristically, when questions are raised about the validity of standards and norms that are to serve as the basis for criticism, Gadamer tells us that they too are handed down to us and need to be recovered from tradition. But this response is not adequate. Consider again what Gadamer highlights in his appropriation of *phronesis* – the distinctive type of mediation of the universal and the particular. Let us focus on the *universal* element that is mediated in *phronesis*. Gadamer's meaning is illustrated by his interpretation of the role of natural law in Aristotle. In the realm of *praxis*, natural law is not to be thought of as a law that is eternal, immutable, and fully determinate. He tells us, "For according to Aristotle, the idea of an immutable natural law applies only to the divine world, and he declares that with us humans natural law is in the last analysis just as inconstant as positive law."[26] While natural law is not to be reduced to or confused with positive law, it requires interpretation and specification in concrete particular situations of *praxis*. Finding justice in a concrete situation demands perfecting law with equity (*epieikeia*): "It follows, then, according to Aristotle that the idea of natural law serves only a critical function. Nothing in the idea authorizes us to use it dogmatically by attributing the inviolability of natural law to particular and concrete juridical contents."[27] The claim that Gadamer makes about Aristotle's understanding of natural law (the *universal* element) which is essentially open to interpretation and is only concretely specified when related and mediated in a concrete ethical situation is paradigmatic for the application of all ethical principles and norms. But what Aristotle stresses and Gadamer realizes is that what is required for the exercise of *phronesis*, and what keeps it from degenerating into the mere cleverness of the *deinos*, is the existence of such a *nomos* in the *polis* or community. Given a community in which there is a living shared acceptance of ethical principles and norms, then *phronesis* as the mediation of such universals in concrete particular situations makes sense. But what has become so problematic for us today, what is characteristic of our hermeneutical situation, is that there is so much confusion and uncertainty (some might even say chaos) about what are the norms of the "universals" which ought to govern our practical lives. What Gadamer himself realizes – but I do not think he squarely faces the issues that it raises – is that we are living in a time when the very conditions required for exercise of *phronesis* – the shared acceptance and stability of universal principles and laws – are themselves breaking down. Furthermore, Gadamer does not adequately clarify the type of discourse that is appropriate when questions about the validity of basic norms (or universals) are raised. When pressed on these questions, Gadamer deals with a different issue. He typically stresses that such universals are inherited from tradition, that they are essentially open, that they require the type of mediation in which their meaning is specified in the application to concrete practical situations. But this does not clarify the issue of what are the norms that are to serve as the universals which are to be mediated and codetermined in particular situations. Nor does it clarify how we are to evaluate a situation in which we are forced to question the validity of such norms. If we follow out the logic of Gadamer's own line of thought, if we are really concerned with "the sense of what is feasible, what is possible, what is correct, here and now," then this demands that we turn our attention to the question of how can we nurture and foster the types of community required for the exercise of *phronesis*. Indeed, there is a paradox that stands at the center of Gadamer's thinking about *praxis*. For on the one hand, he acutely analyzes the deformation of *praxis* in the contemporary world, and shows how the main problem facing our civilization is one in which the very possibility for the exercise of *phronesis* is undermined, and yet on the other hand he seems to suggest that, regardless of the type of community in which we live, *phronesis* is always a real possibility. Just as Aristotle saw the continuity and movement from ethics to politics, one would think that this is a movement necessitated by Gadamer's own appropriation of *phronesis*. But Gadamer stops short of facing the issues of what is to be done when the *polis* or community itself is "corrupt" – when there is a breakdown of its *nomos* and of a rational discourse about the norms that ought to govern our practical lives.[28]

In defense of Gadamer, one can see why he stops short of confronting the practical issues of our hermeneutical situation. We can read his philosophical hermeneutics as a profound meditation on the meaning of human finitude, as a constant warning against the excesses of what he calls "planning reason," a caution that philosophy must give up the idea of an "infinite intellect." Like Heidegger, there is a deep skepticism about the human will and the belief that we can *make* or engineer such communities in which there are shared universal principles. The claims of his philosophical hermeneutics are at once bold and extremely modest. They are bold insofar as hermeneutics has the task of defending practical and political reason against the various attacks and deformations of it in the contemporary world. But hermeneutic philosophy – or any form of philosophy – cannot *solve* the problems of society or politics. It is dangerous to submit to the temptation of playing the prophet. This is the way to dogmatism. But even if one accepts Gadamer's cautions about prophesy and dogmatism, still there is a practical task that confronts us and to which Gadamer's own investigations lead – seeking to nurture the type of dialogical communities in which *phronesis* becomes a living reality.

The major point of this immanent critique of philosophical hermeneutics – that it leads us to practical tasks which take us beyond hermeneutics – can be approached from a different perspective. Thus far we have been concentrating on Gadamer's appropriation of the "truth" in Aristotle's understanding of *praxis* and *phronesis*, but a full-scale analysis of Gadamer's philosophical hermeneutics would require seeing how it represents a blending and appropriation of both Aristotelian and Platonic themes. Here I want to discuss briefly the most important theme that Gadamer appropriates from Plato – the centrality of dialogue and conversation.

A conversation or a dialogue, Gadamer tells us, "is a process of two people understanding each other. Thus it is characteristic of every true conversation that each opens himself to the other person, truly accepts his point of view as worthy of consideration and gets inside the other to such an extent that he understands not a particular individual, but what he says. The thing that has to be grasped is the objective rightness or otherwise of his opinion, so that they can agree with each other on the subject" (*TM*, p. 347; *WM*, p. 363). When Gadamer introduces the concept of play as the clue to ontological explanation, this has its full realization in his understanding of dialogue and conversation.

> Now I contend that the basic constitution of the game, to be filled
> with its spirit – the spirit of buoyancy, freedom and the joy of
> success – and to fulfill him who is playing, is structurally related
> to the constitution of the dialogue in which language is a reality.
> When one enters into a dialogue with another person and then
> is carried further by the dialogue, it is no longer the will of the
> individual person, holding itself back or exposing itself, that is
> determinative. Rather, the law of the subject matter is at issue
> in the dialogue and elicits statement and counterstatement and
> in the end plays them into each other.[29]

Dialogue itself is fundamental for grasping what is distinctive
about hermeneutical understanding. Gadamer is, of course,
aware of the disanalogies between the dialogue that we have
with texts and tradition and that which occurs with other persons. "Texts are 'permanently fixed expressions of life' which
have to be understood, and that means that one partner in the
hermeneutical conversation, the text, is expressed only through
the other partner, the interpreter" (*TM*, p. 349; *WM*, p. 365).[30]
Nevertheless the conversation, questioning, and dialogue with
texts and tradition is like a living conversation or dialogue "in
that it is the common object that unites the partners, the text
and the interpreter" (*TM*, p. 349; *WM*, p. 365). The conversation or dialogue that he takes to be the quintessence of hermeneutical understanding always evokes the memory of a living
conversation or dialogue between persons. But consider what
he stresses in his analysis of dialogue and conversation – it
is the mutuality, the respect required, the genuine seeking to
understand what the other is saying, the openness to test and
evaluate our own opinions through such an encounter. And in
Gadamer's distinctive understanding of practical philosophy
he blends this concept of dialogue which he finds illustrated in
the Platonic Dialogues with his understanding of *phronesis*. But
here too there are strong practical and political implications that
Gadamer fails to pursue. For Gadamer can be read as showing
us that what we truly are, what is most characteristic of our
humanity is that we are dialogical or conversational beings.
According to Gadamer's reading of the history of philosophy,
this is the idea that he finds at the very beginning of Western

philosophy and which in our time is again the most central lesson of the philosophic tradition.

But if we are really to appropriate this central idea to our historical situation, then it points us toward important practical and political tasks. It would be a gross distortion to imagine that we might conceive of the entire political realm organized on the principle of dialogue or conversation, considering the fragile conditions that are required for genuine dialogue and conversation. Nevertheless, if we think out what is required for such dialogue based on mutual understanding, respect, a willingness to listen and test one's opinions and prejudices, a mutual seeking of the objective rightness of what is said, then this provides us with a powerful regulative ideal that can orient our practical and political lives. If the quintessence of what we are is to be dialogical – and this is not just the privilege of the *few* – then whatever the limitations of the practical realization of this ideal, it nevertheless can and should give practical orientation to our lives. We must ask, what is it that blocks and distorts such dialogue, and what is to be done, "what is feasible, what is possible, what is correct, here and now" to make such genuine dialogue a living reality?[31]

Let me conclude by underscoring the main point of my critique of Gadamer's philosophical hermeneutics. I do think that one of his profoundest insights has been the linkage (or fusion) of hermeneutics and *praxis*, and his claim that all understanding involves appropriation to our own concrete historical situation. But if we pursue the logic of his own argument, if we probe what he means by truth and criticism, or the common ethical and political principles required for the virtue of *phronesis*, or the type of *polis* or community that it demands, or the implications of what he has to say about dialogue or conversation, then the thrust of his reflections is to lead us beyond philosophical hermeneutics. They lead us – with a deepened understanding of human finitude – to the genuinely practical task of concretely realizing what he has so nobly defended as being central to our humanity.

4

Nietzsche or Aristotle?
Reflections on Alasdair MacIntyre's
After Virtue[1]

I

Alasdair MacIntyre's *After Virtue*[2] reads like a brief but extremely dense novel: its plot gradually unfolds; it has its moments of suspense and discovery; there are climaxes and anti-climaxes. Indeed, it is written in that very genre of dramatic narrative that MacIntyre tells us is so vital for understanding human life and action. This should not be mistaken for a criticism, for if MacIntyre is right, this is precisely the genre required for understanding moral philosophy, and for appreciating the tradition of the virtues which he seeks to defend. Like the English novels he so admires, it is crammed full with "characters" (who sometimes make rapid entrances and exits) and intricate "sub-plots," but so much so, that it is easy to lose the thread of the main plot. Since MacIntyre's primary intention is to provide a rational vindication of "the moral tradition to which Aristotle's teaching about the virtues is central" (p. 238), it is essential to outline the main story line – even at the risk of neglecting the extraordinary richness of detail as his narrative unfolds.

The book consists of eighteen chapters and reaches its first major dramatic climax at its very center: Chapter 9, entitled "Nietzsche or Aristotle?" In his Prologue, MacIntyre introduces a "disquieting suggestion." In our so-called moral practice and language, a "catastrophe" has occurred, a catastrophe that he likens to one of those science fiction tales where somehow the whole tradition of natural science is destroyed, and where we are left with incoherent fragments which are no longer genuine science but only the *simulacra* of science. He hypothesizes that a point is reached where no one (or hardly anyone) realizes the nature of the catastrophe which they have suffered. People act and talk *as if* what they were calling science still made sense, still is coherent and rational, but in fact their actions and talk are radically incoherent. Embellishing his tale, MacIntyre's hypothesis is that it is not a fiction, but precisely what has happened in the modern period with the language and practice of morality, both in regard to the way in which ordinary people talk, think, and act, *and* in regard to the way in which so-called moral philosophers talk about morality. The language of morality is no longer intelligible, coherent, or rational – even though almost everybody thinks it is.

Like those novels which begin with the present and then work back into the narrative history of the present, MacIntyre begins by rehearsing some characteristics of contemporary moral disagreement, and by presenting certain claims embodied in contemporary emotivism. He maintains that contemporary moral disagreements have an interminable character and are based upon conceptually incommensurable premises. While MacIntyre argues that emotivism is false as a theory about the *meaning* of the sentences which are used to make moral judgments, he does allow that it can properly be understood as reflecting a correct sociological hypothesis about the way in which people now act, think, and talk.

> For one way of framing my contention that morality is not what it once was is just to say that to a large degree people now think, talk and act *as if* emotivism were true, no matter what their avowed theoretical stand-point may be. Emotivism has become embodied in our culture. But of course in saying this I am not merely contending that morality is not what it once was, but also and more importantly that what once was morality has to

some large degree disappeared – and that this marks a degeneration, a grave cultural loss. (p. 21)

What follows will strike many as both shocking and scandalous. For what MacIntyre seeks to show, in what may be called his genealogical unmasking, is that despite the "rationalistic pretentions" of post-Enlightenment moral philosophy, it is nothing but a disguised expression of the emotivism which has become embodied and well entrenched in modern society and culture. The central "characters," or ideal types, of this culture are the aesthete, the bureaucratic manager, and especially the therapist. The panorama MacIntyre portrays is extraordinarily rich in detail but this part of his story reaches its climax in Chapter 9. The "hero" of *this* part of the story is Nietzsche. Why Nietzsche? Because he is the one "moral philosopher" of the modern period who had the perspicacity to reveal the false pretentions of modern "moral" life and philosophy.

> For it was Nietzsche's historic achievement to understand more clearly than any other philosopher – certainly more clearly than his counterparts in Anglo-Saxon emotivism and continental existentialism – not only that what purported to be appeals to objectivity were in fact expressions of subjective will, but also the nature of the problems that this posed for moral philosophy. . . . In a famous passage in *The Gay Science* (section 335) Nietzsche jeers at the notion of basing morality on inner moral sentiments, on conscience, on the one hand, or on the Kantian categorical imperative, on universalizability, on the other. (p. 107)

But the point for MacIntyre is not to vindicate Nietzsche (except in the sense of endorsing his insight into the pretentions and self-deceptions of modernity), but to confront us with a dramatic, grand Either/Or.

> *Either* one must follow through the aspirations and the collapse of the different versions of the Enlightenment project until there remains only the Nietzschean diagnosis and the Nietzschean problematic *or* one must hold that the Enlightenment project

was not only mistaken, but should never have been commenced
in the first place. There is no third alternative. . . . (p. 111)

In short, "Nietzsche *or* Aristotle?" When we reach this climax,
we realize just how high the stakes are. For the alternative posed
by MacIntyre is not just one view of morality versus another –
it is, rather, morality versus no morality.

Like the good storyteller that MacIntyre is, he has dropped
hints about what he means by the Aristotelian tradition of the
virtues and what is required to defend it rationally, but he has
done this in the sketchiest and most preliminary manner. What
follows (Chapters 10 through 13) is a *tour de force*. In a little
more than fifty pages, MacIntyre sweeps through his narrative history of the tradition of the virtues from Homer to
Classical Athens, to Aristotle, culminating in the medieval
contribution to this tradition. MacIntyre's historical sketch is
so dazzling – and is so filled with illuminating and provocative
insights – that it can divert us from the main point of his story.
For by using historical and philosophical arguments, MacIntyre intends – to use his own words – to argue "the rational
case that can be made for a tradition in which the Aristotelian
moral and political texts are canonical" (p. 289).

Indeed, there is something troubling about MacIntyre's
historical sketch of the virtues. He speaks of it as a "relatively
coherent tradition of thought" but points out that "there are
just too many different and incompatible conceptions of virtue
for there to be any real unity to the concept or indeed to the
history" (p. 169). One might even have the uneasy feeling that
the differences within this tradition are as great, as incompatible, and as incommensurable as anything MacIntyre has
located in "the Enlightenment project." One might even claim
that what MacIntyre has shown us *thus far* really supports
Nietzsche's case; that MacIntyre decoded is the champion of
Nietzsche. Why? Because he not only shows that there are incompatible and incommensurable lists and theories of virtue,
but has failed *thus far* to show how we can "rationally" ad-
judicate among rival claimants.

It is important to appreciate the depth of these differences. For it is not just that we are confronted with different (and frequently incompatible) lists and descriptions of the virtues, and that each of these lists embodies "a different theory about what virtue is" (p. 171), but that each of these theories is itself deeply embedded in different and clashing theories about the nature of the human species (typically, man), our *telos*, and the essential moral character of the universe in which we live. As MacIntyre himself emphasizes again and again, what is essential in the tradition of the virtues is that moral and evaluative statements "can be called true or false in precisely the way in which all other factual statements can be so called" (p. 57). The truth or falsity of such judgments presupposes *true* beliefs about "the concept of *man* understood as having an essential nature and an essential purpose or function" (p. 56). But what MacIntyre has not yet done is to show us how rival and incompatible claims to truth about what we essentially are, what is our true nature, what are our genuine ends, what is the moral character of the universe in which we live, are to be rationally evaluated.

To claim as he does, for example, that medieval thinkers "marked a genuine advance" (p. 168) in the tradition of the virtues without confronting the question of whether their understanding of the virtues is based upon a true understanding of what we essentially are and the character of the universe in which we live our moral lives is at best ingenuous, and at worst downright inconsistent with what MacIntyre himself claims must be shown to justify any adequate theory of the virtues. The trouble and perplexity are even worse than this. Much of the polemical and rhetorical force of MacIntyre's critique of the Enlightenment project derives from his emphasis on how it leads to competing and irreconcilable concepts of what is right and just. But MacIntyre himself shows that we have a structurally analogous situation when we consider the virtues. Thus, for example, when he discusses the virtues in classical Athenian culture, emphasizing the competing conceptions of the virtues in the Sophists, Plato, Sophocles, and Aristotle, he portrays Sophocles' vision as one where the human situation is essentially tragic in the *strong* sense that "there *is* an objective moral order, but our perceptions of it are such that we cannot bring rival moral truths into complete harmony with each other" (p. 134).[3] But this is just the essential truth claim, which according to MacIntyre, both Plato and Aristotle categorically reject. Who is right? What are the standards or criteria for making a rational judgment about these rival and clashing claims to truth? It begins to look as if what MacIntyre's *own* narrative history of the virtues reveals is – contrary to his claim of the three stage model of moral decline – that it is a "fiction" to believe that there ever was "a first stage at which evaluative and more especially moral theory and practice embody genuinely objective and impersonal standards which provide rational justification for particular policies, actions and judgments and which themselves in turn are susceptible of rational justification" (p. 18). The major point I want to make does not concern the specific merits of MacIntyre's analysis of Sophocles, Plato, Aristotle (or any other exemplar of the tradition of the virtues). It is, rather, to underscore what is MacIntyre's fundamental point, i.e., any conception of the virtues (what they are, how they are to be described, what is one's theory of virtues) *necessarily* makes a claim to truth – to truth about what we really are, what are our ends, and what is the essential moral character of the universe in which we live. Unless we seek to clarify and justify these truth claims, we will find ourselves in a situation that is analogous to the "interminable" conflicts that MacIntyre locates in the Enlightenment project. Or, we might say that if MacIntyre is really to answer Nietzsche and not play the role of his champion, he must face up to Nietzsche's own deep questioning of, and challenge to, the very idea of a "moral truth."

MacIntyre is well aware of what I have stated above. (He frequently raises the hard questions which arise in the reader's mind as one follows his dramatic narrative. This does not mean that he *answers* these questions.) He reviews just the sorts of difficulties and threats to his position that I have mentioned. Indeed, he even lists further difficulties. (See pp. 169–74.) So, we come to what I shall call the second dramatic climax of *After Virtue*, which is indicated by MacIntyre's own question: "are we or are we not able to disentangle from these rival and various claims a unitary core concept of the virtues of which we can give a more compelling account than any of the other accounts so far?" (p. 174). And we know what the failure to give such an account entails. Given MacIntyre's grand Either/Or, it means that Nietzsche "wins." So, we come to Chapters 14 and 15, which, according to MacIntyre himself, contain "the rational case that can be made for a tradition in which the Aristotelian moral and political texts are canonical" (p. 239). Here we must slow down his narrative and closely scrutinize his "complex argument."[4]

II

MacIntyre's account of a "unitary core concept of the virtues" proceeds in three stages. He tells us:

> The first stage requires a background account of what I shall call a practice, the second an account of what I have already characterised as the narrative order of a single human life and the third an account a good deal fuller than I have given up to now of what constitutes a moral tradition. Each later stage presupposes the earlier, but not *vice versa*. (p. 174)[5]

Let us take up each of these stages in order.

A. *The Concept of a Practice*

To appreciate why the concept of a practice is so important for MacIntyre, it is necessary to cite what he calls his "first, even if partial and tentative, definition of a virtue."

> *A virtue is an acquired human quality the possession and exercise of which tends to enable us to achieve those goods which are internal to practices and the lack of which effectively prevents us from achieving any such goods.* (p. 178)

What then is a practice? What is meant by "goods which are internal to practices?" A practice is defined as:

> any coherent and complex form of socially established coopera-
> tive human activity through which goods internal to that form
> of activity are realised in the course of trying to achieve those
> standards of excellence which are appropriate to, and partially
> definitive of, that form of activity, with the result that human
> powers to achieve excellence, and human conceptions of the
> ends and goods involved, are systematically extended. (p. 175)

Consider some of the activities that MacIntyre includes in the range of practices: chess, football, portrait painting, farming, architecture, "enquiries in physics, chemistry, biology," "the work of the historian," even the "making and sustaining of family life."

Practices are to be distinguished from technical skills which may be required for a specific practice, but do not constitute a practice. Throwing a football is a technical skill, but the game of football is not just a set of technical skills. Institutions may be required to sustain practices (and they can corrupt practices), but are not to be confused with practices. A chess club or a university is a social institution where certain practices may take place, but are not themselves practices. Practices always have a historical dimension, so of course there are histories of practices, histories which can relate their rise and fall.

To illustrate what he means by internal goods, MacIntyre cites the example of teaching an intelligent child the game of chess. I may initially "bribe" the child to play with me by offer- ing him or her candy (this is an external good), but there may come a time when the child "will find in those goods specific to chess, in the achievement of a certain high peculiar kind of analytical skill, strategic imagination and competitive intensity, a new set of reasons . . . for trying to excel in whatever ways the game of chess demands" (pp. 175–6). These are the internal goods of the practice of chess playing. They are internal because we can only identify them in terms of the game of chess and because they can only be "identified and recognized by the experience of participating in the practice in question. Those who lack the relevant experience are incompetent thereby as judges of internal goods" (p. 176). Furthermore, a "practice in- volves standards of excellence and obedience to rules as well as the achievement of goods. To enter a practice is to accept the authority of those standards and the inadequacy of my own performances as judged by them" (p. 177).

Now it is important to realize just how wide the range of practices is. For while not everything is a practice, there do not seem to be any apriori limitations on what may become a practice. Given his own "definition" of a practice, spying, smuggling, safecracking, the art of the executioner, and (despite MacIntyre's suggestion to the contrary) even torturing may become practices. (Indeed, the types of practices that Foucault analyzes in his own genealogical unmasking of modernity – and which he claims constitute the "disciplinary society" or the "carceral archipelago" – appear to satisfy MacIntyre's definition of a practice.)[6] The fact that there may be external goods associated with these practices does not disqualify them as practices. In each case we can discriminate "internal goods" characteristic of these practices. They have histories. They require technical skills, but do not simply consist of sets of technical skills. And they are not institutions. Practitioners can justly claim that "those who lack the relevant experience are incompetent thereby as judges of internal goods." If one is to excel in those practices, one must accept the authority of the standards of the "practice," standards which may themselves be criticized and refined.

Let us remember that the concept of a practice is introduced in order to give a tentative definition of a virtue. Considering the extraordinary range of actual and possible practices, one might think that the next step would be to ask, in regard to a specific practice: what are the acquired human qualities the possession and exercise of which tend to enable us to achieve those goods internal to the relevant practice? Thus, in the case of chess, we may discover that in order to achieve its internal goods, one needs to cultivate one's powers of memory, concentration, ability to anticipate possible strategies, etc. These then would be, according to MacIntyre's definition, the virtues required to excel in chess. There is no reason to believe that the "acquired human qualities" – virtues – required for one practice will be the same as, or even relevant to, those required by other practices; and, indeed, what is a "virtue" for one practice may well be a defect or a vice for another practice.

But this is not the "conclusion" that MacIntyre draws. He says:

> It belongs to the concept of a practice as I have outlined it . . . that its goods can only be achieved by subordinating ourselves to the best standard so far achieved, and that entails subordinating ourselves within the practice in our relationship to other practitioners. We have to learn to recognize what is due to whom; we have to be prepared to take whatever self-endangering risks are demanded along the way; and we have to listen carefully to what we are told about our own inadequacies and to reply with the same carefulness for the facts. (p. 178)

So far, so good. This applies to anyone who aspires to excel in chess, safecracking, or spying. But MacIntyre immediately goes on to claim: "*In other words we have to accept as necessary components of any practice with internal goods and standards of excellence the virtues of justice, courage and honesty*" (p. 178, italics added). Now this seems to be a "leap of faith," or less generously, a non sequitur. For MacIntyre has not shown or argued that these "virtues" – "these acquired human qualities" – are required for every (and any) practice. On the contrary, given his definition of a practice, this assumption is counterintuitive. A practitioner who seeks to excel in espionage may well need to cultivate the acquired human quality of lying, or feigning honesty in appropriate situations. MacIntyre's "leap" becomes even more dubious when we see how he immediately goes on to characterize justice: "justice requires that we treat others in respect to merit or desert according to uniform and impersonal standards" (p. 179). Where has MacIntyre shown that such an "acquired human quality" is required to excel in chess, poker, football, or portrait painting? Furthermore, even if we interpret what MacIntyre is saying in the most favorable way, do we have any reason to believe that the sort of "self-endangering risks" required to excel in chess, football, or spying have any relation to each other? They may well be very different human qualities. Indeed, MacIntyre seems to violate one of the conditions he has laid down for the virtues – the ability to "exercise" the appropriate human quality in a variety of novel contexts. Certainly a master chess player is one who knows when and where to take risks in playing chess, but may completely lack this "virtue" for any other practice.

At times it seems that MacIntyre is developing a very different argument concerning the virtues and practices, i.e., that the virtues are required or presupposed in order to *sustain* practices. He tells us: "Every practice requires a certain kind of relationship between those who participate in it. Now the virtues are those goods by reference to which, whether we like it or not, we define our relationships to those people with whom we share the kind of purposes and standards which inform practices" (p. 119). Or again: "I take it then that from the standpoint of those types of relationships without which practices cannot be sustained, truthfulness, justice and courage – and perhaps some others – are genuine excellences, are virtues in the light of which we have to characterize ourselves and others, whatever our private moral standpoint or our society's particular codes may be" (p. 179). But there are several perplexing features about these claims. Presumably we are living in a time when there has been a "decline" in the virtues. Yet, many of the practices that MacIntyre specifies thrive. But it practices cannot be sustained without truthfulness, justice, and courage, then the very existence of practices such as chess, farming, architecture, and enquiries of physics, chemistry, and biology should count as evidence for the flourishing of the virtues. Furthermore, although practices are coherent and complex forms of socially established cooperative human activities, I can engage in some of these without the *direct* participation of other persons, while other practices require other participants. I paint portraits by myself. I can even go off and farm by myself. But I cannot play football by myself. There is some plausibility in claiming that without truthfulness, justice, and courage, the type of relationships among participants required in order to play football cannot be sustained. But it is extremely dubious to claim that these virtues are required to excel in portrait painting or farming. What MacIntyre characterizes as practices

include what Aristotle calls *poesis* and *praxis*. But while MacIntyre can draw support from Aristotle in claiming that all *praxis*
involves or requires the virtues, it is not clear how and why
poesis (making) involves or requires the virtues.

MacIntyre himself is aware of some of these difficulties
– only he does not quite see them as difficulties. He admits that
there *may* be practices "which simply *are* evil" and that "as a
matter of contingent fact many types of practice may on particular occasions be productive of evil" (p. 186), (although he
never tells us how evil is to be characterized or how we determine whether or not a practice is or may be productive of evil).

What is the basic problem here? Once again MacIntyre con-
cisely states it himself. The range of actual and possible practices is so broad that if we limited ourselves to the conception of
virtue sketched so far, "there are *too many* conflicts and *too much*
arbitrariness" (p. 187). "The claims of one practice may be incompatible with another in such a way that one may find
oneself oscillating in an arbitrary way . . ." (p. 188). It may
even seem "that the goods internal to practices do after all
derive their authority from our individual choices" (p. 188). It
looks as if this account of practices and virtues suffers from
many of the same defects that MacIntyre takes to be characteristic of modernity. Certainly there is nothing he has shown
thus far which would present any serious obstacles to Nietzsche. On the contrary, MacIntyre and Nietzsche look like close
companions. For Nietzsche himself portrays for us a variety of
practices, their internal goods, and what is required to excel in
these practices. And Nietzsche might well endorse MacIntyre's
suggestion that there is "too much arbitrariness" and that the
goods internal to practices "derive their authority from our individual choices."

So we must move to the second stage of MacIntyre's
analysis. For "without an overriding conception of the *telos* of a
whole human life, conceived as a unity, our conception of certain individual virtues has to remain partial and incomplete"
(p. 188). "Partial and incomplete" is a gross understatement.
For the account thus far is in danger of being at once empty
and completely relativistic – empty because it does not set any

limits on what "acquired human qualities" are required to achieve the internal goods of specific practices; relativistic because there is no reason to believe that the acquired human qualities required to excel in one practice are the same as, or even similar to, those required for other, incompatible practices. What is lacking is any standard or principle for ordering and evaluating the confusing array of practices. Or to quote MacIntyre again, "unless there is a *telos* which transcends the limited goods of practices by constituting the good of a whole life, the good of a human life conceived as a unity, it will *both* be the case that a certain subversive arbitrariness will invade the moral life *and* that we shall be unable to specify the context of certain virtues adequately" (p. 189).

B. *The Narrative Account of a Single Human Life*

So we now have to face the crucial claim that there is a "*telos* of a whole human life" which transcends the limited goods of practices. At first it might seem that MacIntyre is leading himself (and us) into a cul-de-sac. For MacIntyre deprives himself of the types of considerations which enabled Aristotle to confront this question. Earlier MacIntyre succinctly identified the three elements required for an Aristotelian moral scheme: "untutored human nature, man-as-he-could-be-if-he-realized-his-*telos* and the moral precepts which enable him to pass from one state to the other" (p. 52). Without the second element the entire scheme falls apart; to use MacIntyre's own expression, it becomes "unintelligible." But how did Aristotle himself attempt to justify the second element? By an appeal to what MacIntyre calls his "metaphysical biology." Aristotle's *Ethics* and *Politics* cannot be excised from his metaphysics, his understanding of living organisms, his psychology, and indeed from his cosmology. The human species has a determinate nature (which, of course, allows for rational choice) and it has a *telos*.[7] But MacIntyre thinks we can give an account of the virtues that "does not require any identification of any teleology in nature, and hence it does not require any allegiance to Aristotle's metaphysical biology" (p. 183). I suspect that both Aristotle and Nietzsche would agree that *if* one calls into question what MacIntyre labels Aristotle's "metaphysical biology," then the entire traditional moral scheme of the virtues falls apart – and Nietzsche "wins." But MacIntyre does not think this follows, so let us turn to his understanding of, and argument for, a human *telos.*

The considerations that enter into the second stage of MacIntyre's analysis are so intricate, complex, and challenging that one can easily lose sight of the main point. In order to clarify, explain, and justify what he wants to say, he needs to explore the concepts of selfhood, action, intelligible action, personal identity, the character of a narrative history and why this is the basic and essential genre for characterizing human actions, what is meant by a "genre," accountability, and a good deal more. For these concepts form a network within which they mutually support and presuppose each other. But to facilitate a grasp of what is going on here, let me turn directly to the denouement, which comes swiftly in three paragraphs (pp. 203–4); then I can discuss what is required to make sense of it. MacIntyre writes:

> It is now possible to return to the question from which this enquiry into the nature of human action and identity started: In what does the unity of an individual life consist? The answer is that its unity is the unity of a narrative embodied in a single life. To ask "What is the good for me?" is to ask how best I might live out that unity and bring it to completion. To ask "What is the good for man?" is to ask what all answers to the former question must have in common. But now it is important to emphasize that it is the systematic asking of these two questions and the attempt to answer them in deed as well as in word which provide the moral life with its unity. The unity of a human life is the unity of a narrative quest. Quests sometimes fail, are frustrated, abandoned or dissipated into distractions; and human lives may in all these ways also fail. But the only criteria for success or failure in a human life as a whole are the criteria of success or failure in a narrated or to-be-narrated quest. A quest for what? (p. 203)

Let us provisionally bracket this last question and grant what this passage presupposes – that it makes sense to speak of the unity of an individual life, that its unity is the unity of a narrative embodied in a single life, etc. How does this bring us any closer to answering the questions: Is there a *"telos* of a whole human life"? What is the character of this *telos*? and How does this *telos* limit the range of practices and virtues that constitute a moral life? What constraints are there in answering the question "What is the good for me?" Can I not answer this by saying the good for me is to become the greatest chess player, football player, or espionage agent? I cannot do this, of course, if I do not have the talents and develop the technical skills required to excel in the endeavor I might choose. But can I not say that I am willing to neglect friends, family, political responsibilities, etc., in order to achieve this good, "the good for me," that I will order all my life and deeds to strive for this goal? I may fail, I may be distracted, but this is and will be my narrative quest. And, what reason is there to believe that there *must* be, or is, anything in common with the way in which I answer the question "What is good for me?" and the way in which anyone else answers this question? If this is what MacIntyre means by a "telos," it is a "telos" in a very quixotic sense.

While there are constraints on how I can answer the question "What is the good for me?," this does not prevent a wide diversity of answers, each of which may clash with, and be incompatible with, others – may require participation in practices incompatible with others, and may even require incompatible virtues. This conception of a human good does not limit "the subversive arbitrariness" that can invade "the moral life"; on the contrary, without further qualification it easily leads to and endorses such an arbitrariness.

It may be objected that I am placing an undue emphasis on what one can "say" to oneself and to others. But this ignores the stress that MacIntyre places on what one *does* ("it is the systematic asking of these . . . questions and the attempt to answer them in *deed* as well as in word which provide the moral life with its unity" [p. 203, emphasis added]). The unity, then, will not be given merely by what one says, but discovered in setting out to achieve one's goals. In short, the unity to which one aspires will be discovered *performatively*. And such a performance cannot be a solitary act; others will have to make sense of the narrative of the performance. Critical judgments regarding the "good for man" will be brought to bear on the account that one gives of the quest one is attempting. Furthermore, such critical judgments are not only "external" to the agent, they must be appropriated and consequently work internally for the moral agent as well. He or she must give a narrative account designed to show that his or her quest exemplifies and illuminates the human good.[8]

But once again, even if one places the stress on deeds, actions, and practices, it is difficult to see how this significantly limits the wide range of (incompatible) quests and ends pursued by agents. One can agree with MacIntyre that it is false to think that *any* goal can serve as a "telos of a whole human life" and that a genuine narrative quest must be located within specific social practices informed by communal traditions. But since MacIntyre himself tells us that some practices may be evil and suggests that there are traditions which are oppressive and/or mistaken, then the "unity of a narrative embodied in a single life" may require an acceptance *or* a rejection of the practices and traditions that have thus far shaped one's life. There is no reason to believe that the moral life of a revolutionary who seeks to overcome oppressive traditions is any less unified than the moral life of a "conservative" who seeks to preserve a tradition.

Perhaps if we answer the question of a "quest for what?" we can achieve some further determinacy. MacIntyre continues:

> It is in looking for a conception of *the* good which will enable us to order other goods, for a conception of *the* good which will enable us to extend our understanding of the purpose and content of the virtues, for a conception of *the* good which will enable us to understand the place of integrity and constancy in life, that we initially define the kind of life which is a quest for the good. . . .
> It is in the course of the quest and only through encountering and coping with the various particular harms, dangers, temptations and distractions which provide any quest with its episodes

and incidents that the goal of the quest is finally to be understood. A quest is always an education both as to the character of that which is sought and in self-knowledge. (p. 204)

Now it is difficult not to be sympathetic with much of what MacIntyre says here. But it is also difficult to see how it helps very much to specify a "*telos* which transcends the limited goods of practices by constituting the good of a whole human life." Unlike Plato, MacIntyre does not claim that there is *the* good which every soul desires and dimly apprehends. Unlike Aristotle, MacIntyre does not want to claim that there is a *telos* or good for human beings which is grasped (at least in outline) when we understand the *nature* of what it is to be a human being (i.e., an Athenian free male citizen). Unlike Sophocles, with his "argument" for the strong tragic view of life, MacIntyre has not shown us that there *is* an "objective moral order" which compels us to acknowledge the authority of incompatible moral claims made upon us. Unlike the medieval thinkers MacIntyre so admires, he has not confronted the claim that we are creatures of a Divine Creator that *the* "good for man is . . . supernatural and not only a natural good, but supernature redeems and completes nature" (p. 172). When we decipher MacIntyre's provisional conclusion about the good life for man – "the good life for man is the life spent in seeking for the good life for man, and the virtues necessary for the seeking are those which will enable us to understand what more and what else the good life for man is" (p. 204) – it looks like, despite his intentions, he is making the case for the type of "decisionism" that he finds so objectionable in Nietzsche or Weber.

C. *A Moral Tradition*

MacIntyre is aware that thus far there is something excessively individualistic about his account of the virtues, the good life, and the human *telos*. This is presumably rectified in the third stage of his analysis of a "core concept of a virtue." For he tells us "I am never able to seek for the good or exercise the virtues only *qua* individual" (p. 204). It is not just that individuals live in different social circumstances; we are also "bearers of a particular social identity. I am someone's son or daughter, someone else's cousin or uncle; I am a citizen of this or that city, a member of this or that guild or profession; I belong to this clan, that tribe, this nation" (p. 204). Whether we recognize it or not we are all bearers of tradition, we function within, and gain our social identity through, membership in communities. Against the type of modern theory of individualism which speaks as if each of us is a separate and discrete individual (where even every decision or choice is discrete and separable), MacIntyre is helpful in reminding us of our historical situatedness and social identities. These *do* provide constraints on what I am and may become, on what can be my narrative quest. But does this really illuminate the *character* of the "*telos* of a whole human life" or my narrative quest? After all, MacIntyre himself is sharply critical of the concept of tradition that thinks of it as simply the dead weight of the past. Traditions "when vital embody continuities of conflict" (p. 206). "When a tradition is in good order it is always partially constituted by an argument about the goods the pursuit of which gives the tradition its particular point or purpose" (p. 206). Sometimes, to keep a tradition alive what may be required is a revolution. But then this means that while we live our lives within traditions, roles, and social identities which characterize what we are, they do not determine what we must become. They set the context for my quest; they do not define it. I may decide that my narrative quest requires giving up my bourgeois comforts and dedicating my life to helping the poor, or that my life can only be unified if I join a revolutionary guerilla group, or perhaps try to opt out of the present *imperium* and join with others to construct "new forms of community within which the moral life could be sustained so that both morality and civility might survive the coming ages of barbarism and darkness" (p. 224). While the traditions, roles, and social identities that constitute what we are do characterize the setting for a narrative quest, they do not determine what is (or ought to be) our *telos*, the good for which we should strive, the good that can provide unity to our lives. The primary issue here is not one of demanding rules (in the Kantian sense) for specifying what is a *telos*. I agree with MacIntyre in the emphasis that he places on the role of *phronesis* in all moral judgment and choice. Nor is it one of expecting MacIntyre to endorse that caricature of the concept of a *telos* where one thinks of a *telos* as a fixed goal to which we are drawn by ineluctable necessity. Rather, what I want to underscore is the need to elucidate the concept of a *telos* with sufficient determinacy so that one at least has some notion of what does and does not count as a possible *telos* of a human life.

Ironically, even here – in the third stage of the analysis of the core concept of a virtue – MacIntyre is much closer to Nietzsche than he realizes. For Nietzsche could well agree with MacIntyre that "an adequate sense of tradition manifests itself in a grasp of those future possibilities which the past has made available to the present" (p. 207). After all, Nietzsche himself uses the genre of dramatic narrative to illuminate what he takes to be the "moral" condition of modern European man. This is the way his *Genealogy of Morals* is structured. Of course, what Nietzsche means by an "adequate sense of tradition" differs radically from what MacIntyre intends. Once we uncover that underlying the ascetic ideal there is "really" the will to nothingness, we also grasp "those future possibilities which the past has made available to the present." MacIntyre might reply that Nietzsche's narrative is not a true narrative, but is only a fiction. (Nietzsche would not consider this a criticism!) But this only brings us back to a question that MacIntyre does not squarely confront: how are we to distinguish *true* or *correct* narrative histories from those which are only fictions or illusions?

Furthermore, in this third stage of the development of the core concept of a virtue – the stage in which "living traditions" are emphasized – MacIntyre tells us that what sustains and strengthens traditions is in part the exercise of the relevant virtues.

> The virtues find their point and purpose not only in sustaining those relationships necessary if the variety of goods internal to practices are to be achieved and not only in sustaining the form of an individual life in which that individual may seek out his or

her good as the good of his or her whole life, but also in sustaining those traditions which provide practices and individual lives
with their necessary historical context. (p. 207)

But however sympathetic one may be with the recovery of
the concept of a living tradition, there is a danger here of a type
of romanticism where we are tempted to think of a tradition as
something which is intrinsically good (unless it is corrupted).
But if MacIntyre concedes that there may be practices "which
simply *are* evil," he ought to recognize that there also may be
traditions "which simply are evil," or which at least undermine
the exercise of the virtues. Do we not have to recognize that
there have been vital traditions that have been used to legitimate the moral inferiority of the poor, women, and minorities?

III

Something clearly has gone wrong. MacIntyre has been osten-
sibly trying to show us why Nietzsche is mistaken, why he does
not "win" – it has not been his intent to present an *apologia* for
Nietzsche. What then has gone wrong? For *After Virtue* contains
brilliant insights and it does touch a sensitive moral nerve.
Some may think that the real difficulty stems from MacIntyre's
refusal to take seriously the foundation of Aristotle's understanding of the virtues, i.e., Aristotle's "metaphysical biology"
and his cosmology. For as MacIntyre tells us (when referring to
Plato, Aristotle, and Aquinas), "the presupposition which all
three share is that there exists a cosmic order which dictates the
place of each virtue in a total harmonious scheme of human
life. Truth in the moral sphere consists in the conformity of
moral judgment to the order of this scheme" (p. 135). But
without a serious attempt to "rationally vindicate" the *truth* of
their claims about the nature of the human species and the
cosmic order, it is not possible to make the rational case for this
tradition. Others may feel that MacIntyre is really at war with
himself and has misstated his Either/Or. He is not really
defending Aristotle. For his deepest sympathies seem to fluctuate between a strong tragic understanding of the virtues

(which is closer to Sophocles than it is to Aristotle) and a medieval conception of the virtues (where our *telos* or good is "supernatural"). Still others may accuse MacIntyre of attempting to synthesize and integrate what is fundamentally incompatible – the type of metaphysical understanding of human nature characteristic of Greek philosophic thought with the type of historicism, or historicity, which only makes sense in a modern, post-Hegelian setting.

I think there is some truth in all these suggestions, but I would like to propose a different analysis and at the same time clarify what I think is the "true" narrative which underlies *After Virtue*. For I want to argue that not only is the exclusive disjunction of Nietzsche or Aristotle systematically misleading (MacIntyre's new version of the quarrel between the ancients and the moderns), but it obscures and betrays what MacIntyre himself has accomplished.

MacIntyre's attack on the Enlightenment project is itself part of the present mood which might be called "the rage against the Enlightenment, or modernity." Much of what he says is compatible with, and echoed by, a variety of disparate voices with whom MacIntyre has little sympathy – we find similar motifs in Heidegger, Adorno and Horkheimer, and Foucault. But there is "overkill" in these totalizing critiques – to use a Hegelian turn of phrase, there is also a "truth" in the Enlightenment project which itself needs to be reclaimed and preserved. Ironically, MacIntyre, who is so sensitive to how every "moral philosophy has some particular sociology as its counterpart" and must itself be understood in its historical social context, distorts the social context in which the Enlightenment project itself emerged. For we do a grave injustice to the Enlightenment if we fail to appreciate the extent to which it was a legitimate protest against hypocrisy and injustice, if we fail to appreciate how it was acutely sensitive to the failures of moral and political ideologies that systematically excluded whole groups of human beings from particpating in the "good life" while they "legitimized" political beliefs that masked various forms of domination.[9] But this is not the occasion to defend the emancipatory intentions of the Enlightenment against MacIntyre. Rather, I want to show how much MacIntyre himself *appropriates* from the very project that he tells us "had to fail."

Consider, for example, MacIntyre's own perceptive interpretation of the Kantian principle, "Always act so as to treat humanity, whether in your own person or in that of others, as an end, and not as a means."

> What Kant means by treating someone as an end rather than as a means seems to be as follows . . . I may propose a course of action to someone either by offering him reasons for so acting or by trying to influence him in non-rational ways. If I do the former, I treat him as a rational will worthy of the same respect as is due to myself, for in offering him reasons I offer him an impersonal consideration for him to evaluate. What makes a reason a good reason has nothing to do with who utters it on a given occasion; and until an agent has decided for himself whether a reason is a good reason or not, he has no reason to act. (p. 49)

Now this is a principle that MacIntyre accepts; indeed, it is fundamental for *his* entire project. When he adds "that what Kant enjoins is what a long line of moral philosophers have followed the Plato of the *Gorgias* in enjoining," he passes over, all to facilely, the thrust of Kant's principle – that it is a principle for *all* of humanity and is not just limited to the few included in one's community.

MacIntyre knows (and shows us how) the tradition of the virtues has always been based on *exclusion* – whether the exclusion of those who do not belong to a proper *polis*, barbarians, slaves, women, non-Christians, etc. It is not only that MacIntyre knows this, he categorically rejects the idea that anyone is in principle to be excluded from the "new forms of community within which the moral life could be sustained so that morality and civility might survive . . ." (p. 249). Consider MacIntyre's own description, as well as *criticism*, of Aristotle's concept of political freedom.

> The free self is simultaneously political subject and political sovereign. Thus to be involved in political relationships entails

freedom from any position that is mere subjection. Freedom is the presupposition of the exercise of the virtues and the achievement of the good.

With this part of Aristotle's conclusion we need not quarrel. What is likely to affront us – and rightly – is Aristotle's writing off of non-Greeks, barbarians and slaves [and women –R.J.B.], as not merely not possessing political relationships, but as incapable of them.

This blindness of Aristotle's was not of course private to Aristotle; it was part of the general, although not universal, blindness of his culture. It is intimately connected with another form of limitation. Aristotle writes as if barbarians and Greeks had fixed natures and in so viewing them he brings home to us once again the ahistorical character of his understanding of human nature. (p. 149)

What is implicit in this passage – and it is echoed throughout the book – is that any adequate conception of the good life and the virtues is one that cannot and should not exclude in principle any member of the human species. Furthermore, there is the danger that the appeal to "functional concepts" can *illegitimately* "justify" traditional historical social roles and identities, and thereby exclude some groups – the poor, minorities, and women – as being incapable of a fully embodied good life.

MacIntyre might reply that, of course he is not only defending, but is modifying, and even "strengthening," the tradition of the virtues. After all, a living tradition always involves argumentation and internal criticism. But while this is true, it does not yet speak to the issue of what *principles* and *standards* are the basis for this critique. For MacIntyre himself "universalizes" the tradition of virtues on the basis of principles which were hammered out in the Enlightenment.

Here it is important to comment on MacIntyre's own attack on "universalization." I think he is right in seeing that the result of *one* interpretation of the principle of universalization (and the "demand" for universal equality) has been to obscure and obliterate the particularity and specificity of morality which is grounded in communal traditions. This sense of universality comes close to what Hegel called "abstract universality." But there is another sense of "universality" which

MacIntyre himself employs – and which is essential for his argument – but which he fails to make fully explicit. Suppose one endorses the claim that if there are not "local forms of community" where the *participants* have a "shared sense" of the virtues and the good life, then one can be rightly skeptical that moral and political life will flourish. Is this itself a universal principle? Does everyone have the "right" to belong to such a community? Or, if one thinks that the appeal to "right" is the appeal to a moral fiction, one can ask, does not a rationally defensible account of the virtues and the good life *require* that every human being ought to be able to participate in such communities?

At the beginning of *After Virtue*, MacIntyre compares his narrative to what "Hegel called philosophical history" (p. 3). But after this initial reference to Hegel, Hegel is not really discussed and is barely mentioned. This is a curious omission considering the array of thinkers MacIntyre does discuss, the sensitive understanding of Hegel exhibited in MacIntyre's earlier writings, and especially because of the relevance of Hegel to MacIntyre's central concerns. In appealing to Hegel I do not want to suggest that Hegel "solved" the problem of Aristotle versus Nietzsche. But I do want to suggest that Hegel formulated, and perceptively understood, the problem which is really central to MacIntyre's own narrative quest.

There is very little in MacIntyre's critique of the Enlightenment project that was not stated or anticipated in Hegel. In many ways Hegel's criticisms of Kant are far more damaging than any MacIntyre generates. Hegel even detected how the Enlightenment's abstract demand for absolute freedom leads to terror. Hegel's portrait of the "characters" (in MacIntyre's sense), and his portrait of the "moral failures of asocial man" enrich MacIntyre's own description of the "emotivism" which has become embodied in our culture. At the same time there are few "modern" philosophers who can rival Hegel in his deep insight into the "tradition of the virtues" and in his understanding of the necessity of communal life for their flourishing – what Hegel called *Sittlichkeit*. Even MacIntyre's understanding of the tragic moral vision of Sophocles and the use of Diderot's *Le Neveu de Rameau* as a modern subversive text appear to be indebted to (at least bear a strong affinity to) Hegel's analysis in the *Phenomenology of Spirit*. But Hegel was far more perspicacious and forthright about basic problems of modernity. For Hegel well understood that there is no possibility of a return to the "immediacy" of an idealized Greek polis and that there is a "truth" in the Enlightenment aspiration to a universal freedom that encompasses all of humanity. What then is the problem which we confront? It is one of seeking to reconcile these deeply conflicting traditions. It is not clear – even in Hegel – whether such a reconciliation is really possible (despite Hegel's official pronouncements to the contrary). The point I am making, and its relevance to modern democracy, has been succinctly stated by Charles Taylor in a formulation that even MacIntyre might accept.

> Thus Hegel's dilemma for modern democracy, put at its simplest, is this: The modern ideology of equality and of total participation leads to a homogenization of society. This shakes men loose from their traditional communities, but cannot replace them as a focus of identity. Or rather, it can only replace them as such a focus under the impetus of militant nationalism or some totalitarian ideology which would depreciate or even crush diversity and individuality. . . .
>
> . . . one of the great needs of the modern democratic polity is to recover a sense of significant differentiation, so that its partial communities, be they geographical, or cultural, or occupational, can become again important centres of concern and activity for their members in a way which connects them to the whole.[10]

There is no guarantee that this "dilemma" can be resolved. But it defines the space in which we must think about moral and political life today. It makes no historical sense to suggest that the "Enlightenment project was not only mistaken, but should never have been commenced in the first place" (p. 111). To make such a claim, to oppose simply the failures of the "moderns" with the wisdom of the "ancients," is to violate

MacIntyre's own insistence that we cannot escape our historicity, our social identities, nor the traditions which inform our lives – including the tradition of the Enlightenment itself. It is to fail to recognize how much MacIntyre himself appropriates from this tradition in his critical reconstruction of the virtues: his implicit appeal to a concrete determinate universality; his defense of the principle of freedom where every participant can share in the type of communal life required for living a good life; his emphasis on the *shared* vision of a moral life by the *participants* in such communities; his demand that we treat all other human beings with respect and recognize every agent's capacity to act rationally.

The problem today is how we can live with the conflict and tension between the "truth" implicit in the tradition of the virtues and the "truth" of the Enlightenment. This is what MacIntyre's own narrative reveals. This is our narrative quest – for no one knows, nor can know, how this quest will turn out. This is the deepest problem with which we must live *after virtue*.

5

Why Hegel Now?[1]

During the past decade there has been an explosion of interest in Hegel. One can barely keep up with the new editions, translations, commentaries, and articles that have been appearing throughout the world. The reasons for this burst of scholarly activity vary in different cultural milieus, but the question is especially perplexing in the context of Anglo–American philosophy. If there is one philosopher who had been thought to be dead and buried, who embodied all the vices of the wrong way of philosophizing, who seemed to have been killed off by abuse and ridicule, it was Hegel. In order to begin to answer the question of why so many Anglo–American thinkers are finding Hegel so fascinating and worthy of careful study, it is necessary to review briefly the history of the influence of, and the fight against, Hegel in the English-speaking world.

I

It is frequently forgotten just how important Hegel was on the American scene during the post-Civil War period when American philosophy was in its formative stages. Stimulated initially by the immigration of German intellectuals, there were informal "Hegel Clubs" and groups such as the St. Louis and Ohio Hegelians. The first professional philosophic journal in America, *The Journal of Speculative Philosophy*, was founded by the Hegelian W. T. Harris, who later became US Commissioner of Education. Although the journal published articles by

Dewey, Peirce, and James, one of its primary purposes was to encourage the exploration of Hegelian themes.

Even more important was the influence (positive and negative) of Hegel on the "classic" American philosophers, especially Dewey, Peirce, James, and Royce. Dewey discovered Hegel when he was a graduate student at Johns Hopkins. In his autobiographical sketch published in 1930, Dewey tells us what Hegel meant to him at the time.[2]

> There were . . . "subjective" reasons for the appeal that Hegel's thought made to me; it supplied a demand for unification that was doubtless an intense emotional craving, and yet was a hunger that only an intellectualized subject matter could satisfy. It is more than difficult, it is impossible, to recover that early mood. But the sense of divisions and separations that were, I suppose, borne in upon me as a consequence of a heritage of New England culture, divisions by way of isolation of self from the world, of soul from body, of nature from God, brought a painful oppression – or, rather, they were an inward laceration. My earlier philosophic study had been an intellectual gymnastic. Hegel's synthesis of subject and object, matter and spirit, the divine and the human, was however no mere intellectual formula; it operated as an immense release, a liberation. Hegel's treatment of institutions and the arts, involved the same dissolution of hard-and-fast dividing walls, and had a special attraction for me.

Gradually, Dewey "drifted away" (to use his own expression) from Hegel. Darwin was soon to replace Hegel as a source of inspiration, although the mark of Hegel is evident throughout Dewey's intellectual career.[3] It is as if Dewey sought to domesticate Hegel, to incorporate what he took to be sound in Hegel and show how it was compatible with a robust naturalism.

The story of Peirce is more complicated. His primary philosophic interests and, even more important, his philosophic temperament were poles apart from Hegel. Peirce was contemptuous of what Hegel and the Hegelians called "logic." He forcefully fought what he took to be its pernicious influence.

But increasingly Peirce came to recognize the affinities between his own pragmaticism and Hegelianism (although he always emphasized what he took to be sharp differences). Commenting on the relation between his own categories of Firstness, Secondness, and Thirdness and Hegel's philosophy, he wrote: "The truth is that pragmaticism is closely allied to the Hegelian absolute idealism, from which, however, it is sundered by its vigorous denial that the third category (which Hegel degrades to a mere stage of thinking) suffices to make the world, or is even so much as self-sufficient. Had Hegel, instead of regarding the first two stages with his smile of contempt, held on to them as independent or distinct elements of the triune Reality, pragmaticists might have looked up to him as the great vindicator of their truth."[4]

William James's allegiances were always much more with the empiricist tradition rather than with the "heavy Germans" (although he was one of the most acute critics of the atomistic tendencies of traditional empiricism). Provoked by his junior colleague at Harvard, Josiah Royce, and his formidable adversary across the Atlantic, F. C. Bradley, James "took on" Hegel and the absolute idealists. At the age of sixty-five, despite his failing health, he could not resist the "professional challenge" of entering enemy territory and delivering a series of lectures at Oxford on "The Present Situation in Philosophy." Oxford had been the center of Absolute Idealism in the Anglo-Saxon world. In these lectures, published in 1908 as *A Pluralistic Universe*, James announced, "Oxford, long the seed-bed, for the English world, of the idealism inspired by Kant and Hegel, has recently become the nursery of a very different way of thinking. . . . It looks a little as if the ancient English empiricism, so long put out of fashion here by nobler sounding germanic formulas, might be repluming itself and getting ready for a stronger flight than ever."[5] With all his grace, wit, and philosophic charm, James ridiculed and exposed what he took to be the excesses and absurdities of the infatuation with the Absolute. But a close reading of these lectures reveals just how complex his attitude was. There is a marked difference between his treatment of Hegel and some of Hegel's followers, who lost themselves in "bloodless abstractions." Despite Hegel's "abominable habits of speech," James claims that he was "a naively observant man" who "plants himself in the empirical flux of things and gets the impression of what happens."[6] He extols Hegel for his keen awareness of the quality of the world as alive, and involving a dialectic movement in things. "Concepts were not in his eyes the static self-contained things that previous logicians had supposed, but were germinative, and passed beyond themselves into each other by what he called their immanent dialectic."[7] "Merely as a reporter of certain empirical aspects of the actual, Hegel, then is great and true."[8] But, according to James, Hegel was not content to be an "empirical reporter," he was "dominated by a notion of a truth that should prove incontrovertible, binding on everyone, and certain, which should be *the* truth, one, indivisible, eternal, objective and necessary, to which all our particular thinking must lead as to its consummation."[9] Hegel then sowed the seeds for, and himself succumbed to, the "vicious intellectualism" that dominates the absolute idealism of his British disciples.

But despite James's capacity to be sympathetic with what he took to be "great and true" in Hegel, the primary effect of *A Pluralistic Universe* was to help kill off philosophic interest in Hegel. After James's apparently devastating attack, it was difficult for any American philosopher to take Hegel seriously.

Josiah Royce was the American philosopher who was most deeply affected by Hegel. He was a sensitive interpreter of German idealism, and one of the first major American thinkers to appreciate the importance of Hegel's *Phenomenology*. His translations, lectures, and own creative philosophic work might have opened Hegel to others and shown what was "living" in him. But unlike Dewey, James, and Peirce, who did exercise a great influence on the course of American philosophy, Royce unfortunately has always been a much more marginal figure who exerted almost no direct influence on subsequent philosophic discussion.

The characteristic feature of this first flowering of Hegel in America was the shared sense that Hegel was, at the very

least, a worthy opponent. Dewey, James, Peirce, and Royce
– for all their differences – sought to state and clarify their own
philosophic positions over and against Hegel. A philosopher
"lives" as long as such an attitude prevails. He dies when it is
no longer thought necessary to argue with him.

One of the reasons why the classic American philosophers
took Hegel so seriously – if only to "refute" him – was because
of the prestige of Absolute Idealism in England. As Dewey
reports, "The 'eighties and 'nineties were a time of new ferment
in English thought; the reaction against atomic individualism
and sensationalistic empiricism was in full swing."[10] The
dominating figure of the English Idealists was F. C. Bradley,
who forcefully argued in support of the Absolute. But the relation between the English Idealists and Hegel is a complex and
curious one. The version of Absolute Idealism produced in
England was quite un-Hegelian and even anti-Hegelian.
Hegel's vivid sense of history, and of the dialectical struggle by
which *Geist* realizes itself, played almost no role for the English
Idealists. Hegel's *Logic* was considered to be the primary text,
not his *Phenomenology* or his writings about Objective Spirit.
The theme that fascinated the Absolute Idealists was the way in
which Hegel presumably had shown that everything is intern-
ally related into a single absolute whole. Like so much of
English philosophy before and after this brief flourishing of
Absolute Idealism, it was decidedly ahistorical.

When James went to Oxford in 1907, Absolute Idealism was
already on the wane, although McTaggart was yet to publish
his commentary on Hegel's *Logic*. But the demise of Idealism
was due primarily to the growing influence of two "young
Turks": Bertrand Russell and G. E. Moore. Both had breathed
the heady atmosphere of Idealism and both, after a brief infatuation, were repelled by it. When read against the
background of Bradley, we can see how Russell's epistemological use of his theory of descriptions, his insistence on
knowledge by acquaintance, and his ontological claims about
particulars were motivated by the desire to refute and answer
Idealism.[11] Moore's paper, "The Refutation of Idealism,"
became something of a minor classic.[12] Moore attacked all

forms of Idealism. Russell – and in a very different way, Moore too – set out to show that what the Idealists claimed to be absurd and contradictory was actually sound and true.

The English form of Absolute Idealism passed away from its dominant position almost as quickly as it had arisen. It was soon looked upon as a temporary aberration in the long tradition of British empiricism. Within a few short years after the early attacks by Russell and Moore, young English philosophers were no longer "refuting" Absolute Idealists, they simply did not read them.

To complete this sketch of the demise of Hegel among Anglo–American philosophers, two other events must be mentioned: the impact of logical positivism and the enormous influence of Karl Popper's *The Open Society and Its Enemies*. Although the members of the original Vienna circle were not directly reacting against Hegel, nevertheless the type of philosophizing represented by Hegel is what they so deeply opposed and sought to eliminate. They claimed that it was little more than high sounding verbiage which when unmasked turns out to be empty and cognitively meaningless. So Hegel was not simply mistaken, advocating a false position which had to be refuted. Rather, his pseudo-propositions were the epitome of metaphysical nonsense. One needed to start afresh, to set the standards of meaning, clarity, and argumentation so rigorously that one could rule out from the beginning the Hegelian mode of pseudo-philosophizing. As the doctrines of the positivists – and more generally the positivist spirit – moved across England and the United States, the verdict which had been reached independently by James, Russell, and Moore was reinforced.

None of these attacks on Hegel was directed primarily at his social and political philosophy. It was his metaphysics, the holistic thrust of his thinking, and his philosophic method (or lack of it) that were taken to be so objectionable. But with the appearance of Karl Popper's *The Open Society and Its Enemies* in 1946, the prejudices of liberal Anglo–American thinkers were confirmed. Even if they had not read Hegel, Popper presumably had, and he had shown once and for all that Hegel's doctrines led directly to the closed totalitarian society which was the very antithesis of what was best and most cherished in the liberal tradition.

These several vehement reactions to Hegel – the triumph of pragmatism, the new forms of analysis practiced by Russell and Moore, the growing influence of the positivist movement, and the attack by Popper – complemented and reinforced each other. A generation of American and English philosophers was taught that Hegel represented the excesses and emptiness of speculative philosophy. He was now thoroughly discredited in favor of new demands for unpretentious meticulous analysis. I recall vividly that when I first studied Hegel in the early 1950s, the prevailing professional opinion in America was that one was either a fool or a madman (or both) to think that Hegel was an important philosopher. It would be naive to suggest that all this has changed. Old entrenched attitudes die hard, and the mention of Hegel can still evoke abuse and snickers in many professional philosophic circles.

II

How then are we to account for the revival of interest in Hegel? What, if anything, does it tell us about our present situation in philosophy? What is there that is still "alive" in Hegel and relevant to contemporary philosophic discussions? Walter Kaufmann (whose own translations and writings on Hegel have helped to combat prevalent myths about Hegel and to make his work more accessible) has recently offered the following explanation:[13]

> First, Hegel is immensely interesting. Once that was shown, many academics with widely different interests found it worth their while to study him and write on him. Secondly, he provides a striking alternative to all kinds of positivism and to the mainstream of Anglo–American philosophy. Thirdly, the immense growth of interest in Hegel reflects student interests. All three factors also help to account for the extraordinary growth of interest in Nietzsche. But in Hegel's case we must add a fourth point: the explosion of interest in Marx.

The trouble with this "explanation" is that it does not really explain, or at best merely scratches the surface. Hegel *is* "immensely interesting" and there have always been some thinkers who have recognized this. But the quality of being "interesting" is not simply an intrinsic property of a philosopher's work, but reflects the interests of those who study and write about him. What then are these new interests? And why Hegel, rather than some other thinker, like Plotinus, who is also "immensely interesting?" True enough, Hegel is a striking alternative to all kinds of positivism, but what accounts for the growing intellectual need for such an alternative, and why this one? No doubt students in many places have organized their own study groups and demanded that Hegel be taught, but why? Many have been led to Hegel through the fascination with Marx, but this only pushes the issue back one step further. Why the explosion of interest in Marx? I think we can penetrate more deeply than Kaufmann does.

Consider Kaufmann's last two points: student interest and the revival of Marx. There have been many attempts to account for the international student activism and protest during the 1960s – ranging from those who see it as a result of permissive child training to those who want to classify it as one of those periodic outbursts of energy of the young against the old. But if we focus on the self-understanding that some of the more articulate members of the New Left had of themselves, they were protesting against the cool inhumanity, the latent violence, the systematic insensitivity to the plight of the poor and oppressed, the disparity between the American dream and the underlying social reality, and the self-destructive artificiality of so much of contemporary life in advanced technological societies. There was a strong moral and even moralistic tone to their protest. There was a deep sense of revulsion against mainstream intellectual orientations which had become so entrenched in academic institutions. For these orientations did not provide an adequate basis for understanding what was going on in society, or offer any guidance for changing it. The "official" liberalism of so many academics seemed to be perfectly compatible with a "do nothing" policy about the roots of social injustice. It seemed to many that the sacred cows of academic life – "objectivity," "impartiality," and "value-neutrality" – were in fact value-saturated and vehicles for an ideology that failed to recognize itself as an ideology. And finally, in the name of increasing "rationality," society seemed to be heading in a direction that was hopelessly irrational. It is in this context that Marx was rediscovered by young radicals. But the Marx who was rediscovered and spoke directly to contemporary concerns was not the Marx whose views had become dogmatized by communist ideologists. Rather, it was the humanistic strain in Marx, which emphasized that bourgeois society is based upon and furthers alienation and exploitation that struck such a resonant chord. It was Marx who spoke of revolutionary *praxis* and demanded human emancipation that was found so appealing. To the extent that Marx himself was actually read and studied, it was the twenty-six-year-old Marx who had written the 1844 Paris manuscripts, who became the new cultural hero. Marx appeared to provide what tired liberal formulas failed to provide – an orientation, a set of categories for coming to grips with the deep internal conflicts and contradictions of advanced capitalist societies, and – many believed – a basis for changing the world through revolutionary *praxis*.

Against their professors who confidently reassured them that Marx was dead and had been empirically refuted, many students saw Marx as more alive and relevant than ever. Gradually, it was not just Marx who was being rediscovered and re-interpreted, but also a tradition of Western Marxism that had been scarcely known in the Anglo–American world. One of the keys for understanding the immense popularity of Marcuse at the height of student activism was the way in which he became an entrée into Marx. With the translations of Lukács, Korsch, the Frankfurt School, Gramsci, and others, it was increasingly appreciated that there had been a long and vital tradition of Marxism which had stressed the same themes that captured the imagination of so many young radicals. There was a common theme running through many of these variants of Marxism – the emphasis placed on the Hegelian origins of Marxism. After reading Lukács, Marcuse, Adorno, Horkheimer, no one could

think of Hegel as a simpleminded idealist who had everything
upside down. To gain a deep understanding of Marx, one had
to "take on" Hegel. This is true even of the countermovement
to the so-called Hegelianized reading of Marx most forcefully
represented by Althusser and his associates. Getting clear
about the relation of Hegel and Marx is much more than an
interesting scholarly exercise. It has political and practical consequences. It has become a means for clarifying what one takes
to be essential and still alive in Marxism.

Gradually, then, as in the title of George Lichtheim's last
collection of articles, there has been a movement of thought,
From Marx to Hegel. This movement itself reflects – as Lichtheim
perceptively observed – how after an initial frustration about
"changing the world" there has been a growing need for a
deeper and more penetrating interpretation of the world.

These factors – the cultural source of student interest, the
revival of Marxism as a live option, and the study of Hegel in
order to deepen and clarify one's grasp of Marx – were all external to mainstream currents in analytic Anglo–American
philosophy. Up until the early 1960s, there were scarcely any
philosophy departments in the Anglo–American world dealing
with Hegel and Marx. There is still a prevailing cynical attitude that it is permissible to teach Marx and Hegel to attract
undergraduate students, but not quite respectable for serious
graduate study. But there are also internal factors in the
development of analytic philosophy that are creating a more
favorable climate for the study of Hegel.

One of the primary reasons for the revival of any philosopher
is the realization that there is a basic affinity between the problems that are in the foreground of current philosophic discussion
and those with which the relevant philosopher was struggling.
Thus, in the early days of logical positivism, the one philosopher
singled out as worthy of study was Hume. Hume was read (or
more often misread) as a proto-positivist – as seeing through
a glass darkly what logical positivists saw so clearly. Or, to put
the issue from their own perspective, logical positivists claimed
that the dramatic advances in logic now enabled them to carry
out a program that Hume and other empiricists had struggled

to articulate. When conceptual analysis replaced the dominance of the reductive analysis of earlier logical positivists and logical atomists, Kant replaced Hume as a source of inspiration. Strawson's commentary, for example, has the clear intention of salvaging what he takes to be worthwhile in Kant and showing its affinity with the "newer" form of conceptual analysis. Wilfrid Sellars, who has presented his philosophic position by commenting on Kantian themes, remarked a few years ago: "now that philosophy had gone 'back to Kant' for the second time, can a Hegelian 'trip' be far behind?"[14] There is something much more serious at stake than the faddish revival of past philosophers. I can show this by turning to a field of inquiry that initially might seem to be quite remote from Hegel: contemporary philosophy of science.

The philosophy of science in our time is more than a subspeciality of philosophy. It has become the locus of some of the most exciting and controversial epistemological and metaphysical disputes The field is alive with controversy and strident polemics but, in this context, I want to stress a number of common themes in what Mary Hesse has called the postempiricist philosophy and history of science.[15]

First, there is common agreement that the "image of science" projected and endorsed by early logical positivists and empiricists is not only simplistic but distortive of the nature of science. The facile distinctions between observation and theory, the context of discovery and the context of justification; between historical issues and philosophic issues about science; between science as activity and science as knowledge break down under close scrutiny. Whatever value these distinctions have in illuminating science, they cannot be taken as hard and fast dichotomies.

Secondly, there has been a much greater emphasis on the need to "look and see" how science actually works. This means studying case histories and classic instances of scientific change in order to clarify *philosophic* issues about science. One reason why the history of science has become so important for philosophers of science is because of the realization that all attempts to specify the criteria for scientific verification, falsification, or confirmation, which are abstracted from historical context, have ended in failure.

Thirdly, the motor force of scientific change – anomalies; conflict; the clash of one paradigm, theory, or research program against another – has come to play a prominant role in understanding science.

Fourthly, (although this is one of the most hotly debated issues) there is a growing consensus that many of our traditional conceptions of rationality are simply inadequate to illuminate the sense in which scientific activity is (or is not) a rational activity, and there are gropings toward developing a more adequate theory of rationality.

Fifthly, until recently philosophers have paid little or no attention to the social context in which science takes place and the social consequences of science, but this is becoming an issue of much greater concern. Here, too, it was once thought that epistemological issues concerning the nature of science and empirical issues concerning the sociology of science could be neatly separated and assigned to different disciplines, but the distinction has become increasingly criticized and blurred.

Every one of these themes and new emphases has a parallel with Hegel. I do not think this can be explained by any sort of direct influence. Rather, I am claiming that there has been an internal dialectic within the philosophy of science which has brought us to a point where we can recognize the deep affinities with Hegel's orientation toward the growth and development of knowledge. There are even some philosophers, like Paul Feyerabend, who have shocked their colleagues by emphasizing this affinity.[16]

If I am right that the philosophy of science is representative of much more general and pervasive epistemological and metaphysical themes, then we ought to find the same type of turning in these areas of philosophic inquiry. A sympathetic reader of the first part of Hegel's *Phenomenology,* viz., *Consciousness (Bewusstsein)*, who makes the appropriate translations, discovers a remarkable parallel between the stages of development that Hegel portrays and the actual historical development of analytic epistemology in the twentieth century. Hegel begins the *Pheno-*

menology with the portrayal of sense certainty. This corresponds to attempts by early phenomenalists to ground all empirical knowledge in discrete sense data which we presumably know by direct acquaintance. Many of the reasons advanced for exposing the defects of phenomenalism and for showing the failures of reductive analysis correspond to the reasons that Hegel gives for the necessity to pass beyond this stage of sense certainty. There is even a correspondence between the way in which the appeal to material objects or the "thing language" superseded phenomenalism and Hegel's analysis of how the stage of perception supersedes sense certainty. This stage in the development of analytic epistemology also led to internal conflicts and problems. Transcending the split that took place among analytic philosophers between those who favored the techniques of ordinary or conceptual analysis and those who favored the construction and reconstruction of artificial languages and formal systems, there was a shared agreement that to focus on the single term or even the isolated sentence as the basic epistemological unit or building block was inadequate. One needed to take a more holistic approach in which the "language game" or the "conceptual framework" was treated as primary and fundamental. This third stage corresponds to what Hegel calls "Understanding." A close reading of this chapter reveals how many of the arguments that have been developed to show how and in what sense language games and conceptual schemes must be taken as primary were anticipated by Hegel. Even this stage of philosophic inquiry is unstable. The very talk of alternative conceptual schemes or frameworks seems to make sense only if we presuppose that there is a "world" or a "given" which can be understood or known in alternative ways. As some philosophers, such as Davidson and Rorty, have shrewdly argued, the very distinction between a "something" that is known and the various ways of knowing it – which has its roots in the Kantian problematic – is incompatible with the devastating attacks on the "myth of the given." [17] As long as we stay within a quasi-Kantian framework, there seems to be no satisfactory way of dealing with the question: what is the "it" or the "world" that is known via alternative conceptual schemes? What sense can even be given to the notion of an "alternative" conceptual scheme? Rorty himself, who focuses on this difficulty, recognizes that what he is claiming sounds very much like Hegel. Hegel, of course, was not struggling with the problems of alternative conceptual schemes as they have been treated by contemporary analytic philosophers, but he was perhaps the most brilliant and ruthless critic of the latent ambiguity in Kant which is the origin of this contemporary dilemma. Hegel argued – rightly, I believe – that Kant cannot have his cake and eat it too, that one cannot at once insist that there is a given or an unsynthesized manifold that grounds all phenomenal knowledge *and* insist that what plays this vital epistemological role is intrinsically nonconceptual and unknowable in itself (because *all* knowledge involves synthesis). This is closely related to the instability of claiming that there *must* be a *Ding-an-sich* that grounds all phenomenal knowledge, but that we cannot know anything about this *Ding-an-sich*.

I do not think that these parallels between Hegel and the development of analytic epistemology are happy coincidences – or moves in the tiresome game of showing how between any two thinkers or philosophic movements there are always some points of similarity. Rather, I believe that Hegel had a profound insight into the dialectical movement of thought, and an uncanny ability to show how various positions or "shapes of consciousness" harbor internal conflicts which require us to pass beyond them. The actual historical development of analytic philosophy exhibits this dialectical movement.[18] Furthermore, while analytic philosophers have not been (in the main) directly influenced by Hegel, over and over again one discovers that the arguments and strategies employed to show why some earlier position is unsatisfactory are similar to those employed by Hegel.

In addition to the philosophy of science, ...d analytic epistemology, there is another central area of analytic philosophy in which we have begun to see the relevance of Hegel. This is the theory of action. By the theory of action, I do not mean anything so neat as a hypothetical-deductive system that purports to explain human action, but the philosophic reflection on the description and explanation of action, how action is to be distinguished from physical movement, the relation of the concept of action to meaning, purpose, intention, motive, reason, and cause. In another context, I have attempted to give an account of how and why the theory of action has become so important in analytic philosophy and to indicate how the changing views on action reflect and are intimately tied up with the development of analytic philosophy.[19] But here, I want to mention two major contributions to this discussion: Charles Taylor's *The Explanation of Behaviour*, and George H. von Wright's *Explanation and Understanding*. Both of these studies have sought to defend the autonomy and nonreducibility of the teleological explanation of human action. Both have been concerned to show the implications of the analysis of action for clarifying the nature and function of the social disciplines. Both have emphasized the similarities between post-Wittgensteinian discussions of action and the tradition of hermeneutics in Continental philosophy. Although Taylor argues his case employing the analytic idiom, Hegel hovers in the background of his work. Von Wright, who is among the most respected and eminent analytic philosophers of our time, introduces his study of explanation and understanding with a review of the two main competing traditions concerned with the "conditions an explanation has to satisfy in order to be scientifically respectable": the Aristotelian and the Galilean. Von Wright says the following about Hegel:[20]

> it seems to me true to say that Hegel is the great renewer – after the Middle Ages and therefore in opposition to the platonizing spirit of Renaissance and Baroque science – of an aristotelian tradition in the philosophy of method. For Hegel, as for Aristotle, the idea of law is primarily that of an intrinsic connection to be grasped through reflective understanding, not that of an inductive generalization established by experiment. . . . For both philosophers, explanation consists in making phenomena teleologically intelligible rather than predictable from knowledge of their efficient causes.

The importance and relevance of Hegel for the theory of action is not that he obscurely said something that vaguely resembles what is now being said by some analytic philosophers. Rather, contemporary philosophers have come to appreciate the difficulties and distortions that result from the attempt to impose a Galilean model of the explanation of action (a model which in our time has taken the canonical form of a deductive-nomological schema). In attempting to account for what is distinctive about human action (or at least some types of human action), it is necessary to examine the ways in which actions themselves are constituted by rules, practices, and institutions. Understanding rules and practices is itself essential for the description and explanation of (human) actions. Few philosophers have equaled Hegel in the passion with which he argued that the character and dynamics of human action must be understood within the context of intersubjective interactions. Furthermore, Hegel focuses on issues which have only begun to be asked by analytic philosophers, although these issues are highlighted by their own analyses. For if there are intersubjective rules and practices that are constitutive of human actions, then it becomes essential to gain some understanding of how such practices emerge, what sustains them, and how they pass away. These are the very issues that are in the foreground of Hegel's philosophy.

While contemporary analytic philosophy was originally based on a total rejection and repudiation of Hegel, the internal development of the closely knit dialectic in the philosophy of science, analytic epistemology, and the theory of action has brought us to a stage in which we can recognize more than superficial resemblances with Hegel – the very issues that are now at the center of discussion are those with which Hegel was struggling. Furthermore, in each of these three areas, the types of difficulties that have brought us closer to the Hegelian problematic are similar. For in each area it is problems dealing with process and change – whether scientific change or conceptual change, or changes in the practices that are constitutive of actions – that have required philosophers to ask in a new way the very questions that Hegel poses.

Thus far I have dealt with some of the external and internal reasons for the renaissance of Hegel. But there are two other factors – which, although difficult to pin down, are no less important. One of the deep convictions of many analytic philosophers has been that the proper way to do philosophy is by piecemeal analysis. If we are serious about clarifying, solving, and dissolving problems, then this can only be accomplished if we are modest in our ambitions and careful about details. The motto has virtually been: In order to conquer we must divide and subdivide. Such an attitude is based upon the presupposition that we can *isolate* discrete philosophic problems and make progress in solving them. Indeed, part of the rhetorical force of the term "analysis" has been to insist on this new way of philosophizing. But the consequence of the serious attempt to carry out such a project has frequently been the very opposite of what was intended. This is not to say that analytic philosophy is based on a mistake or has ended in failure. But in the relentless pursuit of what might initially seem to be a single and discrete issue, our analyses spill over to other issues and other domains. We cannot make much progress on epistemological issues unless we squarely confront metaphysical issues; if we want to get clear about reference and denotation, we must also deal with ontology; whether we start with problems in the theory of knowledge or the theory of value, we discover how we are forced to get clear about problems in what might initially seem to be remote domains.

It is commonly thought – this is one of the myths about Hegel – that his primary concern was with a global approach to philosophy. But the truth is that he always demanded specificity or what he called concreteness (this is not to say that he always practiced what he preached). Only when we attempt to be absolutely specific and deal with what is determinate do we come to the realization that carrying out such a project necessitates a movement to a more general or synoptic perspective. The actual development of analytic philosophy bears out one of Hegel's most important and central claims. Some contemporary philosophers, such as Wilfrid Sellars, have self-consciously made this very same point – that there is a perfectly legitimate sense in which clarifying or solving a single problem in philosophy demands that progress be made on all relevant

philosophic issues. Philosophers are learning or relearning a
lesson that Hegel taught so brilliantly. Few philosophers have
been so critical of the type of abstract general claims that lack
determinateness and specificity. This is the primary defect of
knowledge that Hegel called Understanding (*Verstand*), which
is to be contrasted with the concrete, determinate knowledge of
Reason (*Vernunft*). If something is true, then it must be shown
to be true in detail, it must be pursued in all its determinateness and specificity. It is only by attempting to carry out
such a project that one comes to grasp what is genuinely universal. Hegel, then, would not have opposed the spirit that
animates so much of analytic philosophy; he would have endorsed it. The growing realization, which is now being experienced by many analytic philosophers, of the defects of
piecemeal analysis and the necessity to explore the dialectical
web of interrelations among what initially appear to be discrete
and separable issues is precisely what is to be expected.

The final consideration that I want to discuss in answering
the question, "Why Hegel Now?" has to do with our present
cultural experience. Philosophers – especially analytic philosophers – are resistant to, and suspicious of, any attempt to
approach philosophic activity from the perspective of the cultural context within which it is practiced. To do so seems to
raise the muddy issues of the sociology of knowledge and to
confuse historical and philosophic issues. But it is more than an
empty truism that in addition to being professional philosophers, we are also living in and influenced by our historical
situation.

Enlightenment ideals about the efficacy of reason in clarifying and helping us to solve social and political problems – ideals
which have shaped so much of modern thought – are becoming
increasingly thin and unconvincing. Hegel wrote at a time
when many of the tendencies that have shaped the contemporary world were beginning to become manifest. He was
perhaps unduly optimistic about the power of Reason and
Spirit to resolve the latent contradictions that characterized
social, political, and cultural life. But Hegel did provide us
with an incisive *analysis* of the conflicts, dilemmas, and tensions

that became manifest in the post-French revolutionary period. Although many of his claims about civil society and the state are outdated, nevertheless contemporary societies have not resolved the conflicts and crises that he detected. These have become at once sharper and more confused. Hegel, in his description of the dynamics of modern society, was one of the first to describe the inherent conflicts and instability of the forces, institutions, and practices that have shaped modern society. So, even if we reject Hegel's "solutions," there is still much to be learned from him in our own attempts to comprehend the cultural conflicts and crises of our own time.[21]

III

Charles Taylor has written the most ambitious book on Hegel which has yet appeared in English. In its 580 pages, he seeks to explore the aims of Hegel's epoch; to sketch his intellectual development; to provide an overview of Hegel's most central concept – self-positing Spirit; to explicate and evaluate the *Phenomenology, Logic*, and Hegel's contributions to the study of objective and absolute spirit, including history, politics, art, religion, and philosophy, and to conclude with a discussion of the relevance of Hegel today. There are few philosophers who are as qualified to write a definitive study of Hegel which will speak to the concerns of contemporary Anglo–American philosophers. Taylor was trained at Oxford during the period of post-Wittgenstein philosophy when the theory of action was becoming a dominant concern. He has a fine grasp of contemporary Continental philosophy. His own contributions to social and political thought have focused on Hegelian themes that have become central as a result of the internal dialectic of contempory discussions. Yet the *total* effect of this book is confusing. Despite its length one frequently has the sense of being rushed through complex issues. At times the style is frenetic. The major source of these difficulties is not only Taylor's attempt to cover so much ground but also his combining of so many different types of scholarly approaches in a single volume

– ranging from essays in the history of ideas to detailed commentaries on obscure passages. It is not a book that will satisfy
scholars of Hegel, because Taylor glosses over knotty issues.
But contrary to Taylor's primary intention of making Hegel
accessible and intelligible to those who have not studied Hegel
carefully, his study may have the effect of confirming the biases
of those who think that Hegel is sloppy, careless, and arbitrary.
Yet there is a great deal here that is fresh, original, and sound.
It would be a great pity if the virtues of Taylor's interpretation
were ignored because of some of the defects of this book.
Although there are unifying themes that run through this
study, I suggest that it can be more profitably read as a series of
loosely related essays or lectures on Hegel. Indeed, I do not
think we are confronted with a single book, but with the
material that might have served as a basis for half a dozen
books on Hegel. In my critical discussion, I want first to consider some of the perplexities raised by Taylor's analysis, and
then turn to its major contributions.

The first part of this book, "The Claims of Speculative
Reason," is divided into three chapters: "Aims of a New
Epoch," "Hegel's Itinerary," and "Self-positing Spirit." To
understand the unity of this part, we must appreciate how
Taylor structures his analysis. He seeks to delineate "a central
problem, which insistently demanded solution of the thinkers
of this time" (p. 3) to explore why it became so urgent, how
some of Hegel's contemporaries struggled with and failed to
solve it, how this problem itself underwent transformation in
the course of Hegel's intellectual development ("Hegel's
Itinerary"), and finally how Hegel's concept of self-positing
Spirit was intended to provide a comprehensive and adequate
solution to it. The problem "concerned the nature of human
subjectivity and its relation to the world. It was a problem of
uniting two seemingly indispensable images of man, which on
the one level had deep affinities with each other, and yet could
not but appear utterly incompatible" (p. 3).

Taylor organizes his discussion in a typically Hegelian
fashion; he locates a deep tension, a basic incompatibility or
contradiction that Hegel's own philosophy – in particular, the

idea of self-positing Spirit – was intended to resolve. Taylor does what Hegel himself tells us must be done if we are genuinely to comprehend a philosophic position – to explore how it grows out of, reflects, and seeks to resolve the deepest cultural conflicts and aspirations of its own time. Performing this task for Hegel is especially important because Anglo–American philosophers are almost totally ignorant of the cultural and intellectual context in which Hegel's thought was formed – that post-Kantian period in German thought that was shaped by Herder, Goethe, Lessing, Fichte, and Schelling.

In order to specify the problem and the source of the incompatibility of the competing images of man, Taylor presents a broad sketch of a three-stage model of changing conceptions of human subjectivity – of changes in the basic categories by which we understand the self. The first stage has its roots in classical thought and persists through the Middle Ages. The central theme of this classical understanding of the self is that the entire universe, including the individual self, expresses or reflects a cosmic order of Ideas. The subject is defined in relation to this cosmic order, and consequently self-knowledge or self-presence is identified with attaining a rational vision of the cosmic order. The world itself is understood to be intrinsically meaningful (for it expresses this cosmic order), and it can be approached as a text in which the philosophic task is to decipher and comprehend this cosmic order.

According to Taylor, although the modern conception of the self was already foreshadowed by the Epicureans and the Skeptics, it really came into its own in the seventeenth century. What seemed so plausible and rational from a classical point of view was now seen as a form of indulgence and distortive anthropomorphism – a projection of human teleological meanings onto a world which is essentially non-teleological and devoid of any intrinsic meaning. This is the age of the great dualisms where, in one form or another, the human subject is contrasted with an "objective" order that is devoid of meaning and purpose, and which can best be understood as functioning according to mechanistic laws. Taylor characterizes this modern conception of the subject as "self-defining." Corresponding to

this view of the self is the conception of the world as "objecti-
fied," or "disenchanted."

This modern philosophical anthropology which culminates
in the Enlightenment was the point of attack "of the two major
tendencies in German thought whose reconciliation was the
key problem of Hegel's generation" (p. 11). On the one hand,
there was the groping toward a new conception of the self which
would overcome the ontological and epistemological dichotomies that plagued so much of modern thought – a new anthropology that Taylor labels "expressivism." There is a danger of
misreading this movement of thought as a return to a classical
position, but Taylor argues that to do so is to miss its distinctiveness and power. Using Herder as an exemplar of expressivism, Taylor claims that not only was a new conception
of the self being developed, but a new sense of "expression"
which is closely related to the "sense in which we speak of expression as giving vent to, a realizing in external reality of
something we feel or desire" (p. 14). Expression here is not
something that is accidentally or incidentally related to *what* is
being expressed. It is the embodiment of what is expressed; it
at once determines and clarifies what is expressed. Taylor
argues that this new orientation leads to a new theory of
language and art, and a new appreciation of the centrality of
language and art for understanding the human subject.
Neither language nor art are to be interpreted from the point of
view of how they *represent* or *refer* to the world, but rather from
the perspective of how they *express* and *realize* human life. The
thrust of this expressivist orientation is of primary importance
for understanding Hegel for three reasons: it is strongly anti-
dualist, it makes freedom as authentic self-expression a central
value of human life, and it contains an inspiration toward a
union and harmony with nature that was jeopardized by the
Enlightenment.

On the other hand, there was another powerful reaction
against the modern dichotomy of a "self-defining" subject confronting an "objective" world. Originally, the self was conceived
of (in Descartes, for example) as standing over and against an
objective physical world; it was categorically distinct from such a

world. But the tendency toward objectification threatened the autonomy of the self. What grounds, if any, are there for thinking that the human subject is not just another part of an objective world – a complex physical system differing in degree and not in kind from other physical systems? It is this threat to the autonomy of the self that Kant so brilliantly detected, and one can read much of his philosophy as a serious attempt to meet the challenge posed by the forms of materialism and naturalism in order to defend the autonomy and freedom of the moral self. But the price paid by Kant's apologia of moral freedom was a severe one! For Kant's "solution" to the problem of the autonomy of the moral self did not overcome the dualisms of modern philosophy, it required the acceptance of a set of even more rigid dualisms between the theoretical and the practical, between man as moral agent and man as natural being. In short, Kant's understanding of the human subject was in direct contradiction to the expressivist aspirations of the time.

The central problem of the epoch became one of finding some successful solution or synthesis of conflicting demands between "radical freedom and integral expression" (p. 43). Hegel differs from his contemporaries because "he pushed to the end in a uniquely consistent way" (p. 43) such a synthesis – a synthesis that demanded postulating a cosmic spirit, who lives as spirit only through individuals who *express* this spirit in their thoughts and deeds. Through this self-expression, individuals realize their *own* authentic radical freedom.

This portrait of changing conceptions of human subjectivity and of the problem that became so pressing in Hegel's time is suggestive and helpful for gaining a purchase on what Hegel is "up to." Taylor's description of expressivism can serve as a heuristic device for making that leap into Hegel's world. Using Taylor's schema, we may say that much of analytic philosophy operates in a framework that shows far more affinity with Taylor's second stage of understanding human subjectivity than with expressivism. Indeed, while expressivism affected the literary movement of romanticism, it has had only a marginal influence on mainstream currents in Anglo-American philosophy.

But Taylor's sketch of changing conceptions of human subjectivity is also quite elusive and raises a number of troubling issues. It would be ungenerous to demand more precision of Taylor's introductory sketch than is warranted. But even with this proviso, it does not seem quite right. For example, to characterize the modern understanding of the subject as "self-defining" is not only misleading, but appears to be mistaken. For all their differences, Descartes, Locke, Hume, and indeed most seventeenth and eighteenth-century thinkers did not think of the human subject as *self*-defining. The self or subject has a nature, structure, or at least a set of fixed mental capacities. The philosophic task became one of stating what these faculties or capacities are, and how they could enable us to understand the nature and limits of human knowledge. It is not a *pre*-Hegelian, but a *post*-Hegelian theme that questions this framework assumption, and raises the possibility that the self creates or defines what it is. It is only with Nietzsche, Kierkegaard, and later with Sartre, that such a conception of the self is fully articulated.

Or, even more important, consider what Taylor has to say about expressivism. He seeks to distinguish it from the classical conception of the human subject, but I do not think he is always successful in pinning down just what is the central difference. He says, for example:

> To talk about the realization of a self here is to say that the adequate human life would not just be a fulfillment of an idea or plan which is fixed independently of the subject who realizes it, as in the Aristotelian form of a man. Rather this life must have the added dimension that the subject can recognize it as his own, as having unfolded from within him. This self-related dimension is entirely missing from the Aristotelian tradition. (p. 15)

Not only does this seem to be a caricature of Aristotle, but it reveals that when Taylor contrasts expressivism with the classical conception of the self he is thinking primarily of the tradition of *theoria* and the self engaging in the journey of attaining theoretical knowledge. Much of what Taylor says about expressivism can be used to illuminate what Aristotle meant by *praxis*, the form of activity involved in leading a virtuous life. Taylor ignores or slights the tradition that Aristotle himself initiated in his characterization of *phronesis* and practical wisdom, a tradition reflected in Cicero, the great period of classical rhetoric, and in Vico (who has been read as a progenitor of "modern expressivism"). Consider how Taylor's claims about expressivism can be used to clarify what Aristotle means by virtuous activity.

> Thus the notion of human life as expression sees this not only as the realization of purposes but also as the clarification of these purposes. It is not only the fulfillment of life but also the clarification of meaning. In the course of living adequately, I not only fulfil my humanity but clarify what my humanity is about. (p. 17)

My intention is not to argue that there are some notable exceptions to Taylor's three-stage model, or to suggest that one can tell a very different story about changing conceptions of human subjectivity. Rather, my primary point is that I do not think that Taylor has succeeded in doing what he has set out to do, viz., to clarify precisely what is distinctive about these different conceptions of human subjectivity.

It is to Taylor's credit that he does not flinch from taking the notion of "self-positing Spirit" as Hegel's most central theme. He boldly attempts to show that we can make sense of what Hegel is saying without succumbing to the temptation of thinking that Spirit is some non-substantial mystical force, or simply a mystified way of speaking about species being or humanity. In explicating what Hegel means by Spirit and the role that it plays, it is absolutely essential to clarify what Hegel means by necessity. As Taylor properly emphasizes, Hegel consistently claims that Spirit must *necessarily* embody itself, and that the dialectical process by which Spirit realizes itself involves *necessity*. But what precisely does Hegel mean by necessity? Here, one might think there would be an excellent opportunity to show how Hegel's understanding of necessity is related to the current interest in necessity by analytic philosophers. But although Taylor has a great deal to say about necessity, and returns to the theme over and over again, we do not find a clear analysis of the meaning (or meanings) of necessity in Hegel.

Taylor's most focused discussion of necessity as it pertains to *Geist* occurs in his chapter on "Self-positing Spirit." He tells us that "starting from finite reality, Hegel claims to be able to demonstrate the existence of a cosmic spirit who posits the world according to rational necessity" (p. 97). But this is not Hegel's ultimate starting point, for "the existence of this finite reality can itself be demonstrated" (p. 98). So we are led to speak of the "Hegelian circle of necessity" which, according to Taylor, has nothing to do with circular argument.

There is an "ascending dialectic from a finite reality" (p. 98), and the circle is closed "by showing that this finite reality necessarily exists. 'Necessity' has a different meaning in the phases" (p. 99). In the ascending dialectic, the necessity is one of the "necessity of inference" but in the descending dialectic the notion of necessity is changed: "It is ontological necessity" (p. 99).

Summing up, Taylor writes:

> Our ascending movement thus starts with a postulate and proceeds by necessary inference. But what it infers to is ontological necessity, the proposition that everything which exists is posited by *Geist* according to a formula of rational necessity. The circle is thus not a single stream of inferences. Rather it involves a reversal of starting point. We begin with the ascending movement which is the movement of discovery. Our starting point is finite existence which is first in the order of discovery. But what we reveal is a pervasive ontological necessity, and this shows that our original starting point is really secondary. Finite reality is itself posited by *Geist*, God, the Absolute. This is the real starting point in the order of being. (p. 99)

Taylor is raising some of the most controversial issues in philosophy. For when he speaks of the "necessity of inference" in the ascending dialectic, he is alluding to a type of transcendental argument. Characterizing precisely what is involved in transcendental arguments and determining whether there can be legitimate philosophic arguments that take this form has proven to be one of the most intractable problems in contemporary philosophy. Furthermore, for many philosophers, the very notion of ontological necessity seems to be a category mistake or absurdity. But what is most disturbing in Taylor's presentation is that he fails to clarify or analyze what is *meant* by "necessity" when we speak of the necessity of inference or ontological necessity. When Taylor discusses necessity in the context of the *Logic*, he effectively criticizes some of the standard misinterpretations of what Hegel means. But a positive elucidation of this central and slippery concept still eludes us. Throughout the book we are confronted with a bewildering variety of the uses of this slippery concept. Taylor speaks of "real necessity," "absolute necessity," "unconditioned necessity," necessity which is "self-conditioned," "external necessity," the "truth of necessity," "free necessity," etc.

The lack of clarity about the meaning (meanings) of necessity is not a localized difficulty. It affects Taylor's analysis of the *Phenomenology* and the *Logic*. After Taylor concludes his outline of what Hegel means by self-positing Spirit, he tells us that it is not sufficient to present Hegel's system; it must be demonstrated, for "its only adequate presentation is a demonstration" (p. 122). "A demonstration *must* be able to take us from our ordinary understanding of things, and show that this is untenable, that it *must* give way to Hegel's vision of things" (p. 122, italics added). Taylor then turns to exploring the three primary routes or demonstrations that we find in Hegel: the *Phenomenology*, the *Logic*, and that which "occupies the philosophy of nature and the philosophy of spirit" (p. 122).

In speaking of these demonstrations, Taylor is clearly employing the notion of necessity. Yet when we turn to what he actually does, he seems virtually to abandon any claim to necessity. Thus in the *Phenomenology*, as we follow what Hegel called the highway of despair, we presumably follow the stages or the forms of consciousness which begin with natural consciousness and culminate in absolute knowledge.

Although almost one hundred pages of Taylor's book deal with the *Phenomenology*, one is left with a confusing impression of what he seeks to show. He begins by presenting an overview

and then proceeds to what may appear to be an explication of
the major sections of the *Phenomenology*. But not only is his
analysis highly selective, he rapidly skips over large sections of
the *Phenomenology*. He advances a theory about two different
types of dialectic in the *Phenomenology*: "strict dialectics, whose
starting point is or can reasonably claim to be undeniable" (p.
218), and "interpretative or hermeneutical dialectics, which
convince us by the overall plausibility of the interpretation they
give" (p. 218). It is difficult to discern what principles guide
what Taylor does and does not discuss. Taylor does say that the
Phenomenology is too rich to go through systematically, and tells
us "What I should like to do is examine certain sections only
which throw light on his position, and simply give the general
direction of argument in the others in order to show the movement of the whole work" (p. 140). But then it would seem that
Taylor is not seriously interested in explaining and evaluating
in what sense the *Phenomenology* is (or is not) a demonstration.

I certainly do not think that a commentator must uncritically
accept or identify himself with the position of the philosopher
he is explicating. One wants to see what are the crucial
strengths and weaknesses. Taylor is frequently acute in both
defending and criticizing Hegel. It is clear that he thinks that, as
a demonstration, the *Phenomenology* fails, although this does not
detract from its importance and power. But one would expect
that there would be some clear indication of what precisely
Hegel thought he was doing in the *Phenomenology*, and an assessment of the ways in which he fails to fulfill this intention.
Taylor does speak to all these issues but he does so in a way
that can be very confusing. It is not always clear whether he is
explicating what Hegel said, what Hegel should have said, or
what Taylor thinks about a particular issue. While there are a
number of brilliant insights about themes and specific discussions in the *Phenomenology*, Taylor's mode of analysis has the
consequence of making the *Phenomenology* seem like much more
of a hodgepodge than it really is. A reader who is unfamiliar
with the original would gather the impression that it is a rather
disjointed mixture of loosely related discussions that pretend to
be connected by a necessary dialectic. What one misses is a

sense of the power, coherence, and thematic consistency of the work.

Taylor's almost informal approach to the texts, picking up what he thinks is worthy of discussion and playing down or skipping over other sections, is even more disturbing when he turns to his analysis of the *Logic*. In his preface, Taylor tells us that for ". . . anyone who wants to understand how Hegel's philosophy was authenticated in his own eyes, and, indeed, how this philosophy and its authentication are inseparable for Hegel, the *Logic* remains indispensible" (p. vii). In the first two hundred pages of this book, Taylor frequently creates the impression that the *Logic* is the only real candidate for the role of strict dialectical proof. "The *Logic* is in fact . . . the only strict, self-authenticating dialectic of Hegel's system" (p. 221).

But as soon as Taylor begins his analysis – which again is extremely perceptive in some of its explications – he does not take his own claims seriously. Or rather, it is clear that whatever Hegel thought he was doing, Taylor thinks there are many gaps, unexplained transitions, unwarranted claims about what has been shown. Taylor says, "The *Logic* thus presents the chain of necessarily connected concepts which give the conceptual structure of reality" (p. 231). But in commenting on the very first transition in the *Logic*, Taylor says:

> But the derivation of Becoming here is not as solid as *Dasein*. This is the first, but not the last place in the *Logic* where Hegel will go beyond what is strictly established by his argument, because he sees in the relation of concepts a suggestion of his ontology: here the universality of movement and becoming in the relation of Being and Non-Being. But of course as probative arguments these passages are unconvincing. They fail, as strict conceptual proof, however persuasive they are as *interpretations* for those who hold Hegel's view of things on other grounds. (p. 233)

Taylor does not accept Hegel's own self-understanding of what he was doing, or Hegel's conception of philosophy as system. This is perhaps the clue to why Taylor has so much difficulty in explaining what Hegel means by necessity. Rather than demonstrations, we find in Hegel an ontological vision which can be supported only with suggestions, indications, and arguments that are at best persuasive rather than demonstrable. Many passages in this book indicate that this is Taylor's own understanding of the philosophical enterprise, that philosophy is essentially a hermeneutical discipline which cannot achieve the type of closure that Hegel thought he achieved. Taylor's book would have been far more persuasive if he had clearly stated and defended this view from the very beginning. Then instead of being seduced into thinking that we will find logically tight demonstrations, and judging Hegel a miserable failure, we would read Taylor as a guide to what he takes to be powerful interpretative dialectics.

I essentially agree with Taylor that – despite some of Hegel's manifest claims to the contrary – many of Hegel's arguments and unconvincing, his transitions forced, and, perhaps most important, a number of his central concepts such as necessity are not clearly articulated and defended. Taylor – unlike some other commentators – does not gloss over these difficulties. He writes both sympathetically and critically about Hegel. Nevertheless, I do think that if Taylor had clarified his own point of view from the very beginning, specified his principles of interpretation, and clearly indicated when he is explicating Hegel and when he is criticizing Hegel, then the entire study would have been more forceful and focused.

I can approach this difficulty from a slightly different perspective. Taylor's conception of philosophy which emerges from this book and from his other writings is not Hegel's conception of philosophy. Indeed there is a fundamental clash. If we change our own orientation, if we reject Hegel's self-understanding of what he is doing, if we make less stringent demands on Hegel's mode of argumentation – if, in short, we see that Hegel's strength lies in his "interpretative dialectics," then a rich terrain opens up to us. Given this interpretative model of philosophy, we can then turn our attention to assessing the strengths and weaknesses of competing interpretations. While Taylor does not think there can ever be final closure to the hermeneutic process, there can be a *rational* assessment of conflicting interpretations.

Taylor does think this is the most illuminating way of approaching the *Phenomenology*. He says that the *Phenomenology* "is more impressive and persuasive as interpretation of certain passages of political and religious history than it is as argument" (p. 216). Furthermore, Taylor also thinks this is the proper way to approach the *Logic*. He sees its force as an "interpretation for those who hold Hegel's view of things." Commenting on what Hegel says about finitude, Taylor writes:

> We have here a second and much more important case in which Hegel forces his argument beyond what it can strictly yield, and ends up with what is really an interpretation of things powerfully suggestive of his ontology, rather than a strict demonstration of it. (p. 23)

Once we realize that Taylor himself is engaging in "interpretative or hermeneutical dialectics, which convince us by the overall plausibility of the interpretation they give" rather than "strict dialectics whose starting point is or can reasonably claim to be undeniable," then we may read his study in a very different light. We may focus on those themes that Taylor takes to be among Hegel's most important and lasting contributions to philosophy. The most pervasive theme, one to which Taylor returns again and again, is that of embodiment. Consider some of Taylor's representative claims about the meaning and centrality of embodiment.

> Thus man does more than reflect a nature complete in itself, rather he is the vehicle whereby the cosmic spirit brings to completion a self-expression the first attempts at which lie before us in nature. Just as on the expressivist view man achieves his fulfillment in a form of life which is also an expression of self-awareness. But this is not achieved in some transcendent realm beyond man. If it were, then union with the cosmic spirit would require that man subordinate his will to a higher being, that he accept heteronomy. Rather spirit reaches his self-awareness in man. (p. 44)

It was a basic principle of Hegel's thought that the subject, and
all his functions, however spiritual were inescapably embodied;
and this in two related dimensions: as a rational animal that is
a living being who thinks; and as an expressive being, that is,
a being whose thinking always and necessarily expresses itself
in a medium.

This principle of necessary embodiment, as we may call it, is
central to Hegel's conception of *Geist*, or cosmic spirit. (p. 83)

. . . once we see the world as posited by *Geist*, a spirit whose life
is thought, then we see the categories of thought as necessarily
embodied, as 'going over', as it were, into their embodiment.
(p. 226)

To be embodied means to be in a particular time and place, and
hence to be finite. But finite spirit must go beyond an identification of himself as particular, and this is why the existence of
many men and their life together in society plays an essential
part. Man is raised to the universal because he already lives
beyond himself in a society, whose greater life incorporates his.
(p. 336)

In the *Phenomenology*, the *Logic*, and the realms of objective
and absolute spirit, Taylor pursues and explores variations on
the theme of embodiment. This is the movement from the
abstract to the concrete. Embodiment is not a mere filling out
of what already exists. It is the process of determination and
clarification itself. Not only does Hegel see this process of embodiment working itself out in both history and logic, it is the
key to the master strategy which Hegel employs to show how
the fundamental dichotomies that have plagued so much of
philosophy are to be overcome (*aufgehoben*). Whether we focus
on mind and body, thought and action, form and matter,
Hegel in each case seeks to show that these dichotomies are
abstract "moments" when they are taken to be separate and
distinct. This even applies to the dichotomy of idealism and
materialism. Rather than classifying Hegel as an "idealist,"
Taylor wants us to see how Hegel overcomes the traditional
problematic in which we distinguish idealism from materialism.

If idealism is thought of as claiming an ontological primacy for what is spiritual or mental as *over against* what is physical or material, then Hegel is *not* an idealist. Spirit or mind is a barren abstraction unless it is concretely embodied. For Hegel, Spirit must be materialized, and what is taken to stand in opposition to Spirit, whether nature or matter, must itself be permeated by Spirit.

By focusing on this theme of embodiment, Taylor suggests a way of seeing the relevance of Hegel to recent developments in analytic philosophy of mind and phenomenology. Both of these movements have attacked the Cartesian framework that has shaped so much of modern philosophy. Both movements, in different ways, stress how language and subjectivity are concretely embodied in the activities that constitute human life.

One of the most effective contexts in which Taylor follows out the consequences of the theme of embodiment is in coming to grips with Hegel's social and political philosophy. Some of the best pages in this study deal with the elucidation and significance of what Hegel means by "objective spirit."

To grasp what Hegel means by "objective spirit," we must overcome the "atomistic prejudices" which have such a powerful hold on us: "when we think of a human being, we do not simply mean a living organism, but a being who can think, feel, decide, be moved, respond, enter into relations with others; and all this implies a language, a related set of ways of experiencing the world, of interpreting his feelings, understanding his relation to others, to the past, the future, the absolute, and so on. It is the particular way he situates himself within this cultural world that we call his identity" (p. 380). Consequently, it is "no extravagant proposition to say that we are what we are in virtue of participating in the larger life of our society" (p. 381). The institutions and practices which make up the public life of a community are not merely external constraints on what we are. For they themselves are expressions of what we are. This, according to Taylor, is the basis for understanding "alienation." Alienation occurs when the norms, as expressed in public practices, cease to hold our allegiance, when there is a growing sense of the disparity of what we take ourselves to be and forms of public life in which we find ourselves. This recurring experience of loss of a sense of identity and the attempts to find a new form of cultural identity in the community is the story of objective spirit – a story which promises a possibility of a successful identification between the individual and the community. Hegel's "thesis of the primacy of *Sittlichkeit*, and the related notion of the community as 'ethical substance,'" can be expressed "in three propositions, put in ascending order of contestability" (p. 386). "First, that what is most important for man can only be attained in relation to the public life of a community, not in private self-definition of the alienated individual. Second, this community must not be merely a partial one. . . . It must be co-terminous with the minimum self-sufficient human reality, the state" (p. 386). And thirdly, "the public life of the state has this crucial importance for man because the norms and ideas it expresses are not just human inventions. On the contrary, the state expresses the Idea, the ontological structure of things" (p. 386).

Taylor finds this last claim to be the most dubious, viz., that man in his political life is "the vehicle of cosmic spirit, and the corollary, that the state expresses the underlying formula of necessity by which spirit posits the world" (p. 387). Nevertheless, while skeptical of Hegel's "solution," Taylor does think that Hegel has incisively posed a dilemma that still lies at the heart of modern societies, especially modern democracies.

> Thus Hegel's dilemma for modern democracy, put at its simplest, is this: The modern ideology of equality and of total participation leads to a homogenization of society. This shakes men loose from their traditional communities, but cannot replace them as a focus of identity. Or rather, it can only replace them as such a focus under the impetus of militant nationalism or some totalitarian ideology which would depreciate or even crush diversity and individuality. (p. 414)

> . . . one of the great needs of the modern democratic polity is to recover a sense of significant differentiation, so that its partial communities, be they geographical, or cultural, or occupa-

tional, can become again important centres of concern and activity for their members in a way which connects them to the whole. (p. 416)

It certainly would be a distortion to suggest that Hegel was primarily concerned with the fate of modern democracies. And this is not Taylor's primary point. But the mode of interpretation that he adopts in dealing with Hegel's understanding of social and political reality is one where Taylor is clearly interested in showing how Hegel still "speaks to us," that there is a way of understanding what he has to say about "objective spirit" and *Sittlichkeit* that provides a richer orientation and set of categories for coming to grips with our own attempts to understand and interpret present social and political reality. Hegel scholars may feel uncomfortable with the way in which Taylor departs from Hegel's text, or by the way in which he attempts to "translate" Hegel into a contemporary idiom. But I believe that herein lies Taylor's distinctive strength as an interpreter. For in dealing with Hegel's social and political philosophy, Taylor approaches Hegel not primarily as a self-effacing commentator, but rather as a philosopher engaged in dialogue with another philosopher – seeking to show what we may learn from him in our attempts to understand the world. It is at such moments that Taylor's interpretation becomes vibrant and "powerfully suggestive" – opening up new possibilities for answering the question "Why Hegel Now?"

6

Negativity: Theme and Variations[1]

Negativity is the deepest, most persistent, and most pervasive theme in Marcuse's work. It is a leitmotif that is in the background of almost everything that he wrote. It connects his varied interests in Hegel, Marx, Freud, and the radical critique of contemporary culture. My aim is to sound the depths of this theme, to explore some of its primary variations, and to show how it is the key for understanding the power – what Marcuse himself might have called the "explosive quality" – of his critique. I also want to show that the theme of negativity is not only the source of Marcuse's strength as a thinker, but harbors what I take to be crucial weaknesses in his "project." The spirit of my own analysis is to do what Marcuse so effectively did with other thinkers – to engage in an immanent critique.[2] The first task of such a critique demands that we grasp adequately what is being criticized.

The logical place to begin is with Marcuse's interpretation of negativity in Hegel. For it is Hegel – even more than Marx and Freud – who most profoundly shaped Marcuse's thinking. Or to be more precise, it is Marcuse's distinctive emphatic interpretation of Hegel that provides the essential clue for understanding what he means by negativity. We can trace this back to Marcuse's earliest writing on Hegel, but it is also vividly and forcefully articulated in his first full-length book in English, *Reason and Revolution: Hegel and the Rise of Modern Social Theory*. There is scarcely a page of his Hegel interpretation that does not explicitly or implicitly refer to negativity. On the opening page of the preface – in his typical dialectical manner – Marcuse tells us that Hegel's system "could well be called a *negative philosophy*, the name given to it by its contemporary opponents. To counteract its destructive tendencies, there arose, in the decade following Hegel's death, a positive philosophy which undertook to subordinate reason to the authority of established fact."[3] For Marcuse, the battle between negativity and positivity is the most consequential and decisive battle in the contemporary world. It is not only a battle that takes place between competing philosophical or intellectual orientations. We are threatened with the triumph of positivity which infects every aspect of culture and social reality, a positivity that reflects a basic impotence in the face of what is given, what appears as existing historical social fact. Everything Marcuse *said* and *did* was motivated by the basic desire to expose and combat the invidious consequences of positivity.

> Hegel's philosophy is indeed what the subsequent reaction termed it, a negative philosophy. It is originally motivated by the conviction that the given facts that appear to common sense as the positive index of truth are in reality the negation of truth, so that truth can only be established in their destruction. The driving force of the dialectical method lies in this critical conviction. Dialectic in its entirety is linked to the conception that all forms of being are permeated by an essential negativity, and that this negativity determines their content and movement. The dialectic represents the counter-thrust to any form of positivism.[4]

For Marcuse, as for Hegel, it is crucial to distinguish sharply "abstract negativity" that results in emptiness, nothingness, in "mere" denial, from "determinate negation" by which the truth is revealed. Marcuse stresses the theme that shines forth in the following passage from the Preface to the *Phenomenology*.[5]

> The life of Spirit is not the life that shrinks from death and keeps itself untouched by devastation, but rather the life that endures it and maintains itself in it. It wins its truth only when, in utter dismemberment, it finds itself. It is this power, not as something

positive, which closes its eyes to the negative, as when we say of something that it is nothing or it is false, and then, having done with it, turn away and pass on to something else; on the contrary, Spirit is this power only by looking the negative in the face, and tarrying with it. This tarrying with the negative is the magical power that converts it into being.

I want to stress, as Marcuse does, the two-dimensionality of this concept of negativity. There is negativity, opposition, critical judgment in the tension between the demands of Reason (*Vernunft*) and the positivity of an untrue, distorted, existing social reality. "The realization of reason is not a fact but a task."[6] For Marcuse, this first dimension of negativity has been the dominant characteristic of the tradition of philosophic thought which has opposed and implicitly condemned "the given facts that appear to common sense as the positive index of truth." This aspect of negativity is embodied in the role that the concepts of "essence" and "universality" have played in philosophy from Plato through Hegel. In this respect, Hegel *is* the culmination of, and embodies the "truth" of, the history of philosophy – just as Hegel claimed for his system. But Hegel's distinctive genius is to be found in the move that he made from thought to being. Negativity does not simply exemplify itself in the way in which philosophy and critical thinking have opposed the positivity of existing fact, but Hegel saw that the power of negativity lies at the heart of being in all its forms. It is being itself, and *a fortiori* social reality itself, that contains negativity – contains its own opposition, and the seeds for its own ineluctable destruction and transformation. "*All things are contradictory in themselves.*"[7] Herein lies the primary significance of Hegel's joining of Reason and History. With extraordinary perspicacity and persistence, Marcuse shows how this two-dimensional quality of negativity is revealed in every aspect of Hegel's philosophy.

Even in the abstract formulations of the *Logic* we can see the concrete critical impulses that underlie this conception. Hegel's dialectic is permeated with the profound conviction that all immediate forms of existence – in nature and history – are "bad," because they do not permit things to be what they can be. True existence begins only when the immediate state is recognized as negative, when beings become "subjects" and strive to adapt their outward state of their potentialities.[8]

The actualization of these potentialities demands the destruction, the negation, of everything that inhibits them from their full realization. It is only by negation that Reason and Freedom can be realized.

But for all Hegel's insight into the power of negativity and the way in which it is *immanent* in being in all its forms, it is negativity that ultimately defeats Hegel himself. The consequences of Hegel's dialectic lead to the realization that "the inherent potentialities of men and things cannot unfold in a society except through the death of the social order in which they are first gleaned."[9] It is not that Marx simply refuted and negated Hegel; for Marcuse it is more accurate and revealing to claim that it is "History and social reality themselves that 'negate' philosophy."[10] This is what Marx discovered. "In Hegel's system all categories terminate in the existing order, while in Marx's they refer to the negation of this order."[11] This is a transition to an "essentially different order of truth." We can locate here the movement from philosophy to Critical Theory which has the practical intent of fostering the destruction of a repressive, alienating, and dominating social reality in order to further the struggle and realization for genuine freedom and happiness.

Consequently it is the "working out" of negativity that leads us from philosophy to Critical Theory. Critical Theory is like philosophy insofar as "it opposes making reality into a criterion in the manner of complacent positivism. But unlike philosophy, it always derives its goals only from the present tendencies of the social process. Therefore it has no fear of the utopia that the new order is denounced as being. When truth cannot be realized within the established social order, it always appears to the latter as mere utopia."[12] Critical Theory claims to comprehend present existing social reality. This theory can grasp the negativity that is implicit in social reality: it can focus on those very tendencies that can negate the existing order and have the power to bring about the full realization of human potentialities – potentialities which when realized culminate in the triumph of Reason, Freedom, and Happiness.

In 1937, Marcuse raised the basic question that confronts Critical Theory.

> What, however, if the development outlined by the theory does not occur? What if the forces that were to bring about the transformation are suppressed and appear to be defeated? Little as the theory's truth is thereby contradicted, it nevertheless appears then in a new light which illuminates new aspects and elements of its object. . . . This situation compels theory anew to a sharper emphasis on its concern with the potentialities of man and with the individual's freedom, happiness and rights contained in all its analyses.[13]

This passage takes on greater poignancy when we remind ourselves of the context in which it was written. It appeared at a time when fascism was gaining in ominous power, and when the Frankfurt thinkers were in exile in New York writing in German to an unknown audience. Furthermore, consider the significance of this passage against the background of the Marxist legacy. For Marx, as Marcuse himself had argued, the power of negativity was embodied in the proletariat, the potentially revolutionary class that can destroy the existing social order and bring about its radical transformation. But increasingly, Marcuse, like the other Frankfurt thinkers, was not only becoming skeptical about the *real* possibility of a proletarian revolution, but also about the adequacy of the framework of the critique of political economy for coming to grips with the negativity and the "*real*" potentialities of the contemporary world. But if one rejects, or is skeptical about, the Marxist conception of the role of the proletariat, and yet holds on to the conviction that the fundamental task of Critical Theory is to discover the form of negativity that can effect a radical transformation, then the hard question becomes: where does one discover this movement and negativity? Critical Theory makes sense in a concrete situation where the "forces that were to bring about the transformation are suppressed and appear to be defeated." But it makes no sense if there is an absence of negative forces at work, and no evidence of hidden tendencies that can bring about a revolution. From the mid-1930s on, Marcuse's primary project became one of answering the very question he raised, of probing and searching for the power of negativity that lies hidden in existing social reality. It is precisely this project that enables us to understand Marcuse's attraction to and dialectical use of Freud in *Eros and Civilization*.

Before passing on to the extraordinary use that Marcuse makes of Freud, I want to pick up on another variation of the theme of negativity, which is implicit in what I have already said, and sheds light on a significant aspect of Marcuse's style of thinking. Given Marcuse's understanding of negativity, we can appreciate why he was so hostile to the "sociology of knowledge," and suspicious of what he took to be positivistic reductions of the concept of ideology, which even proved seductive for many who thought they were following Marx. In 1937, reviewing some of the discussions that had appeared in the *Zeitschrift für Sozialforschung*, Marcuse wrote:

> Several fundamental concepts of philosophy have been discussed in this journal: truth and verification, rationalism and irrationalism, the role of logic, metaphysics and positivism, and the concept of essence. These were not merely analyzed sociologically, in order to correlate philosophical dogmas with social loci. Nor were philosophical constructs "resolved" into social facts. To the extent that philosophy is more than ideology, every such attempt must come to nought. When critical theory comes to terms with philosophy, it is interested in the truth concept of philosophical concepts and problems. It presupposes that they really contain truth. The enterprise of the sociology of knowledge, to the contrary, is occupied only with the untruths, not the truths of previous philosophy.[14]

Marcuse not only said this, it is precisely what he *did* throughout his work. His interpretations of the philosophical tradition are self-consciously one-sided and frequently brilliant. He practiced a type of depth hermeneutics of negativity in which he sought to uncover the hidden truth implicit in these thinkers and their concepts – a hidden truth that almost always focused on their negativity. This is the way in which he interpreted Aristotle (who next to Hegel was Marcuse's favored philosopher), Plato, the Hedonists (including the Cyrenaics and Epicureans), Kant, and Schiller. This is also why he was relentless in his criticism of all forms of empiricism and positivism, and why he turned upon phenomenology itself, especially Husserl – for he claimed that the consequence of Husserl's thought was to empty the concept of essence of its negative power.[15] Just as Marx began with a critique of religion and philosophy which sought to discover the latent truth implicit in them as well as the ways in which they mystify reality, so too was this what Marcuse sought to do with philosophy. Marcuse also argued that when philosophy came to an end (as it did with Hegel), one could no longer turn to philosophy to discover the expression of negativity and truth. For our time, phantasy and art become the forms in which the repressed dreams of freedom and happiness are expressed – albeit in a distorted form. It was Marcuse's search for the deepest and most powerful forms of negativity that led him to and shaped his interpretation of Freud – an interpretation in which Marcuse sought dialectically to use Freud against himself.

Eros and Civilization is Marcuse's most perverse, wild, phantasmal, and surrealistic book. (I am not using these adjectives in a pejorative, but in a *descriptive* sense.) It is the book in which Marcuse probes the theme of negativity to its very extremity. It is strangely Hegelian and anti-Hegelian, Marxist and anti-Marxist, Nietzschean and anti-Nietzschean, and these oppositions are held together in an explosive tension. With an almost perverse, tabooed delight, Marcuse seizes upon those very aspects of Freud's thought which many thinkers, including the neo-Freudians, take to be the most dubious, unfounded, and speculative hypotheses: the late theory of instincts – the struggle between Eros and the death instinct; and Freud's reconstruction of the prehistory of mankind from the primal horde through patricide to civilization. Why? Because it is precisely in these apparently outrageous speculations – when properly deciphered – that the deepest level of "truth" latent in Freud is to be discovered. The drama that unfolds in Marcuse's analysis is anti-Hegelian in the sense that the development of civilization is not seen as the development of the stages or forms of consciousness, each embodying the truth of the preceding stages, and each contributing to the progressive realization of Reason and Freedom. And yet the mythic story that Marcuse presents *is* Hegelian insofar as in a world of increasing totalitarianism, alienation, repression, and domination, the "return of the repressed" and the liberation of Eros *demand* the destruction and negation of the *"performance principle*: the prevailing historical form of the reality principle."[16] The drama is structured as a grand, cataclysmic dialectic of negativity. It is anti-Marxist in the sense that there is scarcely any concern with the critique of political economy, the role of the proletariat, the conflict of classes, or the dialectical, historical development of modes and relations of production. And yet, Marcuse accepts and presses the Marxist thesis that it is precisely the development of capitalism – and more generally, advanced industrial societies – that creates the material conditions for a total and radical transformation of society.

Reason as it appears in *Eros and Civilization* is *not* primarily the Hegelian *Vernunft*, but rather the "logos of domination" which deeply fears, suppresses, and represses the ineradicable instinctual demand for gratification and happiness. "Civilization has to defend itself against the specter of a world which could be free. If society cannot use its growing productivity for reducing repression (because such usage would upset the hierarchy of the *status quo*), productivity must be turned *against* the individuals; it becomes itself an instrument of universal control. Totalitarianism spreads over the late industrial civilization wherever the interests of domination prevail upon productivity, arresting, and diverting its potentialities."[17]

As Marcuse probes the hidden message of Freud, and dialectically transforms Freud, he begins to sound more and more like Nietzsche (and yet also anti-Nietzsche):

Nietzsche speaks in the name of a reality principle fundamentally antagonistic to that of Western Civilization. The traditional

form of reason is rejected on the basis of being-as-end-in-itself
– as joy (*Lust*) and enjoyment.[18]

The vision that Marcuse projects is one in which our deepest
subterranean memories keep alive the dream of liberation,
where "the *recherche du temps perdu* becomes the vehicle of future
liberation,"[19] and where "the consummation of being is, not
the ascending curve, but the closing of the circle: the *re-turn*
from alienation."[20] The image of the closed circle which can be
found at the beginning and the end of philosophy is no longer
Aristotle's *nous theos* or Hegel's absolute idea, but the eternal
return of the finite:

> Nietzsche envisages the eternal return of the finite exactly as it
> is – in its full concreteness and finiteness. This is the total
> affirmation of the life instincts, repelling all escape and negation.
> The eternal return is the will and vision of an *erotic* attitude
> toward being for which necessity and fulfillment coincide.[21]

The message and the rhetoric of *Eros and Civilization* are
deeply disturbing. Marcuse's language is cataclysmic and
apocalyptic – the language of "explosion," "total destruction,"
and "shattering" of the hardened, deadening, repressive crust
of existing social reality. But it is also a revealing book because,
as Marcuse pursues negativity into the hidden recesses of our
unconscious, he touches on those themes which are the most
central ones of his own distinctive vision – the aesthetic, phantasy, play, imagination, and art.

I think we fundamentally misunderstand and distort Marcuse's
vision if we think that he was merely concerned with the aesthetic as one dimension of human life or one aspect of culture.
On the contrary, his vision is essentially and *intrinsically* an
aesthetic one. Aesthetic categories permeate every aspect of
Marcuse's thinking. The centrality of the aesthetic was already
evident in Marcuse's early brilliant and ecstatic review of
Marx's *1844 Economic and Philosophical Manuscripts*. Marcuse
was one of the first to declare that the publication of the *Manuscripts* "must become a crucial event in the history of Marxist

studies."[22] In *Eros and Civilization* there is an almost playful use of the Heideggerian technique of philosophical etymology where Marcuse seeks to demonstrate "the inner connection between pleasure, sensuousness, beauty, truth, art, and freedom – a connection revealed in the philosophical history of the term *aesthetic.*"[23]

Phantasy "plays a most decisive function in the total mental structure: it links the deepest layers of the unconscious with the highest products of consciousness (art), the dream with the reality; it preserves the archetypes of the genus, the perpetual but repressed ideas of the collective and individual memory, the tabooed images of freedom."[24] Sometimes Marcuse writes – and I believe that this is one of his core beliefs – that in our time not only is philosophy dead, but that Critical Theory itself is no longer adequate for keeping alive the "tabooed images of freedom." The Great Refusal, "the protest against unnecessary repression, the struggle for the ultimate form of freedom,"[25] can *only* find proper expression in phantasy and art – surrealistic and irrealistic art which inverts what we normally take to be reality. It is only phantasy – whose "logic" works beneath the control and domination of consciousness – that is uncompromising in its demands. This emphasis on phantasy and its expression in art even shows up in Marcuse's analysis and condemnation of "Soviet Marxism." It might seem strange that some of Marcuse's most incisive remarks about the role of art in society should appear in *Soviet Marxism.* But it is not at all strange when we grasp what Marcuse takes to be the essential "political force" of art:

> But art as a political force is art only in so far as it preserves the images of liberation; in a society which is in its totality the negation of these images, art can preserve them only by total refusal, that is, by not succumbing to the standards of the unfree reality, either in style, or in form, or in substance. The more totalitarian these standards become, the more reality controls all language and all communication, the more irrealistic and surrealistic will art tend to be, the more it will be driven from the concrete to the abstract, from harmony to dissonance, from content to form. Art is thus the refusal of everything that has

been made part and parcel of reality. . . . The Soviet state by administrative decree prohibits the transcedence of art; it thus eliminates even the ideological reflex of freedom in an unfree society. Soviet realistic art, complying with the decree, becomes an instrument of social control in the last still nonconformist dimension of human existence.[26]

The dialectic of negativity – the theme that Marcuse shared with Adorno – reaches its extremity and deepest human level in phantasy and art – "the last still non-conformist dimension of human existence." *Eros and Civilization* ends with a vision of the possible union of instinct and reason where a liberated Eros even triumphs over death – Thanatos. But this is not Marcuse's last word.

One-Dimensional Man is Marcuse's most ambiguous book. But its ambiguity is rooted in the concrete social situation that Marcuse is addressing. Marcuse himself indicates this ambiguity when he tells us:

> *One-Dimensional Man* will vacillate throughout between two contradictory hypotheses: (1) that advanced industrial society is capable of containing qualitative change for the foreseeable future; (2) that the forces and tendencies exist which may break this containment and explode the society.[27]

But even this formulation does not accurately represent what Marcuse explores. For the first hypothesis that he lists still speaks of a society that "is capable of *containing* qualitative change." This presupposes that the power of negativity is still operative – still implicit in what we are, and still demands realization. Yet the specter that haunts Marcuse's analysis is one where in advanced industrial societies human nature – even our instinctual nature – is being so drastically transformed that there is nothing left to be "contained" – that the power of negativity itself is being undermined and eliminated. Marcuse's inferno is one in which human beings are being so thoroughly desublimated that there is not even the possibility of the "instinctual revolt against the established reality principle," a nightmarish world in which "the last still nonconformist dimension of human existence" is being systematically eliminated, a world where even radical critics of society like Marcuse end up with their picture on the covers of slick magazines that titillate a society that "loves" its critics and renders them completely harmless. It is the world in which – to use Philip Reiff's term – there is the triumph of the therapeutic – where we treat ourselves and others treat us as ministering "cures" and "false" gratifications to "false" needs. This is a world that is *beyond* total alienation, repression, and domination. When there is nothing left to be repressed, the concept of repression itself loses all sense. It is perhaps evidence of "the cunning of Reason" (*die List der Vernunft*) that Marcuse's most pessimistic analysis of the fate of Western society, which raises the possibility that we may be living in a world where Critical Theory itself loses its meaning, was read by many as the great liberating tract of the 1960s. But the reason for this is not difficult to discern when we consider the second more muted hypothesis that Marcuse explores – the hypothesis "that the forces and tendencies exist which may break the containment and explode the society." Marcuse still holds out for the possibility of that improbable configuration of tendencies and forces which will bring about a total revolution. We have not yet quite reached "the end of man," the end of the instinctual demand for liberation and happiness. No longer can we share Marx's confidence about the emergence of a class – proletariat – which becomes the agent of revolution. But there is still a chance for "qualitative change." The full ambiguity of Marcuse's position – one which reflects the ambiguity of our situation – emerges sharply in the concluding sentences of *One-Dimensional Man*.

> But the chance is that, in this period, the historical extremes may meet again: the most advanced consciousness of humanity, and its most exploited force. It is nothing but a chance. The critical theory of society possesses no concepts which could bridge the gap between the present and the future; holding no promise and showing no success, it remains negative. Thus it wants to remain loyal to those who, without hope, have given and give their life to the Great Refusal. At the beginning of the fascist era, Walter Benjamin wrote:

Nur um der Hoffnungslosen willen ist uns die Hoffnung gegeben.

It is only for the sake of those without hope that hope is given to us.[28]

Marcuse's writings after *One-Dimensional Man* fluctuate between his two contradictory hypotheses: between the rhetoric of believing that we are on the verge of seeing the revolution come to life and the warning that we are left with only the (impotent?) Great Refusal.

But he never gave up hope; he never submitted to the despair of thinking that the power of negativity could not assert itself. He searched – in what sometimes seems like a desperate manner – for the signs of those social movements and tendencies that were progressive and liberating. He was open to new possibilities and enthusiastically supported them in speech and deed. He never accepted the lament over the death of the New Left, and he claimed that the women's movement may yet turn out to be the most radical movement of our times. To the end he encouraged and personified the demand for happiness and liberation. In all his activities he was "life affirming."

I have been primarily focusing on Marcuse as a negative thinker, as one of the most persistent radical critics of our time, but what was so beautiful about Marcuse (and I am using "beautiful" in a way in which he would have used it) is that there was a deep harmony between Marcuse as a thinker and Marcuse as a man. Those who knew him even slightly were deeply affected by his charm, his humor, his playfulness, his sheer zest and delight in living, his own capacity for the pleasure of being alive. It is this quality that evoked such profound resonances among those who were inspired by him, and so much hostility and *resentment* among those who envied him.

It is not my intention to deliver a eulogy, and I think that he would be impatient and disdainful of such academic rituals. Rather I have tried to present the strongest and most sympathetic case for Marcuse because I want to carry the spirit of negativity one step further and sharply criticize him. I want to explore the gaps and omissions in his powerful vision.

Every strong thinker has his or her insight and blindness. In critically assessing a thinker it is sometimes more revealing to focus upon what he or she ignores, does not explore, and does not say. So with Marcuse there are crucial problems for his own project that never quite come into the foreground – that are like a penumbra, hovering in partial obscurity. These are the themes and problems related to the nature of community, communication, intersubjectivity, and the nature of practical rationality in which individuals are oriented to working together to achieve a rational consensus concerning the norms that are to govern their lives. It would be a slander to suggest that Marcuse was unaware of these themes. There is plenty of evidence that he envisioned new ways in which individuals might communicate with each other and with nature, and which would overcome repression and domination. But there is little evidence that he ever subjected these themes to careful, systematic analysis. They certainly do not play the dominating role that the triad of Reason, Freedom, and Happiness plays in his critical thinking. Yet I want to suggest that without a proper analysis of these concepts, there is the real danger that Marcuse's triad remains abstract and "false," it lacks "determinate negation."

Consider the concept of Reason and the central role that it plays in Marcuse's thought. It certainly makes sense in interpreting Hegel to emphasize in the strongest possible way the contrast between abstract *Verstand* and concrete *Vernunft* – and to stress the dynamic quality of Reason that works through history and demands realization – a realization that entails Freedom. Marcuse is extraordinarily incisive about the shrinkage and distortion of "reason" in advanced industrial societies – and the ways in which reason becomes "the Logos of domination." We can appreciate his forceful critique of Weber's concept of *Zweckrationalität* and be sympathetic when he declares, "It is difficult to see reason at all in the ever more solid 'shell of bondage' which is being constructed. Or is there perhaps already in Max Weber's concept of reason the irony that understands but disavows? Does he by any chance mean to say: And this you call 'reason'?"[29] But we cannot leave matters here if our intention is to explore the possibility of developing concepts that are adequate for a critique of our contemporary situation. We cannot avoid the deep question that has been posed in theory and practice: Is there an alternative to "bourgeois reason"? Is there an alternative to the narrow economic sense of reason where we think of reason as simply the effective or efficient means to pregiven ends? I do not believe it is intellectually viable simply to invoke some variant of Hegelian *Vernunft* without a serious attempt to explicate this concept and to justify a more adequate and comprehensive understanding of rationality. Otherwise we are confronted with the danger that Hegel himself saw so well where "On bare assurance is worth just as much as another."[30] Without engaging in such a project, then, the very basis of a critical theory of society is threatened.

Nor do I think it is satisfactory to project an ideal of a "new *rationality of gratification* in which reason and happiness converge,"[31] where reason and instinct can unite, where the sensuous becomes rational and the rational becomes sensuous. What concretely does this mean? If we are to take seriously (or even playfully) the suggestion that the qualitative difference between "socialist society as a free society and the existing society" is to be found in the "aesthetic-erotic dimension,"[32] then we must not only comprehend what we are talking about, but ask ourselves what type of social institutions in a "postindustrial" world can embody such a "rationality of gratification." We are confronted here not only with the danger of vacuity, but the more ominous danger where the demand for absolute liberation and freedom turns into its opposite – absolute terror.

This is not the place to sketch what I mean by a comprehensive understanding of rationality that gives a prominent place to the type of practical rationality that can be institutionalized in a free society. But at least let me indicate that such a concept of rationality is not only intrinsically dialogical and communicative but places upon us the *practical* demand to work toward that form of democratic socialism in which the material conditions exist whereby individuals can confront each other as equals and jointly participate in open communication. It is my own conviction that we find the seeds for such a dialogical conception of practical rationality in the best work of the pragmatic thinkers – including Peirce, Dewey, and Mead[33] – a theme that has been taken up and extended in new ways by Apel and Habermas.

One of the great blind spots of Marcuse – and indeed the older Frankfurt thinkers – was the failure to see this and to misjudge the pragmatic movement as being only one more variant of the positivism that they abhored and detested.

An analogous failure of "determinate negation" turns up in the meaning and role of the concept of potentiality – especially human potentiality. Marcuse is extraordinarily perceptive about the fundamental character of potentiality in Hegel, Marx, and even Freud. We cannot begin to grasp the distinctive power of Hegel and Marx unless we realize how they revitalized the concept of potentiality – a revitalization that represents a dialectical appropriation of the Greek, especially the Aristotelian, concept of potentiality which is so intimately related to *energia* and *dynamis*. Marcuse even tells us that "since ontology is the doctrine of the most general forms of being and as such reflects human insight into the most general structure of reality, there can be little wonder that the basic concepts of Aristotelian and Hegelian ontology were the same."[34] The deep motivation for Marcuse's relentless attack on all forms of positivism and empiricism is that they mutilate and abandon the concept of potentiality. If the real is mistakenly identified with the historically given, then we can no longer speak of a "true" human potentiality which has been suppressed and repressed by a "false" existing reality. We can no longer speak of the power of negativity that lies at the heart of all being and demands realization. The fate, indeed the very intelligibility, of Critical Theory depends on a viable concept of human potentiality. Marcuse emphasized this over and over again. But this very insight reveals a basic dilemma. For as Marcuse himself tells us, we can no longer accept the ontology and metaphysics of Aristotle and Hegel. And yet their concepts of potentiality are intimately bound up with their ontology and metaphysics.

So the acute problem becomes, how are we to "reconstruct" the concept of potentiality? How are we to appropriate the vitally important idea that there is a "true" human potentiality which is being defeated by an "untrue" repressive reality without illicitly smuggling in an ontology and metaphysics that are no longer viable? How are we to negate the abstract concept of human potentiality and give it "determinate negation"? How are we to meet the challenge that relying on the concept of "true human potentiality" has become an intellectual crutch which lacks justification or warrant? This is not a rarified philosophical or intellectual problem when we remind ourselves that however much we condemn totalitarianism and fascism as "untrue" and "evil," they are *also* realizations of human potentialities.

The type of failure or inadequacy that I have been pointing out in the appeal to the concepts of Reason and potentiality can also be seen in Marcuse's use of the concepts of Freedom and Happiness. I do not think that one finds in Marcuse the resources to make the subtle and crucial discriminations between *individual* and *public*, communal, freedom and happiness – the type of freedom and happiness that only comes into existence and can be sustained through the sharing and interactions of individuals in their plurality. What always seems to be missing in Marcuse is not "Man" or "human potentialities," but *men* – or better, human beings in their plurality who only *achieve* their humanity in and through each other. I want to reiterate that Marcuse is certainly aware of what I am trying to stress. I think he was remarkably perceptive about the communal joy and happiness that is experienced when individuals join together and act together to oppose repression, domination, and exploitation. My criticism is that he failed to develop for us the concepts and theoretical orientation required to comprehend these phenomena.

It may seem outrageous, but I am tempted to suggest that Marcuse's deepest flaw was his failure to appreciate what is concretely involved in social and political life. After all, the emphasis on the primacy of the social dimension of human life is the primary legacy of Marx and Hegel. And yet, we never find in Marcuse a careful analysis of what precisely constitutes the sociality and inter-subjectivity of human beings. For all Marcuse's emphasis on "social reality" and the negativity that lies at the core of "existing historical social reality" – expressions that are repeated over and over again in his work – he does not probe what is the meaning and "essence" of a "*social* being."

Hegel, at the beginning of the famous discussion of Lordship and Bondage, announces the theme of Recognition (*die Anerkennung*) – a theme that sets the task and indicates the *telos* of the rest of the *Phenomenology*. "Self-Consciousness exists in and for itself when, and by the fact that, it so exists for another; that is, it exists only in being acknowledged."[35] We know what the end of this journey requires for Hegel. For "Self-Consciousness" can only come to rest, can only complete its journey and thereby become what it truly is – infinite and free – when it is recognized by another "Self-Consciousness" that is itself infinite and free. The concrete realization of freedom can only be achieved in and through the freedom of the "others" that I confront. The realization of freedom makes no sense when it is thought of as an individual project which is not bound up with the freedom of "others" – "others" who no longer threaten and oppose me, but achieve and reflect the freedom that we mutually share. For Hegel, as for Marcuse, history thus far has been "the highway of despair," the history of domination and "false consciousness." This is the aspect of the Recognition theme that Marcuse continually emphasized. He agrees with Freud that there has been a "recurrent cycle" of "domination-rebellion-domination," where the "second domination is not simply a repetition of the first one; the cyclical movement is *progress* in domination."[36] If one reads history as Marcuse did, where this recurrent cycle not only has continued to repeat itself, but where we are reaching the dialectical extremity of this cycle, then it makes eminently good sense to focus on this aspect of the Recognition theme. But if we are to demystify this concept of Recognition, if we are to extract the "truth" implicit in this *Begriff*, and come to an understanding of what a society would be like in which the mutual achievement and recognition of freedom are to be realized, then we cannot avoid asking ourselves how is this freedom to be embodied in political and social institutions. Society is not an abstraction; it consists of a complex interlocking set of social institutions and practices. We cannot responsibly avoid the hard questions of how institutions and practices in a socialist society are to embody Reason, Freedom, and Happiness. If Critical Theory is to justify its claim to comprehend and encourage the real tendencies and potentialities that can effect such a revolution, then we must try to understand and engage in the forms of *praxis* that will bring us closer to the "qualitative difference" of a socialist free society.

The essential thrust of Marcuse's thinking and language is toward totality. He never wavered in his thinking that the dominant tendency of our time is toward totalitarianism. If this situation is to be confronted, then nothing less than a total revolution is required – a revolution that totally "negates," "destroys," "shatters," "explodes" the performance principle – "the prevailing historical form of the *reality principle*." It is true, as I have emphasized, that Marcuse was always on the lookout for and encouraged the signs of opposition – whether they were to be found on the streets of Haight-Ashbury or the liberation movements in the Third World – that might yet combine into the configuration that could bring about such a revolution. But even here, what Marcuse was looking for was not piecemeal reform, but *total* revolution.

Although it was not his intention – indeed it was the *opposite* of what he believed and intended – I think that at times he was insensitive to the consequences of the rhetoric of the demand for total revolution: the growing sense of total impotence. Perhaps the greatest failing of the international New Left movement of the 1960s was its naïveté – how once it became clear that the phantasy and dream of a qualitatively different world in which the "rationality of gratification" triumphs was not to be immediately realized, many of those involved were all too ready to seek their gratification in other ways. This situation can certainly *not* be blamed on Marcuse. He fought despair, defeatism, and escapism to the end of his life. Nevertheless it is the dark side of the abstract demand for total destruction and total liberation.

I can well imagine a champion of Marcuse objecting to what I have been saying. Insofar as I criticize Marcuse for a failure of "determinate negation," insofar as I call for the need to try to develop a dialogic conception of rationality, insofar as I want to appeal to concepts such as communication, community, and inter-subjectivity in gaining a theoretical and practical perspective of what is going on in society – it is I who am being innocent and abstract. For I have failed to realize how all these concepts are in danger of being corrupted by "bourgeois reason," and have failed to appreciate the depth of the crisis we are experiencing. Today our plight is one where the whole heritage of philosophical and intellectual concepts in the West has been so thoroughly perverted and distorted, that one must resort to more drastic and radical means to keep the dream of freedom and happiness alive.

I certainly want to concede that all I have done is to make a few suggestions, and that if I take my own demand seriously, it requires "working out" and "working through" – my own project requires "determinate negation." But I would at least like to defend the idea that if there is any hope for Critical Theory, it cannot remain content with the "Great Refusal" and "negative dialectics." And I want to make such an *apologia* by appealing to what is latent in Marcuse himself. For there is a deep tension between what might be called the manifest or "official" theoretical orientation in Marcuse and what is latent and "unofficial." The manifest position is one that tells the story of how everything in Western society has been relentlessly working toward the triumph of totalitarianism in all forms of culture and human life reaching down even to our unconscious instinctual phantasy dream world. It is this very logic of domination that has created the material conditions and the possibility for a total revolution – even though such a revolution may never come to be and may remain only a dream.

But there is a latent, more muted thesis that keeps surfacing in Marcuse and which I think is closer to the "truth." For with the spread of domination and what frequently appears to be the inexhaustible "power" of the so-called Super Powers, there is also the counterthrust – the increasing awareness of impotence,

impotence to deal with national and international crises. We are not simply living in a monolithic, interlocking technocratic society, but a society that keeps creating its own opposition, in which there is breakup: the spontaneous generation of movements of protest where suddenly individuals decide to take their fate into their own hands in the face of what appear to be overwhelming forces opposing them. Throughout the world the impotence of "power" is becoming sharper and more acute together with the creation of those tendencies, incipient movements, and public spaces within which individuals can collectively and communicatively act together to achieve mutually shared goals. It is this latent theme that I think represents Marcuse's true legacy. If we take this seriously, it requires those of us who have been inspired by Marcuse's own intellectual courage and joy to try again and again to comprehend what is going on in the prolonged crisis of our times and to engage in those forms of *praxis* that are still open to us. Not to make this attempt and to give in to defeatism would be to betray what is most vital in Marcuse's legacy – even when it requires us to negate and pass beyond Marcuse himself.

7

Heidegger on Humanism[1]

Heidegger is a thinker who has taught us to be sensitive to mood (*Stimmung*). By attending to, and reflecting upon moods, we can come to a deeper understanding of our being-in-the-world and our comportment with Being (*Sein*) itself. I want to begin (one of several beginnings in order to find a pathway into the thicket of Heidegger's thinking about humanism) by seeking to elicit a mood that is becoming increasingly pervasive in our intellectual, cultural, and everyday lives. To highlight what I mean, it is helpful to contrast the present mood with one that typifies so much of nineteenth-century Continental thought.

Consider the spirit that breathes through such diverse thinkers as Hegel, Marx, and Nietzsche. The mood I want to identify is beautifully exemplified by the passage from the Preface to Hegel's *Phenomenology of Spirit* when he writes about his age as a birth-time and a period of transition. Spirit which is always restless and moving forward is about to burst forth into a new qualitative stage of development – a happening that he metaphorically characterizes as the birth of a child. "But just as the first breath drawn by a child after its long quiet nourishment breaks the gradualness of merely quantitative growth – there is a qualitative leap, and the child is born – so likewise the Spirit in its formation matures slowly and quietly into its new shape, dissolving bit by bit the structure of its previous world. . . ."[2] We find variations on this same metaphor throughout the writings of Marx, especially in his early writings. The mood is one of expectation, hope, of being on the verge of a radical qualitative transformation, a new beginning that emerges out of the womb of an old and dying order – a beginning that at once presupposes what has been, breaks with it, and fulfills and redeems it.

Even Nietzsche – who philosophizes with a hammer, who is the great unmasker, the supreme practitioner of the hermeneutics of suspicion, the penetrating critic of the disease of nihilism which he sees as spreading throughout European culture – tells us that pregnancy is also a disease. There is a mood of exuberance, affirmation, and yea saying. These are thinkers of *Aufhebung* and *Überwindung* where there is at once negativity and destruction, but where there is also "determinate negation," affirmation, the expectation of a new and higher "form of life." Indeed, it is this mood that underlies and nourishes the explicit conceptual forms of teleology that inform their writings.

Contrast this mood with what appears so prevalent and pervasive in our time. There is a sense of entropy, of almost inescapable decline where suspicion, unmasking, and destroying of illusions have been carried so far that there is even an inability and anxiety to "name" what we are living through. We speak of "post-modernity," "post-subjectivism," "post-structuralism," etc., but no one seems to be able to satisfactorily fill in the content of the "post." We hear from all sides about the end of metaphysics, the end of philosophy, and even the end of Western Civilization – but "end" here no longer has any resonances of a *telos*, a fulfillment, accomplishment, or consummation – except in the bitter ironic sense that what has "finally" been revealed is the nihilism that has always been implicit in Western Civilization. This mood is epitomized by Heidegger when he writes:[3]

> The decline of the truth of beings occurs necessarily, and indeed as the completion of metaphysics.

> The decline occurs through the collapse of the world characterized by metaphysics, and at the same time through the desolation of the earth stemming from metaphysics.

Collapse and desolation find their adequate occurrence in the fact that metaphysical man, the *animal rationale*, gets fixed as the laboring animal.

This rigidification confirms the most extreme blindness to the oblivion of Being. But man wills *himself* as the volunteer of the will to will, for which all truth becomes that error which it needs in order to be able to guarantee for itself the illusion that the will to will can will nothing other than empty nothingness, in the face of which it asserts itself without being able to know its own completed nullity.

The decline has already taken place. The consequences of this occurrence are the events of world history in this century. They are merely the course of what has already ended. Its course is ordered historico-technologically in the sense of the last stage of metaphysics. This order is the last arrangement of what has ended in the illusion of a reality whose effects work in an irresistable way, because they claim to be able to get along without an unconcealment of the *essence of Being*. They do this so decisively that they need suspect nothing of such an unconcealment.

The still hidden truth of Being is withheld from metaphysical humanity. The laboring animal is left to the giddy whirl of its products so that it may tear itself to pieces and annihilate itself in empty nothingness.

It is difficult to imagine a more devastating condemnation of the destiny of "metaphysical humanity," or a more bleak portrait of the modern age – although we must not forget that Heidegger frequently cites the evocative lines from Hölderlin: "But where danger is, grows the saving power also. . . ." (I will return to Heidegger's interpretation of these lines later in this essay.)

The mood that I am seeking to elicit discloses itself in what might be called the "rage against Humanism." "Humanism" seems to have become the signifier that names everything that is ominous, dark, and nihilistic in the modern age – and if Heidegger is right, "metaphysical humanism" has its origins already in the beginnings of classical Greek *philosophy*, when "original thinking comes to an end." We shall see, however, that discerning what is meant by "Humanism," discriminating the sense (senses) in which Heidegger condemns humanism, and who can even be read as opening vistas for thinking about a "new" humanism, requires a complex task of unraveling. But before pursuing the question of humanism, let me try out another *Holzwege* into the labyrinth of Heidegger's thinking.

For all of Heidegger's erudition there is no evidence that he ever seriously read or thought about the American pragmatic thinkers. His occasional remarks about "pragmatism" and "America" illustrate what he himself has perceptively characterized as "chatter" (*Gerede*). He would probably shudder at even calling them "thinkers" – if by thinking we mean the type of "original," "meditative," "poetic" thinking that he seeks to elucidate in his later writings.[4] On the contrary, they exemplify the type of calculative, technological thinking that is revealed in the last stages of the decline of "metaphysical humanity." But for someone who has studied and listened to these philosophers, the encounter with Heidegger is at once perplexing and troubling. For one is struck by the deep affinities and resonances, especially with the Heidegger of *Sein und Zeit*. We can witness this most vividly by comparing their critiques of Cartesianism – Cartesianism which Heidegger and the pragmatists took to be at the heart of so much of modern philosophy and culture. Almost every point that Peirce makes in his brilliant attack on Cartesianism in 1868[5] (and which is reiterated by later pragmatic thinkers) is echoed in *Sein und Zeit*: the radical critique of modern subjectivism, epistemological foundationism; the dubious quest for certainty; the "spectator theory of knowledge," the suspicion and de-structuring of the dualisms and dichotomies of modern thought, the decentering of the very idea of autonomous consciousness; the claim that we never fully escape from our prejudices and prejudgments – all of these themes are shared by Heidegger and the pragmatists. Even more important, the sense of our historicity, that we are beings "thrown" into the world, that we are always already *in medias res*, that it is more revealing to understand our *Dasein* by attending to our prereflective practices, and to what is ready-to-hand (*zuhanden*) are motifs common to Heidegger and the pragmatists. Together they share a heroic effort to break with the excesses of subjectivism, individualism, and the false sense of human beings as the sovereign and "lord of beings." But despite these similarities and affinities, one is also struck by the differences of tone, emphasis, and concern. Whatever one makes of Heidegger's famous *Kehre*, there is ample evidence in *Sein und Zeit* that the analysis of *Dasein* is preparatory for encountering the *Seinsfrage*. And in his subsequent writings, Heidegger warns us against a distorted anthropological, humanistic, or existential misreading of *Sein und Zeit*. The one theme – the single thought – to which Heidegger returns again and again is the question of Being itself, and the ontological difference of beings and Being. From Heidegger's perspective, the pragmatists are only further evidence of the oblivion and forgetfulness of Being – at best a minor footnote to the last great "metaphysical" thinker, Nietzsche. The pragmatists might suspect that despite Heidegger's efforts to think through and beyond metaphysics, to overcome metaphysics, he is still entrapped and inscribed in the tradition he seeks to overcome. One way of putting the issue forcefully is to ask where Heidegger and the pragmatists "stand" on the question of humanism, or as Heidegger prefers to phrase it, "the *humanitas* of *homo humanus*." For Heidegger, "the essence of man consists in his being more than merely human, if this is represented as 'being a rational creature'. . . . Man is not the lord of beings. Man is the shepherd of Being" (p. 221).[6] As the "shepherd of Being," man's "dignity" is to be found in being called by Being itself into the preservation of Being's truth. But the pragmatists would certainly be critical of this fateful dichotomy of man as "lord of beings" or the "shepherd of Being." What is left unsaid, what seems to pass into the shadows of the background is what Aristotle called "*praxis*" – the distinctively human form of activity manifested in *ethos* and the life of the *polis*. The type of "action" that becomes dominant in Heidegger's later writings – indeed it is almost obsessive – is the *activity* of thinking itself; thinking which "concerns the relation of

Being to man"; the "thinking that is to come [which] is no longer philosophy, because it thinks more originally than metaphysics – a name, identical to philosophy"; thinking which is a deed "that surpasses all *praxis*," which "towers above action and production, not through the grandeur of its achievement and not as a consequence of its effect, but through the humbleness of its inconsequential accomplishment" (p. 239).

The mention of *praxis*, which is intended to call to mind Aristotle's meaning and more generally the tradition of practical philosophy that he helped to initiate, brings me to my third beginning – a pathway that brings us even closer to the heart of Heidegger's attack on metaphysical humanism. In the early 1920s, before the publication of *Sein und Zeit*, when Heidegger was still teaching at Marburg, he gave a famous seminar on Aristotle's *Nicomachean Ethics*, focusing on the discussion of *phronesis* in Book Six. We know a great deal about that seminar, at least indirectly, because Gadamer frequently refers to it as a decisive event in his own intellectual development.[7] And we know what Gadamer appropriated from Heidegger's *phronesis* interpretation. For at a crucial stage in *Truth and Method*, Gadamer tells us that "if we relate Aristotle's description of the ethical phenomenon and especially of the virtue of moral knowledge [*phronesis*] to our own investigation, we find that Aristotle's analysis is in fact a kind of model of the problems of hermeneutics."[8] It is not just that hermeneutical understanding is a form of *phronesis*, but the theme of *phronesis* becomes increasingly prominent in Gadamer's own thinking – so much so that he tells us:[9]

I think, then, that the chief task of philosophy is to justify this way of reason against the domination of technology based on science. That is the point of philosophic hermeneutic. It corrects the peculiar falsehood of modern consciousness: the idolatry of scientific method and the anonymous authority of the sciences and it vindicates again the noblest task of the citizen – decision making according to one's responsibility – instead of conceding that task to the expert. In this respect, hermeneutic philosophy is the heir of the older tradition of practical philosophy.

But I do not think that we find anything comparable to this eloquent claim in the writings of the later Heidegger. On the contrary, Heidegger tells us that "philosophy is over" and in his *Der Spiegel* interview which was published posthumously he declares:[10]

> Philosophy will not be able to effect any direct transformation on the present state of the world. This is true not only of philosophy but of any simply human contemplation and striving. Only a god can save us now. We can only through thinking and writing prepare to be prepared for the manifestation of god, or the absence of god as things go downhill all the way.

It is *almost* as if Heidegger has completely "given up" on the *humanitas* of *homo humanus*, despairing of even the possibility that man can come into the clearing of Being – although we shall later explore the ways in which this is not quite accurate. But the contrast between Gadamer (and in this respect Gadamer is much closer to the pragmatists) is striking. Gadamer does not think that we have reached a stage where "science has expanded into a total technocracy, and thus brings on the 'cosmic night' of the 'forgetfulness of Being'."[11] As he tells us, in this respect, his "divergence from Heidegger is fundamental."[12] Gadamer's defense and explication of *phronesis*, and the role that it can still play in fostering human solidarity is one of the most subtle and powerful statements of the type of humanism that Heidegger *appears* to condemn. How are we to account for Heidegger's virtual silence about *praxis* and *phronesis* in his later writings? Why is it that this "intellectual virtue" which also reveals *aletheia* seems to drop from our view? What does this mean for Heidegger's own understanding and critique of humanism? These are the questions that I now want to explore.

II

So let me turn directly to Heidegger's *Letter on Humanism* – the *locus classicus* for his discussion of humanism. This is clearly one

of Heidegger's most important texts. Let us recall the circumstances for it being written and published, for these are relevant
to what it says and leaves unsaid. The letter was written in
response to a series of questions posed by a French colleague,
Jean Beaufret – the first of which is: "Comment redonner un
sens au mot 'Humanisme'?" ["How can we restore meaning
to the word 'humanism'?"] Sartre's manifesto, *Existentialisme
est un Humanisme*, had recently appeared, and this text is in the
background of both Beaufret's questions and Heidegger's
response. The *Letter* was an occasion for Heidegger to
disassociate himself as strongly as possible from the existentialism propounded by Sartre – and more generally, from what
Heidegger took to be the distorted reading of *Sein und Zeit*. But
the *Letter* which was published in 1947 is much more. It was an
opportunity for Heidegger to reflect on his own thinking and
writing since the publication of *Sein und Zeit* – especially his
thinking about Nietzsche and Hölderlin. In retrospect, one can
also see that most of the themes of Heidegger's subsequent
writings are mentioned in the *Letter*. We should also remember
that the *Letter* was written at a time when Heidegger was for-
bidden to teach and when he was being severely attacked for
his "role" in Nazi Germany. I mention this because in its style
and content, the *Letter* can be read – in the classical sense – as
an *apologia*. Finally, I do not think it is without significance that
the original German publication of the *Letter* in 1947 appeared
as an "appendix" or "supplement" to the second edition of
Platons Lehre von der Wahrheit. But Heidegger does not begin the
Letter by explicitly taking up Beaufret's questions. Let me cite
the opening:[13]

> We are still far from pondering the essence of action decisively
> enough. [One views] action as causing an effect. The actuality
> of the effect is valued according to its utility. But the essence of
> action is accomplishment. To accomplish means to unfold
> something into the fullness of its essence, to lead it forth into
> this fullness – *producere*. Therefore only what already is can really
> be accomplished. But what "is" above all is Being. Thinking
> accomplishes the relation of Being to the essence of man. It does
> not make or cause the relation. Thinking brings this relation to

Being solely as something handed over to it from Being. Such offering consists in the fact that in thinking Being comes to language. Language is the house of Being. In its home man dwells. Those who think and those who create with words are the guardians of this home. Their guardianship accomplishes the manifestation of Being insofar as they bring the manifestation to language and maintain it in language through their speech. Thinking does not become action only because some effect issues from it or because it is applied. Thinking acts insofar as it thinks. Such action is presumably the simplest and at the same time the highest, because it concerns the relation of Being to man. (p. 193)

The style here is typical of the writings of the later Heidegger with its deceptively simple staccato sentences – a style intended to provoke and call forth thinking, but which also can have and has had a mesmerizing effect on many of Heidegger's disciples. Before we even grasp what is being said here, the progression of key words signifies the pathway of Heidegger's own thinking – from "action," "accomplishment,""Being," "thinking," "Language," "dwells," "guardianship," to the completion of the hermeneutical circle with the claim that thinking is presumably the simplest and highest form of action. This is virtually a catalogue of the major themes of the later Heidegger, and – as I will try to show – without yet mentioning "humanism," this opening passage contains Heidegger's response to the question of humanism.

But let us go over carefully the flow of Heidegger's thinking here and arrest it. The second sentence in German reads: *"Man kennt das Handeln nur das Bewirken einer Wirkung."* Who is Heidegger speaking about when he writes: *"Man kennt . . .?* One might speculate that what he means here is the same as what he means when he speaks of *"Das Man"* in *Sein und Zeit.* But why is this so important? Because Heidegger here already passes over in silence a crucial distinction concerning action. Heidegger is certainly correct in identifying a pervasive and deeply entrenched way of thinking about action in the modern age. We might even label this the "technical" understanding of action – where action is exclusively thought of as making

something happen, as effecting a means to achieve a predetermined end. But this is certainly not the way in which Aristotle,
and those who identify themselves with the tradition of practical philosophy that traces itself back to Aristotle's ethical and
political writings, think of *praxis*. Heidegger is certainly aware
of the distinctions between *poiesis* and *praxis*, *techne* and *phronesis*,
but in this context when he speaks of action (*Handeln*) he passes
over these distinctions in silence. My point is not merely philo-
logical or historical, for it stands at the very center of contemporary concerns with the character and different modes of
action.[14] It is, for example, central for two of Heidegger's most
prominent students: Gadamer and Arendt, as well as being
central for Habermas and the pragmatists. For all of them – in
very different ways – have sought to expose what is at stake in
collapsing all of human activity into the technical sense of
action – a sense of action that departs radically from what
Aristotle meant by both *poiesis* and *praxis*. They would all endorse the claim of Habermas when he seeks to distinguish the
technical and practical senses of action and power:[15]

> The real difficulty in the relation of theory and praxis does not
> arise from this new function of science as a technological force,
> but rather from the fact that we are no longer able to distinguish
> between practical and technical power. Yet even a civilization
> that has been rendered scientific is not granted dispensation
> from practical questions, therefore a peculiar danger arises
> when the process of scientification transgresses the limit of tech-
> nical questions, without, however, departing from the level of
> reflection of a rationality confined to the technical horizon. For
> then no attempt is made to attain a rational consensus on the
> part of citizens concerned with the practical control of their
> destiny. Its place is taken by the attempt to attain technical con-
> trol over history by perfecting the administration of society, an
> attempt that is just as impractical as it is unhistorical.

But this is not the way in which Heidegger understands our
contemporary horizon. Indeed he sees the seeds of the technical
sense of action and calculative thinking already implicit in
Plato and Aristotle. (This is just the thesis that he develops in
Platons Lehre von der Wahrheit.)[16] In what might be called

Heidegger's "strong" reading of the history of philosophy which reveals the history of Being, there has been a relentless, ineluctable drive toward making manifest the concealed technical thrust implicit in the history of metaphysics. What emerges in Heidegger's writings after *Sein und Zeit* is a reiterated series of hidden identities: philosophy = metaphysics = humanism = nihilism = enframing [*Gestell* – the "essence of technology"], culminating in the last stage of metaphysics where there is "the consumption of all materials, including the raw material 'man'." [17]

If we are to be "saved" from this destiny, if man is to find again a dwelling – an *ethos* – so that he can escape from his homelessness, a homelessness which has become so radical in the modern age, it is only by answering the call of thinking – meditative, poetic, original thinking; thinking which does not come to an end with the end of philosophy, but is "in transition to another beginning." [18] "Where enframing reigns," as it does in the modern age, "there is danger in the highest sense." "But where danger is, grows the saving power also." [19] It is not technology itself that is the supreme danger, but the essence of technology – *Gestell*. In this respect there is a point of analogy with the passage we cited from Habermas when he suggests that the danger does not come from the new function of science as a technological force, but rather from our being "enframed" in a technical horizon. But where Habermas (and this move is also characteristic of Gadamer, Arendt, and the pragmatists) emphasizes the difference between a technical and practical horizon, Heidegger appeals to a "poetic revealing." Being is always near and distant. He concludes *The Question Concerning Technology* by *asking* whether a poetic revealing "may expressly foster the growth of the saving power, may awaken and found our vision of that which grants and our trust in it," and by declaring "The closer we come to the danger, the more brightly do the ways into the saving power begin to shine and the more questioning we become. For questioning is the piety of thought." [20]

Heidegger at once portrays our extreme "spiritual decline" – "the darkening of the world, the flight of the gods, the destruction of the earth, the transformation of men into a mass, the hatred and suspicion of everything free and creative" where the "childish categories of pessimism and optimism have long since become absurd,"[21] and yet affirms the possibility of the growth of the saving power through the highest form of action – thinking which concerns the relation of Being to man.

This is why I have said that Heidegger's response to the question of humanism is already implicit in the opening sentences of the *Letter*. *If* we think of humanism as identical with metaphysics and *Gestell*, which is itself the manifestation of the oblivion and forgetfulness of Being, then Heidegger is opposing such humanism in the strongest possible manner. *If* humanism in the modern age "is nothing but a moral-aesthetic anthropology, that philosophical interpretation of man which explains and evaluates whatever is, in its entirety, from the standpoint of man and in relation to man,"[22] then all of Heidegger's pathways are intended to expose, reject, and exorcize this modern "world picture." This is why the distinctions between *poiesis* and *praxis*, *techne* and *phronesis* are so insignificant in the writings of the later Heidegger. "No mere action will change the world," for all *human* action collapses into the "will to will." Our only hope – and it seems to be a feeble hope – is by answering the silent call of Being.

But I want to argue that such a response to the question of humanism is not only totally inadequate, but is itself extremely dangerous – dangerous because it seduces us into thinking that all human activity (other than the activity of thinking) reduces itself – flattens out – into *Gestell*, manipulation, control, will to will, nihilism; dangerous because it virtually closes off the space for attending to the type of thinking and acting that can foster human solidarity and community. Rorty's casual remark may seem tendentious and offensive: "Heidegger decides that since the Nazis didn't work out, only a god can save us now,"[23] but it contains a kernel of "truth." For the focal point of so much of Heidegger's writings after the publication of the *Letter on Humanism* leads us to an Either/Or: *either* we are condemned to metaphysical humanism whose last stage is where "the laboring animal is left to the giddy whirl of its products so that it may tear itself to pieces and annihilate itself in empty nothingness," *or* we can be "saved," return to an *ethos* – a dwelling – through a poetic revealing and meditative thinking.

Let me try to show this by attending to Heidegger's explicit remarks about humanism. When Heidegger takes up the question, "How can we restore meaning to the word 'humanism'?," he begins by wondering whether we should even retain the word "humanism." "Isms" are notoriously misleading and tend to obscure more than they illuminate, "but the market of public opinion continually demands new ones" (p. 195). He briefly reviews the variety of forms of Western humanism, mentioning Roman, Christian, and Marxist humanism. But Heidegger is not concerned with a historical survey of the varieties of humanism, he seeks to "bring forth" the essence of humanism. What then is this essence?

> Every humanism is either grounded in metaphysics or is itself made to be the ground of one. Every determination of the essence of man that already presupposes an interpretation of being without asking about the truth of Being whether knowingly or not, is metaphysical. The result is that what is peculiar to all metaphysics, specifically with respect to the way the essence of man is determined, is that it is "humanistic". (p. 202)

So humanism and metaphysics are inextricably linked together. What then is the essential character and limitation of "metaphysical humanism"? "In defining the humanity of man, humanism not only does not ask about the relation of Being to the essence of man; because of its metaphysical origin humanism even impedes the question by neither recognizing nor understanding it" (p. 202). And what then is the concealed essence of metaphysics? It is itself technology – or more accurately, the essence of technology, *Gestell*. "The name 'technology' is understood here in such an essential way that its meaning coincides with the term 'completed metaphysics'."[24] And lest we think that Heidegger is dealing with "mere words," let us not forget that already in *An Introduction to Metaphysics*, when

Heidegger asks: "Is 'being' a mere word and its meaning a vapor or is it the spiritual destiny of the Western world?" his response is unambiguous:[25]

> This Europe, in its ruinous blindness forever on the point of cutting its own throat, lies today in a great pincers, squeezed between Russia on the one side and America on the other. From a metaphysical point of view, Russia and America are the same; the same dreary technological frenzy, the same unrestricted organization of the average man.

I know that there are many sympathetic interpreters of Heidegger who take such statements as unfortunate lapses, but Heidegger's claims about the consequences of the oblivion and forgetfulness of Being are by no means untypical. Over and over again he seeks to reveal the ineluctable progression from philosophy to metaphysics to the devastating power of the essence of technology – all of which reveal the essence of metaphysical humanism.

Thus far I have been emphasizing and seeking to clarify Heidegger's anti-humanism. But there will be those who say that to leave the matter here is to leave one with a distorted interpretation of Heidegger. It is to miss the point of his critique of metaphysics and humanism. Heidegger is not totally rejecting humanism just as he does not totally reject metaphysics. His project is one of overcoming (*Überwindung*), where he seeks to think *through* the very grounds and origins of metaphysical humanism. Even in the *Letter*, he tells us "the essence of man consists in his being more than merely human" and that metaphysical humanism fails to do justice to man's dignity. To understand Heidegger we must realize that he is leading us to a more primordial way of understanding the *humanitas* of *homo humanus*. It is true that what Heidegger opens up for us "contradicts all previous humanism" and seeks to make a radical break with metaphysical subjectivism, but he does this in order to shock us into thinking about the meaning of the *humanitas* of *homo humanus* in a new (or very old) way.[26] He seeks to awaken a reflection "that thinks not only about man but also about the 'nature' of man, not only about his nature but even more primordially about the dimension in which the essence of man, determined by Being itself, is at home" (p. 225). Furthermore, it may be argued that we need to realize that Heidegger is dealing with questions in a more "primordial," "radical," "fundamental" manner. He clearly sees that modern attempts to "solve" problems turn out to be variations on the same theme – the theme of *Gestell*. They are part of the problem of modernity and its metaphysical humanism. Only if there is some fundamental conversion in our thinking, a thinking that transcends *praxis* and *poiesis*, a thinking that "is neither theoretical nor practical, nor . . . the conjunction of those two forms of behavior" (p. 240) can we be "saved." Read in this way, after we sort out precisely what he is seeking to destroy and overcome, we can interpret Heidegger as opening vistas for a new way of thinking about humanism, as pointing to what might even be called a "meta-humanism."

Let me first emphasize that I do think that this is certainly Heidegger's primary intent – and there is plenty of textual evidence to support such a reading. But my questioning and skepticism concerns the content (*Inhalt*) of this new/old meta-humanism. Following the hermeneutical principle of seeking to give the strongest possible interpretation to what one seeks to understand, I want to proceed with the help of two guides who do read Heidegger in this way: Fred Dallmayr and John Caputo. Neither is uncritical of Heidegger, but both, in different ways, sensitively and perceptively try to show how Heidegger "delineated a new version of humanism"; how his thinking leads to a "recovery of man."

III

There are many virtues in Dallmayr's discussions of Heidegger.[27] As a political theorist he is particularly sensitive to the relevance of Heidegger's writing for rethinking the social and political character of human beings. He carefully reconstructs Heidegger's radical critique of subjectivity. He reviews – and clearly shows – what is misleading about the appropriation and commentary on Heidegger that construes *Dasein* "egologically" as an existentialist adaptation of Husserl's phenomenology, and in particular Husserl's theory of intersubjectivity. He reminds us of the central role of care (*Sorge*), solicitude (*Forsorge*), co-being (*Mitsein*) and Dasein's being-with (*Mitdasein*) in *Sein und Zeit*.[28] He tells us that the crucial experimental trait of *Dasein* is "neither rationality nor will to power but *care* – a term denoting both the anxiety deriving from the lack of a fixed behavioral structure and the capacity for genuine attentiveness reaching beyond subjectively-instrumental pursuits."[29] *Dasein*, as care, is "intrinsically permeated by *world* and others." "Everyday existence, although regularly inauthentic, is not only a defect to be remedied, but a mode of being-in-the-world. As such it is implicitly open to Being and thus contains at least the anticipation of authentic co-being."

Dallmayr's reading of Heidegger, insofar as it pertains to the question of humanism, is eloquently summed up when he writes:[30]

> Emancipatory solicitude – also called anticipative-emancipatory solicitude – is introduced in the section delineating different types of care, especially as a counterpoint to managerial solicitude. In contradistinction to the latter's manipulative thrust, Heidegger writes, "there is the possibility of a kind of solicitude which does not so much displace the Other as anticipate him in his essential potentiality for Being – not in order to take 'care' away from him but in order to restore it to him in a genuine fashion." Involving the dimension of authentic care, that is, the very existence of the Other and not merely the affairs with which he is concerned, this type of solicitude helps the Other to become transparent to himself in his care and to become *free for* it.

And Dallmayr goes on to claim:

> As is apparent, Heidegger's observations carry important normative implications; in fact, his conception of authentic existence and co-being can in my view be seen as a reformulation of the traditional notion of the good life and in particular of the

Kantian postulate of the kingdom of ends. Compared to the latter principle, Heidegger's conception has the advantage not only of increased realism or concreteness but also of greater moral adequacy. Despite its anti-utilitarian intent, the postulate to treat others as ends rather than means contains instrumentalist traces, in the sense that the ego tends to function as a means for others who, in turn, appear as values "for me" or as "my" ends. Authentic co-being, on the contrary, is distinguished by respect for others in their *Dasein* and their "potentiality for Being," rather than in their role as moral goals.

Dallmayr epitomizes this reading of Heidegger – this "new version of humanism" when he says: "authentic *Dasein* does not rule out co-being, but only efforts of interhuman management. Forsaking manipulation and mastery, genuine solicitude manifests itself in *letting be*, in the willingness to let others live their lives and anticipate their deaths – an attitude which is far removed from indifference."[31]

Although Dallmayr bases his interpretation of Heidegger on a careful analysis of *Sein und Zeit*, it becomes clear that he does not think that Heidegger abandons or retracts this understanding of *Dasein*. Rather Dallmayr's understanding of Heidegger's development is one where these themes are deepened and illuminated.[32] But despite the apparent persuasiveness of Dallmayr's attractive interpretation, I do not find it fully convincing.

First, as Dallmayr himself indicates, the "normative implications" that he draws from Heidegger's analysis of *Dasein* are his – not Heidegger's. On the contrary, Heidegger warns us against a "moral-philosophical" or "moral-existentiell" interpretation of such terms as "authenticity" and "inauthenticity." It is almost as if Heidegger fears that any such normative interpretation must be "anthropological" in its pejorative sense, and contaminates the purity of "an 'estatic' relation of the essence of man to the truth of Being" (p. 212).

Secondly, even such rich and evocative terms as "care" and "solicitude" undergo a subtle but decisive turn in Heidegger's later writings. For it is not the authentic care and solicitude of other human beings that is his major concern, but the care of Being and Language itself.

Thirdly, *mitsein* and *mitdasein* also seem to recede into the background. Heidegger is less and less interested in delineating the types of sociality and community – or even in suggesting how "authentic community" might be achieved. Ethics (and politics too) arise as disciplines only when "thinking waned." In the typical Heideggerian move which is always seeking to take us back to what is presumably "primordial," Heidegger tells us that to understand *ethos*, we need to go beyond (and behind) Aristotle, to the tragedies of Sophocles, and ultimately to Heraclitus' three words *ēthos anthrōpōs daimōn* for the essence of *ethos* to come to a clearing. Despite Heidegger's brilliant and imaginative interpretation of this fragment (pp. 232–5), it is difficult to see that it brings us very far in understanding what *ethos* means for our being-in-the-world. Indeed, as Heidegger interprets the fragment, "Man dwells, insofar as he is man, in the nearness of god," it brings us back to thinking, not *praxis*.

Fourthly, despite Dallmayr's claims about Heidegger's "increased realism or concreteness" and his "greater moral adequacy," this is precisely what Heidegger's pronouncements seem to lack. I fail to see how, for all their metaphoric power, Heidegger's "poetic" remarks about dwelling, *ethos*, and letting be, provide any determinate orientation or guidance for how we are to live our lives in "authentic community" – or what such an "authentic community" even means. Typically, when Heidegger speaks of public life or the public realm, he speaks of it in a disparaging tone; for example, when in the *Letter* he mentions "the peculiar dictatorship of the public realm" (p. 197) in the modern age. Once again, what seems to be lacking is any attention to a discrimination of the modes or types of public or communal life. One may even question whether terms like "care," "solicitude," and "authenticity" are the most illuminating for analyzing communal ethical and political life. For they do not "bring forth" the dialogic and communicative dimensions of ethical and political life.

Finally, I think one must be wary of Heideggerian claims about what is truly primordial and concrete when we realize that the reading that Dallmayr gives of *Sein und Zeit* appears to be compatible with the aggressive – almost nationalistic – call for spiritual regeneration characteristic of *An Introduction to Meta-physic* – where terms like "courage," "decision" and "destiny" are so prominent, and the much more resigned (but still active) language of *Gelassenheit* and the *Der Spiegel* interview.[33]

Caputo too has no hesitancy in speaking of Heidegger's *Letter* as presenting us with a "species of humanism," albeit a "humanism of a higher sort." And the title of his essay from which these phrases are cited is intended as a direct challenge to those who speak so facilely of the "end of man": "Hermeneutics as the Recovery of Man."[34] In this essay, and in Caputo's defense of Heidegger against what he takes to be the distortive, reductionist misreading of Heidegger by Derrida and Rorty, he argues passionately for reading Heidegger as providing new insight about the *humanitas* of *homo humanus*. Caputo's thesis is that there are "two philosophies of recovery or retrieval which feed into the hermeneutic strategy of *Being and Time* – the Kierkegaardian notion of existential 'repetition', and the phenomenological return to beginnings in Husserl."[35] According to Caputo, it is "Kierkegaardian repetition that controls and decisively modifies the phenomenological element in *Being and Time*, and hence the hermeneutics which is at work in this book has broken with metaphysics."[36] Contrary to Derrida's (and Rorty's) reading of Heidegger, this type of recovery of origins has nothing to do with a "nostalgia for presence." I cannot go into the details of Caputo's perceptive analysis of these two philosophies of recovery, and the ways in which he argues that Heidegger shows that they belong together. But Caputo's point becomes clear when he writes:[37]

> But authentic *Dasein*, which has the courage for anxiety, recovers the absence which underlies its presence; it breaks the grip of the actual upon its Being and, in so doing, recovers its freedom. The freedom of *Dasein* is that it is no longer held fast by the actual; it is a transcendence beyond things which stretches out into the Nothing.

While Caputo focuses on the existential dimension of Heidegger's thinking – especially Heidegger's appropriation of

Kierkegaardian repetition – he, like Dallmayr, sharply distinguishes this from the metaphysical humanism and subjectivism that Heidegger overcomes. But the "higher species" of Heidegger's "humanism" becomes clear when Caputo tells us:[38]

> Unless the Being in terms of which a being is projected reaches back and articulates a preunderstanding, then it is groundless and uprooted. And that means that the labors of a concrete, working hermenutics must be enlisted in the service of articulating our self-understanding. The interpretation of a past historical epoch, of a work of art, or of a scriptural text, must be governed by their ability to tell us who we are, to say something to us here and now about the beings which we ourselves are or, better, must become. All hermeneutics, on whatever level, is the recovery of man and is governed by the existential imperative to become oneself.

Similar themes are at work in Caputo's spirited critique of what he takes to be Rorty's distorted interpretation of Heidegger. Rorty "has taken up only the 'deconstructive' side of Heidegger, the critique of metaphysics . . . but . . . he remains quite hostile to Heidegger's project of retrieval (*Wiederholung, andenken*)."[39] For the purposes of this essay, I want to bracket the issue of whether Caputo is right in arguing that the "deconstructive" interpretaton of Heidegger by Derrida and Rorty is one that "can only come to grief." Rather I want to concentrate on his portrait of Heidegger and hermeneutics which he wants to distinguish and defend against the deconstructive misappropriation of Heidegger. Caputo epitomizes this when he writes:[40]

> In my view, the point that the continental philosophers have been making, first under the name of "existentialism," then of "phenomenology," and nowadays of "hermeneutics" – all of which, to use Rorty's term, is "edifying" philosophy – is to make of philosophy a concerted effort to put man back in touch with himself. Their attack upon metaphysics has been aimed at reawakening a sense of the human drama, at recovering the lived

quality of our experience and the historicality of the dialogue into which we have all been entered. On this account, everything turns on what Heidegger, following Kierkegaard, called "repetition" or "retrieval" (*Wiederholung*) of a primordial but latent pre-understanding in which we all always and already stand.

I do think that Caputo is right is seeking to recover and retrieve a deep underlying theme in Heidegger's thinking. But we need to turn our attention to what such phrases as "a sense of the human drama" and "recovering the lived quality of our experience" really mean – if these are to be more than mere rhetorical gestures. If a concerted effort is to be made to "put man back in touch with himself," do we not have to recognize that *one* vital dimension of what we truly are is beings of *praxis*? Willy-nilly, we are beings compelled to act in this world. We are, as even Heidegger tells us, inextricably bound up not only with other beings, but with other human beings. If we are "thrown" into this world, then ethical and political action is inescapable. What Caputo has not shown us, has left unsaid, is *how* repetition and retrieval illuminate our *praxis* here and now. Ethics and politics need not be interpreted as asking for blueprints, specific rules of action, methodical procedures to follow in order to "solve" our ethical and political problems. But a "higher" or more "primordial" sense of humanism that does not help to provide any orientation toward our *praxis* comes very close to being empty. Not only is it empty, but it is also dangerous because it can mystify the *content* of such repetition.

We should not forget that one of the most infamous contexts in which Heidegger calls for repetition is when, in 1935, he calls for spiritual regeneration of the German nation.[41]

All this implies that this nation, as a historical nation, must move itself and thereby the history of the West beyond the center of their future "happening" and into the primordial realm of the powers of being. If the great decision regarding Europe is not to bring annihilation, that decision must be made in terms of new spiritual energies unfolding historically from out of the center.

> To ask "How does it stand with being?" means nothing less than to recapture, to repeat [*wieder-holen*], the beginning of our historical–spiritual existence, in order to transform it into a new beginning. This is possible. It is indeed the crucial form of history, because it begins in the fundamental event. But we do not repeat a beginning by reducing it to something past and now known, which need merely be imitated; no, the beginning must be begun again, more radically, with all the strangeness, darkness, insecurity that attend a true beginning.

This too presumably requires "courage" and the imperative to become what we truly *are*. I find lacking in Caputo's explication and defense of Heidegger's "humanism of a higher sort" the same thing that I find lacking in Dallmayr's explication. Both leave us just where we need to begin serious questioning. Both are extremely persuasive in clarifying what underlies Heidegger's critique of "metaphysical humanism" and of the ways in which he seeks to overcome it. But neither is very helpful in revealing the determinate content of this so-called higher humanism. And both seem to side-step Heidegger's increasing skepticism about any positive role that *praxis* and *phronesis* might play in putting us back in touch with ourselves.[42]

IV

Except for my brief remarks at the beginning of this essay, I have not explicitly discussed the pragmatic thinkers, but they have not only been in the background of my probing of Heidegger's anti-humanism and his "meta-humanism," but in the foreground. I indicated that there is a great deal that is shared by the pragmatists and Heidegger. Both share a radical critique of the metaphysics of subjectivity. Both seek to undercut the dichotomy between subjectivism and objectivism that provides the framework of so much of modern thought. Both have a profound sense of our finitude and historicity. Both reject the conception of man as "lord of beings." The pragmatists – especially Dewey – are aware of the danger of limiting ourselves to a technical horizon – of the genuine threat of what

Heidegger calls *Gestell*. And the pragmatists can also be seen as reawakening our sense of the human drama and recovering the lived quality of our experience. But there is a decisive *difference*. For the pragmatists turn our attention to how we can think about our *praxis*, and how we can foster a sense of solidarity and community among human beings. This is why the notion of a critical community without any absolute beginning points or finalities is so fundamental for them – a type of community in which there can be an overcoming of the "eclipse of public life." Our dialogue, and communicative transactions, are not only with Being itself, but with other human beings. And if we are to understand this concretely and cultivate what Aristotle called *phronesis* in *our* historical situation, then we must turn our attention to the ethical and political questions – the practical questions that Heidegger does not directly confront. One need not denigrate what Heidegger has taught us about the onto-logical difference of beings and Being, Language, and Think-ing. One can agree with much of Heidegger's analysis and critique of calculative, manipulative thinking, where human beings are only "human resources." But the dichotomy between "two kinds of thinking, each justified and needed in its own way: calculative and meditative thinking"[43] is too undif-ferentiated. What is paradoxical in Heidegger is that despite his enormous subtlety and powers of discrimination, the pathways of his later thinking lead us to a series of stark con-trasts – contrasts that too easily lead to a view of all "merely" human actions as only variations of *Gestell*. What Gadamer, Arendt, Habermas, and the pragmatists illuminate for us, and try to bring into a clearing – is obscured and left in darkness by Heidegger. For all of them are acutely aware of the "deforma-tion of praxis" in the modern age, and the conceptual and material ways in which *praxis* is assimilated to a fabricating, technical mentality. In this respect too, we can become aware of the dangers of the mood that I sought to elicit at the begin-ning of this essay and which is manifested in so much of Heidegger's writings. For Heidegger's condemnation of the nihilistic humanism implicit in Western metaphysics and his deep skepticism about the modern age easily slide into a form of "totalizing critique" that seductively leads us to the inexorable conclusion that "we can only through thinking and writing prepare to be prepared for the manifestation of god, or the absence of god as things go downhill all the way." The primary issue is not one between "pessimism" and "optimism." It is rather an issue of bringing into a clearing, achieving an orientation concerning what we are to do, how we are to live our lives *together*, what "authentic community" means, and how it can be nurtured. If "questoning is the piety of thought," then this questioning cannot turn away from thinking about our *praxis*. Meditative thinking and poetic revealing may "foster the growth of the saving power," but a "higher species" of humanism or metahumanism that is silent about what human *praxis* means here and now in our concrete historical horizon, will not "save" us – it will only obscure and conceal "the supreme danger."

8

Judging – the Actor and the Spectator[1]

Hannah Arendt frequently remarked about "the fundamental and flagrant contradictions" in the thinkers and writers she admired. She tells us "In the work of great authors they lead to the very center of their work and are the most important clue to a true understanding of their problems and new insights" (*BPF*, p. 25). In this chapter, I want to explore a "flagrant" contradiction that stands at the heart of her work. It is the conflict between her two central concerns – acting and thinking – and it comes into clear focus in her reflections on judging. "The capacity to judge is a specifically political ability" (*BPF*, p. 221). Yet judging is also characterized as the mental activity of the spectator who seeks to understand the *meaning* of the spectacle of human affairs. Judging is at once the faculty par excellence of those who participate and engage in action and the faculty of non-participating spectators. To judge and to act are presumably radically distinct. How are we to make sense of this? By probing this tension we are drawn into the center of her "problems and new insights," into her own distinctive project to make sense of the human condition.

What I propose to do then is first to explore judging (and the closely related concept, opinion) from the perspective of the *vita activa*, and specifically from the perspective of the highest form of human activity – action. Then I will examine judging from the point of view of the *vita contemplativa*, focusing on its autonomy, and its intimate relations with thinking.

Let me begin by reflecting on what Arendt would consider a

truism, but a truism that has all sorts of ramifications once these are teased out. She tells us, almost casually, that "debate constitutes the very essence of political life" (*BPF*, p. 241). Note that in what initially seems to be a rather innocuous claim she does *not* say that the essence of politics is domination, or control of the legitimate means of violence, or that it consists of the ways in which an individual or a class seeks to impose interests on some other individual or class. The essence of politics is debate, and we will see that this has a special meaning for Arendt and presupposes certain conditions about human individuals.

Debate itself is a form of action, and "action," (the term that Arendt uses to designate the distinctive and highest form of human activity), is not to be confused or merged with the other forms of the *vita activa*, labor and work. Man is both *animal laborans* and *homo faber*. Both forms of activity are grounded in the human condition, but neither of these are to be confused with action whereby the distinctive humanity of men is *revealed*.[2] Action is the public disclosure of the agent in speech deed.

> Action and speech are so closely related because the primordial and specifically human act must at the same time contain an answer to the question asked of every newcomer: "Who are you?" This disclosure of who somebody is, is implicit in both his words and deeds . . . . Without the accompaniment of speech, at any rate, action would not only lose its revelatory character, but, and by the same token, it would lose its subject, as it were; not acting men but performing robots would achieve what, humanly speaking, would remain incomprehensible. Speechless action would no longer be action because there would no longer be an actor, and the actor, the doer of deeds, is possible only if he is at the same time the speaker of words. (*HC*, p. 158)

A number of consequences follow from this rich passage about the intimate relation of action and speech. The most important is that human plurality is the basic condition of action and speech; without this plurality, there could not be any action or speech. By human plurality Arendt does not merely mean that there is "otherness," that there is something that thwarts one's desires, ambitions, passions, or goals. Rather there is a unique distinctiveness about each and every human individual. This is the distinctiveness that is revealed, that makes its *appearance* in speech and action. Human plurality understood in this manner is not a state of being: it is an achievement. Or we might say that it is a potentiality which is to be actualized – a potentiality rooted in what is distinctive about the human condition – the capacity to begin, to initiate, to act. For "to act in its most general sense means to take initiative, to begin . . . to set something into motion" (*HC*, p. 157). "A life without speech and without action . . . is literally dead to the world; it has ceased to be a human life because it is no longer lived among men" (*HC*, p. 157). Human plurality is the basic condition of action and speech because they can only take place *in between* men. Labor, work, and even thinking can be performed by solitary individuals, but action and speech require the witness and participation of other men. Already we see how distinctive action is for Arendt, for action is intrinsically political. It is the activity requiring the existence of that public space or polis in which men can encounter and participate with each other.

Given this account of action and speech as essentially political activities requiring the existence of a public space, we can draw out further important consequences of politics. Equality or isonomy among citizens, among members of the political community, is also a condition of politics. Equality is not a natural condition of men, nor a gift by which they have been endowed by a creator. Drawing upon the experience of the Greek polis, she tells us that:

> Isonomy guaranteed (*isotes*) equality, but not because all men were born or created equal, but on the contrary, because all men were by nature not equal, and needed an artificial institution, the polis, which by virtue of its *nomos* would make them equal. Equality existed only in this specifically political realm, where men met one another as citizens and not as private persons. . . . The equality of the Greek polis, its isonomy, was an

attribute of the polis and not men, who received their equality or virtue of citizenship, not by virtue of birth. (*OR*, p. 23)

Returning to the gloss on the truism "debate is the very essence of political life" we see more clearly why Arendt does not think of politics as involving rulership where one person or group dominates another. Rather it involves "no rule," the mutual and joint action grounded in human plurality and the isonomy of citizens where individuals debate and attempt to persuade each other. Persuasion, not force or violence, is the quintessence of political life. Persuasion is not the manipulation of others by image making. Persuasion involves free open debate among equals in which we seek to form, test, clarify, and test opinions.

We can deepen our grasp of Arendt's understanding of action and anticipate the role that judgment plays in political life by seeing how it is related to public freedom. Referring to the *philosophes* of the Enlightenment whose importance lies in their shrewd insight into this aspect of freedom, she writes:

> Their public freedom was not an inner realm into which men might escape at will from the pressures of the world, nor was it the *liberum arbitrium* which makes the will choose between alternatives. Freedom for them could exist only in public; it was a tangible, worldly reality, something created by men to be enjoyed by men rather than a gift or a capacity, it was the manmade public space or market-place which antiquity had known as the area where freedom appears and becomes visible to all. (*OR*, pp. 120–1)

According to the history or story of freedom that Arendt tells, the emergence of this public freedom was coeval with the rise of the Greek polis; it was first experienced before it became a subject of reflection. Freedom only became a *philosophic* problem associated with the will and individual choice once this public freedom disappeared as a distinctively political phenomenon.

Freedom must be sharply distinguished from liberation, for liberation is always liberation *from* something – whether it be liberation from the hardships and necessities of life or liberation

from oppressive rulers. But freedom does not have this negative connotation. It is a positive worldly achievement of human
action and exists only as long as that public space exists in
which men debate and participate in determining public affairs.
The distinction between freedom and liberation is of enormous
significance. They have been confused ever since the French
Revolution. This confusion, Arendt claims, has had the most
disastrous consequences. In what might seem to be a harsh –
but for Arendt was only a realistic pronouncement – she
declares "Nothing we might say today, could be more obsolete
than to attempt to *liberate* mankind from poverty by *political*
means; nothing could be more futile and more dangerous"
(*OR*, p. 110).

It may be thought, and has frequently been claimed, that at
best Arendt is describing what freedom and politics had been,
not what they *are*. But I think this persistent criticism really
misses the mark. Her concern with revolutions (and with the
"revolutionary spirit") is that these have exemplified the all too
brief manifestations of this public spirit, this public freedom.
Such freedom has made its appearance in those unpredictable
spontaneous developments that have followed revolutions but
have rarely been anticipated by "professional" revolutionaries.
It is evidenced whenever individuals create for themselves a
public space in which they can participate as equals in debating
public affairs. It arose in the Paris Commune, the Russian
soviets, the citizens' councils formed in the wake of the Hun-
garian Revolution, and in the beginnings of the civil rights and
anti-Vietnam war movement in America. The tragedy of the
modern age is that these fragile moments of public freedom
have been destroyed almost as soon as they arose. Even the
American Revolution, which she extolled, failed to "solve" the
problem of founding – of creating those institutions in which the
revolutionary spirit and this public freedom could be housed
and preserved. But this highlighting of the appearance of public
freedom across widely divergent historical circumstances and
periods indicates how far her intention was from telling a story
of something that is now only part of the past. Her primary
intention is to help us to understand, clarify, recover, and

remember what is essentially a *permanent* human possibility rooted in the human condition of plurality and human natality.[3]

This characteristic of her thinking about what we are doing, where it becomes manifest that she seeks to *think* in the gap between the past and future, and to recover for us what is still a permanent human possibility, helps to make sense of another leitmotif that pervades her work. In almost everything Hannah Arendt wrote she was carrying out a battle against all those forms of necessitarian arguments – whether they have their roots in Hegelian, Marxist, Weberian, or the new cooler technocratic modes of thought. The belief that there is an underlying logic to history which is ruthlessly working itself out behind the backs of men – a "logic" of history which according to some must lead to progress and the eventual triumph of freedom, and according to others must inevitably result in disaster – is not only false, it is one of the most virulent and dangerous diseases of the modern age. Her attacks on the variety of these doctrines has been sharp and multifaceted, but they are informed with her central vision that ultimately they negate what is most distinctive about human individuals, their capacity to begin, to initiate, to act together. This capacity can be suppressed, repressed, forgotten, and defeated, but it can never be eliminated as long as there is human life.

In sketching Arendt's understanding of political life, I have already anticipated the central role of opinion and judgment. In her remarks about debate, speech, and persuasion we find the germs of what is characteristic of opinion and judgment seen from the perspective of action – for they are the mental capacities which are distinctively relevant to politics. Typically, Arendt seeks to disclose her meaning by making careful distinctions and discriminations. We can grasp what she means by opinion by seeing how she distinguished it from truth. There has been a long history of the battle between truth and opinion, a battle which is as old as philosophy itself. The cognitive attitude, *telos*, and the means of establishing the validity of the claims of the truth seeker, whether the pure philosopher or the empirical gatherer of facts, must be sharply distinguished from the mental capacities and procedures whereby individual opinions are formed, tested, and debated. This is not to deny the relevance of truth and facts to the formation of opinion. But to emphasize the all important relevance of truth to the formation of opinion is no warrant for identifying truth and opinion. There have always been those who have sought to impose the standards appropriate to truth and the peculiar element of coercion that truth carries to the realm of politics – typically with disastrous results. For to impose the procedures, tests of validity, and the demands that are appropriate to truth on politics is in effect to destroy politics with its essential and non-reducible plurality and variability of opinions. Arendt claimed that one of the deepest tendencies in the tradition of political philosophy was not really to understand and do justice to politics, but to be concerned with the relation of politics to philosophy, where either implicitly or explicitly the realm of politics is measured by and judged to be deficient according to the standards of truth. The thrust of her political thinking was to provide an *apologia* for the political life against the claims of the philosophers. In ancient times the battle between truth and opinion was articulated in terms of the *agon* between a rational or philosophic truth (*aletheia*) and opinion (*doxa*). However, in our contemporary world where there is so much skepticism about the very possibility of rational or philosophic truth, there has been a new turn in this battle. This is a characteristic not only of totalitarian forms of government but of those forms of government that are obsessed with image-making and which try to deny or transform the coerciveness of factual truth by blurring the distinction between facts and opinions. There is a tendency to destroy factual truths by treating them as if they were faulty opinions.

Opinions, however, are the very stuff of politics. Individuals do not simply "have" opinions, they *form* opinions. In this respect, opinion formation is representative thinking.

> I form an opinion by considering a given issue from different viewpoints, by making present to my mind the standpoints of those who are absent: that is, I represent them. . . . The more

people's standpoints that I have present in my mind while I am pondering a given issue, and the better I can imagine how I would feel and think if I were in their place, the stronger will be my capacity for representative thinking and the more valid my final conclusions, my opinion. (*BPF*, p. 241)

Opinion formation is not a private activity performed by a solitary thinker. Opinions can only be tested and enlarged when there is a genuine encounter with different opinions. There is no test for the adequacy of an opinion, no authority for judging it, other than the force of the better *public* argument. The formation of opinions, therefore, requires a political community of equals, the imagination to represent other viewpoints, and the courage to submit opinions to public exposure and test. While we seek agreement in opinion, it is not a defect or flaw in opinion formation if we fail to reach agreement – for the variability of opinions is an expression of ineradicable human plurality.[4]

The emphasis on communication, testing, purification, imagination, and the representation of opinions in a public space enables us to see how judgment is involved in the formation of opinion. "Judging," Arendt tells us, "is one, if not the most important activity in which this sharing-the-world-with-others comes to pass" (*BPF*, p. 221). In seeking to clarify what she means by judgment, we find a striking example of Arendt's own imaginative interpretation of the history of philosophy. She claims that among all philosophers it was Kant who provided us with insight about the distinctiveness of judgment, and indeed "what . . . is quite new and even startlingly new in Kant's propositions in the *Critique of Judgment* is that he discovered this phenomenon in all its grandeur precisely when he was examining the phenomenon of taste" (*BPF*, p. 221). I do not want to enter into the scholarly question of the adequacy of Arendt's interpretation of Kant but to focus on what she thought that Kant had "discovered." For Arendt made the striking claim that it is in the first part of Kant's *Critique of Judgment*, where he deals with aesthetic judgments which are normally believed to be the furthest removed from politics, that we find his "unwritten" political philosophy. What she has in mind is Kant's analysis of "reflective judgment," that mode of thinking particulars which does not subsume particulars under general rules but ascends "from the particular to the universal." It involves discriminating and discerning the particular in its particularity. It requires an "enlarged mentality" (*eine erweiterte Denkungsart*) where one is able to "think in the place of everybody else" (*BPF*, p. 220). "The judging person," as Kant says quite beautifully, "can only 'woo the consent of everyone else' in hope of coming to an agreement with him eventually" (*BPF*, p. 222). "Judgment," Kant says, "is valid 'for every single judging person' but the emphasis in the sentence is on 'judging;' it is not valid for those who do not judge or for those who are not members of the public realm where the objects of judgment appear" (*BPF*, p. 221). Arendt claimed that Kant was particularly incisive in basing judgment on taste, but taste is not to be identified with "private feelings"; it is the very opposite. Taste is a kind of *sensus communis*. It is a "community sense" – the sense which fits us into human community. What Arendt is struggling to discriminate and isolate for us is a mode of thinking that is not to be identified with the expression of private feelings, nor to be confused with the type of universality characteristic of cognitive reason. It is a mode of thinking which is capable of dealing with the particular in its particularity but which nevertheless makes the claim to communal validity. For this is precisely the mode of thinking that is essential to political life.

> The power of judgment rests on a potential agreement with others, and the thinking process which is active in judging something is not, like the thought process of pure reasoning, a dialogue between me and myself, but finds itself always and primarily, even when I am quite alone in making up my mind, in an anticipated communication with others with whom I know I must finally come to some agreement. From this potential agreement judgment derives its specific validity. This means, on the one hand, that such judgment must liberate itself from the "subjective private conditions", that is from the

idiosyncracies which naturally determine the outlook of each individual in his privacy and are legitimate as long as they are only
privately held opinions, but which are not fit to enter the
market place, and lack all validity in the public realm. And this
enlarged way of thinking, which as judgment knows how to
transcend its own individual limitations, on the other hand,
cannot function in strict isolation or solitude; it needs the
presence of others "in whose place" it must think, whose
perspectives it must take into consideration, and without whom
it never has the opportunity to operate at all . . . judgment, to
be valid, depends on the presence of others. (*BPF*, p. 221)

It is here that we find the culmination of Arendt's thinking
about action and politics. All the paths of her thinking lead us
to the centrality and distinctiveness of the human capacity to
judge. This is the way in which judging *appears* when we approach it from the perspective of action. It resonates back to
what we have said about debate, speech, publicness, and the
persuasion characteristic of political life. But this is not the
whole story, and I want to turn to some of the paradoxes, perplexities, and "flagrant contradictions" that emerge when we
look more closely at what she says about judging and judgment,
especially when we view it from the *vita contemplativa*.

When we examine more closely what she says, we can see
how even the interpretation of judgment that I have given is
not quite right. It does not fit with everything she says. There
are deep conflicts that seem to be pulling her in different directions. Let me return to the text in which she first provides an
analysis of judgment, "The Crisis in Culture." What is characteristic of her presentation is the ease with which she passes
from Greek thought to Kant's analysis of aesthetic judgment.
She tells us that the Greeks called this capacity to judge "insight," and they considered it the principal virtue or excellence
of the statesman in distinction from the wisdom of the philosopher. The difference between this judging insight and speculative thought lies in that "the former has its roots in what we
usually call common sense, which the latter constantly
transcends" (*BPF*, p. 221). Or again, when speaking of the
wooing characteristic of judgment, she tells us "this 'wooing'

or persuading corresponds closely to what the Greeks called convincing and persuading speech which they regarded as the typically political form of people talking to one another" (*BPF*, p. 222). She even tells us that "culture and politics then belong together because it is not knowledge or truth which is at stake but rather judgment and decision, the judicious exchange of opinion about the sphere of public life and the common world, and the decision what matter of action is to be taken in it, as well as to how it is to look henceforth, what kind of things are to appear in it" (*BPF*, p. 223). Now such passages would lead us to think that judgment is similar to what was called *phronesis* – that form of practical reasoning which deals with the particular which Aristotle sought to discriminate from *episteme* and *techne*.[5] But then what are we to make of the startling claim that it was Kant who behind taste "discovered" the mental ability of judgment? This becomes even more problematic when we realize that Kant not only sought to distinguish sharply the reflective judgment of aesthetics from cognition but also from the legislation of practical reason. Furthermore, as Arendt herself emphasizes, judging is the capacity of the spectator who views and judges human affairs, the human spectacle, not that of the actors who participate. This does seem flagrantly to contradict the claim that judging is itself not only the political ability par excellence but *is* a form of *action* – debate – which Arendt takes to be the essence of politics.

Our perplexities are only increased when we see what she has to say about judging from the perspective of the *vita contemplativa*. In *The Life of the Mind*, she tells us that her preoccupation with the mental activities of thinking, willing, and judging has two rather different origins. She was acutely aware of the deficiency of *The Human Condition* in neglecting the examination of the *vita contemplativa*, even though this was constantly presupposed, and even though the very expression *vita activa* was formulated by those committed to the *vita contemplativa*. But the second origin of her preoccupation with *The Life of the Mind* was her witnessing the Eichmann trial and her attempt to raise the *quaestio juris* about the controversial concept, "the banality of evil." She asked, "Might the problem of good and evil, our faculty of telling right from wrong, be connected with our faculty of thought?" "Could the activity of thinking as such, the habit of examining whatever happens to come to pass or to attract attention, regardless of results and specific content, could this activity be among the conditions that make men abstain from evil doing or even actually 'condition' them against it?" (*LM*, I, p. 5). She came to think that the key to understanding Eichmann was not monstrous motives, or stupidity, but is *thoughtlessness*. She explores these issues with great tentativeness, but the direction of her thinking is clear. For she now characterizes the faculty of judgment not only as the faculty that enables us to say this is beautiful and this is ugly but *this is right* and *this is wrong*. In the parts of *The Life of the Mind* that she completed she only briefly returns to elaborating what might be this interrelation between thinking and judging. This occurs toward the end of the volume of *Thinking*.

> The faculty of judging particulars (as brought to light by Kant), the ability to say "this is wrong," "this is beautiful," and so on, is not the same as the faculty of thinking. Thinking deals with invisibles, with representations of things that are absent; judging always concerns particulars and things close at hand. But the two are inter-related, as are consciousness and conscience. If thinking – the two-in-one of the soundless dialogue – actualizes the difference within our identity as given in consciousness and thereby results in conscience as its by-product, then judging, the by-product of the liberating effect of thinking, realizes thinking, makes it manifest in the world of appearances, where I am never alone and always too busy to be able to think. The manifestation of the wind of thought is not knowledge, it is the ability to tell right from wrong, beautiful from ugly. And this, at the rare moments when the stakes are on the table, may indeed prevent catastrophes, at least for the self. (*LM*, I, p. 193)[6]

There are several extraordinary and perplexing aspects of the claims in this passage. Arendt well knew that, even though she invokes the name of Kant, she was radically departing from Kant. There is no question in Kant that the "ability to tell right from wrong" is a matter of practical reason and *not* the faculty of reflective judgment which ascends from particulars to generals or universals. It is as if Arendt is suggesting that just as the tradition of political philosophy had distorted and misjudged the phenomenon of politics, the same is true of the tradition of moral philosophy when it comes to grasp the quintessence of good and evil. She was deeply skeptical of the role that customs, habits, rules, and universal principles play in moral philosophy. She even said, "the fact that we usually treat matters of good and evil in courses in 'morals' or 'ethics' may indicate how little we know about them, for morals comes from *mores* and ethics from *ethos*, the Latin word being associated with rules of behavior, whereas the Greek is derived from habitat, like our 'habits'" (*LM*, I, p. 5). But the point I want to emphasize that seems to reveal a basic conflict within Arendt's thinking is that she, who always insisted on the need to distinguish politics from morals carefully, and who tells us in no uncertain terms that "the capacity to judge is a specifically political ability" increasingly emphasized the moral implications of judging – judging as the ability to say this is *right* and this is *wrong*. Ironically, it now seems to be the faculty that comes into play when politics breaks down.

We are not at the end of our difficulties and conflicts. This can be seen when we consider the temporal modality of judging. For what is clear when she juxtaposes judgment with *phronesis* is that the temporal modality here is that of the future. When men come together to discuss, exchange opinions and judge, they are oriented toward "the decision what manner of action is to be taken in the sphere of public life," but increasingly she emphasizes the way in which judging is primarily concerned with the past. She ends her volume *Thinking* by telling us:

> Here we shall have to concern ourselves, not for the first time, with the concept of history, but we may be able to reflect on the oldest meaning of this word, which, like so many other terms in our political and philosophical language, is Greek in origin and derived from *historein*, to inquire in order to tell how it was – *legein ta eonta* in Herodotus. But the origin of this verb is again Homer (*Iliad* XVIII) where the noun *histor* ("historian," as it

were) occurs, and that Homeric historian is the *judge*. If judgment is our faculty for dealing with the past, the historian is the
inquiring man who by relating it sits in judgment over it. If that
is so, we may reclaim our human dignity, win it back, as it
were, from the pseudo-divinity named History of the modern
age, without denying history's importance but denying its right
to being the ultimate judge. (*LM*, I, p. 216)

She concludes the volume with the very quotation from Cato
which was to be one of the epigraphs for the section on *Judging*,
"a curious phrase which aptly sums up the political principle
implied in the enterprise of reclamation." "*Victrix causa deis
placuit, sed victa Catoni.*" "The victorious cause pleased the
gods, but the defeated one pleases Cato" (*LM*, İ, p. 216).

But how are we to make sense of these conflicting claims?
How are we to deal with the strain in her thinking that associates judgment with the form of practical reasoning that the
Greeks, and especially Aristotle, call *phronesis* and the claim
that judgment is the mental activity of the non-participating
spectator? How are we to explain that in the context of action
the temporal modality of judging is the future; while from the
perspective of the life of the mind, judging is our faculty for
dealing with the past.

There are a number of facile resolutions which I do not think
really work. One might simply want to claim that she was
changing her mind about the status and nature of judgment.
But a careful reading of her earliest statements about judgment
reflect many of these same tensions and conflicts. In the latest
characterizations of judgment she continued to emphasize its
essential political character. Or one might say that what is
needed is a discrimination of the different types of judgment
such as political judgments, aesthetic judgments, moral judgments, and historical judgments. At times Arendt does speak in
such a manner, but nowhere does she ever try to provide us
with the *differentia* of the types of judgment.[7] On the contrary,
she always emphasizes the unity and autonomy of judging per
se. Indeed, I do not think that she ever reconciled the different
ways in which her own thinking was pulling her. I want to suggest, however, that we find a clue to these conflicting tendencies

by returning again to the origins of her preoccupation with the mental activities of the life of the mind. As I mentioned earlier, she herself indicates different origins – the need to come to grips with the "unfinished business" of what we are doing when we think, and more generally with the *vita contemplativa*; and to probe the hypothesis that the key to understanding Eichmann and the banality of evil was to discern the interrelation between thinking and judging. But there is a third source that underlies these two – and this concerns Hannah Arendt herself. For the only self-description that Arendt ever accepted to characterize what she was doing was that of an independent thinker. She did not think of herself as an "activist," or as a "theorist" laying down prescriptions for what is to be done. To many it seemed perplexing that she who spoke so eloquently and incisively about the meaning and dignity of politics resisted the temptation to indoctrinate others or to try to bridge the gap between thinking and acting. She told us while "there are other people who are primarily interested in doing something I am not. I can very well live without doing anything. But I cannot live without trying to understand whatever happens."[8] At the very center of her being was the need to think but not necessarily to think in the way in which "professional thinkers" think. It was thinking *particularity* that most intrigued her – judging. Throughout her writings she took herself to be a spectator of human affairs – seeking to understand them in their particularity and their "exemplary validity." Throughout her writings she constantly returns to the theme of the primacy of the spectator. She loved to cite the parable ascribed to Pythagoras and repeated by Diogenes Laertius:

> Life . . . is like a festival: just as some come to the festival to compete, some to ply their trade, but the best people come as spectators [*theatai*], so in life the slavish men go hunting for fame [*doxa*] or gain, the philosophers for truth. (*LM*, I, p. 93)

But as she interpreted this parable, it was not the quest for truth that she emphasized; it was the quest for meaning and understanding which is manifested in judgment. Her quarrel with the philosophical tradition, the two-world theory, and the resulting "metaphysical fallacies" was that there was an ineluctable tendency in this tradition to turn away from particularity toward the sky of ideas or some transcendent reality, or to some universals by which we could subsume particularity. Whether the context was political philosophy, or moral philosophy, or the search for some sort of metaphysical truth, she felt that it tended to miss what was most distinctive about our humanity – the capacity to judge. What drew her to Kant's analysis of aesthetic judgment as a model for all judgment is what she took to be his deepest insight – that there is a distinctive mode of thinking which is not to be confused with cognition or with practical reason – both of which are obsessed with universality – a mode of thinking that could deal with particularity as such without subsumption and which would enable us to understand the meaning of this particularity. She also thought that Kant, as she read him, was profoundly right in stressing the intersubjectivity of this mode of thinking – that the spectator is not alone but is always appealing to and needs other judging spectators. Judging, although a mental activity of the life of the mind, never leaves the world of appearances. "The withdrawal of judgment is obviously very different from the withdrawal of the philosopher. It does not leave the world of appearances but retires from active involvement in it to a privileged position in order to contemplate the whole" (*LM*, I, p. 94). This *is* what Hannah Arendt always sought to do. Whether she turned her attention to the study of totalitarianism, or the Eichmann trial, or even to politics itself, she sought to understand and judge phenomena in their particularity and to resist the temptation to misjudge them by relying on concepts, universals, categories that failed to do justice to their distinctiveness and uniqueness. All of her thinking consists in exercises of discernment and discrimination that are characteristic of taste and judgment. This feature of her thinking also helps to explain why she was so intrigued with Cato's statement – "The victorious case pleased the gods, but the defeated one pleases Cato." For even in her attempt to understand judgment in politics and action, she was more interested in those defeated causes in which action and the revolutionary spirit became manifest and tangible than in the claims to "human progress" and the "success of History." It was the "lost treasures" – those moments of "exemplary validity" that she sought to reclaim, understand, and judge. I think we can most deeply understand what she was doing when we realize that this for her was the way – the only way – "to reclaim our human dignity."

Throughout all of Arendt's work, there is a deep tension between acting and thinking, between the perspective of the actors who participate in the human spectacle and that of the spectators who seek to understand its *meaning*. She never reconciled this tension, although at times there is the suggestion of a possible reconciliation. We can see a hint of such a reconciliation in her remarks on Kant's notion of a united mankind.

> It is by virtue of this idea of mankind, present in every single man, that men are human, and they can be called civilized or humane to the extent that this idea becomes the principle of their actions as well as their judgments. It is at this point that the actor and the spectator become united; the maxim of the actor and the maxim, the "standard" according to which the spectator judges the spectacle of the world become one. (*LM*, II, p. 271)

But Arendt barely develops this suggestion; and in the end, it is never quite clear how she herself might have reconciled the conflicting claims about judging when viewed from the *vita activa* and from the *vita contemplativa*. She left us with a whole series of perplexities, riddles, and contradictions. Hannah Arendt thought that the only way in which thinking could be taught was by infecting others with those perplexities that occasion all authentic thinking. This is what she herself so effectively does. But it is important to realize that these were not just *her* perplexities. For the clash and conflict between the *vita activa* and the *vita contemplativa*, the competing claims that they make upon all of us, and the search to find some resolution between the actor and the spectator continues to be one of the deepest problems of our time.

9

Rethinking the Social
and the Political[1]

I

The concepts of "the social" and "the political" are among the most fundamental in Hannah Arendt's thinking. The way in which she develops them and weaves them into her analysis of "the modern age" is extraordinarily provocative and disturbing. I want to show that her analysis is at once highly illuminating and systematically misleading. Indeed, the more we probe, the more we discover how her categorical distinction between the social and the political is unstable and reveals profound tensions. My purpose is not simply to explicate what she means (although this is where I begin), but rather to use her insights and blindnesses to rethink what is at stake in this distinction. And the primary reason for engaging in such an analysis is because I believe that rethinking the distinction of the social and the political has significant theoretical and practical consequences for confronting our contemporary social and political situation.

Although Arendt employed this distinction throughout her writings, it is in *The Human Condition* (*HC*)[2] and *On Revolution* (*OR*) that we find the most detailed discussion of these concepts. *The Human Condition* can be read from a variety of perspectives. Clearly what is most prominent, and what is announced in the opening sentences of the first chapter, is examination of the *vita activa*. "With the term *vita activa*, I propose to designate three fundamental human activities: labor, work, and action. They are fundamental because each corresponds to one of the basic conditions under which life on earth has been given to man" (*HC*, p. 7).[3] The three central chapters are entitled "Labor," "Work," and "Action." But this structural approach to *The Human Condition* ("structural" in the sense that labor, work, and action are the three primary structures or forms of human activity) does not highlight the story that Arendt is telling in her book – a story that centers on giving an account of the rise, character, and *aporias* of what she calls "the modern age." It is in the context of relating this story that the concepts of the social and the political play such a fundamental role. In its barest outlines, the narrative that she relates is one of a series of reversals or inversions. The Latin and medieval notion of a *vita activa* was itself introduced as a contrast to the *vita contemplativa* – a distinction which has a long tangled history going back to the Greek classical age (See *HC*, pp. 12–17). The first reversal began with the inversion that took place when the *vita activa* was taken to have primacy over the life of contemplation (with a growing skepticism about the character and claims of *vita contemplativa*). But Arendt's main concern is with the reversals that have taken place within the *vita activa*. The classical hierarchy of action, work, and labor – where action is the highest form of human activity which is based upon the human condition of plurality and is characterized by the speech and deeds with which men reveal who they are and appear to each other in the public space of the *polis* – has been overwhelmed and distorted by a fabricating mentality (work), and finally by a laboring mentality. Not only has there been a victory of *homo faber* over the life of political *praxis*, but even *homo faber* has eventually succumbed to the triumph of *animal laborans*. What the Greeks took to be the lowest form of human activity which is grounded in biological necessity and is to be hidden from the daylight of the public realm has become for us all pervasive and consuming. We are living in an age – the modern age – in which *animal laborans* has been victorious. And this development itself can also be characterized as the triumph and domination of society over politics.

There are many affinities (as well as differences) with the way in which Arendt characterizes the victory of *homo faber*, and

the analysis of the growth and spread of *Zweckrationalität* that is
so prominent in the analyses of modernity by Weber, Lukács,
and the Frankfurt School; and even deeper subterranean affinities with what Heidegger "names" *Gestell* (Enframing) – "the
essence of technology."[4] Consider the following description by
Arendt:

> among the outstanding characteristics of the modern age from its
> beginning to our time we find the typical attitudes of *homo faber*:
> his instrumentalization of the world, his confidence in tools and
> in the productivity of the maker of artificial objects, his trust in
> the all-comprehensive range of the means-ends category, his
> conviction that every issue can be solved and every human
> motivation reduced to the principle of utility; his sovereignty,
> which regards everything given as material and thinks of the
> whole of nature as of "an immense fabric from which we can
> cut out whatever we want to resew it however we like"; his
> equation of intelligence with ingenuity, that is, his contempt for
> all thought which cannot be considered to be "the first step . . .
> for the fabrication of artificial objects, particularly tools to make
> tools, and to vary their fabrication indefinitely"; finally, his
> matter-of-course identification of fabrication with action. (*HC*,
> p. 305)

But this is not where Arendt's narrative ends. It culminates
with the triumph of *animal laborans* over *homo faber*. "What needs
explanation is not the modern esteem of *homo faber* but the fact
that this esteem was so quickly followed by the elevation of
laboring to the highest position in the hierarchical order of the
vita activa (*HC*, p. 306). We are not even a society of workers,
but a society of laborers. Even within this society there has
been a further degeneration; from a society of producers we
have become a society of job holders and consumers. This is
what happens when society and "socialized man" becomes all
engulfing. Her indictment is put forth forcefully and even
harshly when she declares:

> in the rise of society it was ultimately the life of the species
> which asserted itself. Theoretically, the turning point from the

earlier modern age's insistence on the "egoistic" life of the individual to its later emphasis on "social" life and "socialized man" (Marx) came when Marx transformed the cruder notion of classical economy – that all men, insofar as they act at all, act for reasons of self-interest – into forces of interest which inform, move, and direct society as a whole. Socialized mankind is that state of society where only one interest rules, and the subject of this interest is either classes or man-kind but neither man nor men. The point is that now even the last trace of action in what men were doing, the motive implied in self-interest, disappeared. What was left was a "natural force," the force of the life process itself, to which all men and all human activities were equally submitted . . . and whose only aim, if it had an aim at all, was survival of the animal species man. (*HC*, p. 321)[5]

This "conclusion" brings us full circle to the theme announced in her *Prologue*: "The modern age has carried with it a theoretical glorification of labor and has resulted in a factual transformation of the whole society into a laboring society" (*HC*, p. 4). The final turn of the screw comes when she speculates that what "we are confronted with is the prospect of a society of laborers without labor, that is without the only activity left to them. Surely, nothing could be worse" (*HC*, p. 5).

But what precisely is packed into this notion of the social and society that Arendt typically employs with such disdainful overtones? We can tease out her meaning by considering the time, when as paradoxical as it may sound, there was no distinctive social realm. According to Arendt's depiction of the classical Greek age (which many of her critics have claimed is an idealized and romanticized portrait), there was a sharp distinction between the private and the public, a distinction that corresponded with the different realms of the household (*oikia*) and the *polis*. It is in the communal life of the *polis*, when men appear among their peers, and seek to achieve glory that they engage in the highest form of human activity – action (*praxis*). This is the tangible realm of public freedom where men face each other as equals, and participate in the formation and testing of opinions through public debate. This is the realm of "no rule" – where only persuasion (rather than force and violence) "rules."[6] Participation in public political life requires that citizens have mastered the "necessities of life," but such mastery belongs to the prepolitical realm – the household. Force and violence, which according to Arendt have no place in the political sphere, are justified in the household organization because they are "the only means to master necessity" (*HC*, p. 31). Labor, for Arendt, is always associated with biological necessity and survival – the realm in which we are driven by needs and wants. Unless we are *liberated* from the pressing demands of biological necessity, it makes no sense to speak of engaging in a life of tangible public freedom. But this is the task of the household, the private realm, where even slavery can be "justified" – it is a realm that is at once prepolitical, and yet an essential condition for the very existence of a *polis* where men can engage in action.

But the emergence of the social realm, which only came fully into existence in the modern age, is a "hybrid realm" where the classical distinctions of the private and the public, the household and the *polis* have been completely blurred. It is a realm in which we "see the body of peoples and political communities in the image of the family whose everyday affairs have to be taken care of by a gigantic nation-wide administration of housekeeping" (*HC*, p. 28). The culmination of this development of a hybrid realm of society is the welfare state (a notion which Arendt took to be a virtual self-contradiction). Even the modern conception of the private – what Arendt calls "intimacy" – has nothing to do with the classical private/household and public/political division. Modern privacy is not what it was in classical times – the realm in which men are deprived of genuine political activity, but has itself been "discovered" in opposition to society and the social realm. The great theoretician of privacy/intimacy was Jean-Jacques Rousseau (*HC*, pp. 38–9).

Arendt seeks vividly to portray the disastrous consequences for politics and public life that have taken place with the rise of society in the modern age. "Society has conquered the public realm" and society "excludes the possibility of action." "Instead, society expects of each of its members a certain kind of behavior, imposing innumerable and various rules, all of which tend to 'normalize' behavior to exclude spontaneous action." "As we know from the most social form of government, that is, from bureaucracy (the last stage of government in the nation-state just as one-man rule in benevolent depotism and absolutism was its first), the rule by nobody is not necessarily no-rule; it may, indeed, under certain circumstances, even turn out to be one of its cruelest and most tyrannical versions" (*HC*, p. 40). This picture of the modern age may strike us as extraordinarily bleak, but the full fury of Arendt's attack on modern society only becomes completely manifest in *On Revolution* when she turns to what she calls "the Social Question."

Arendt's thinking, her exercises in political thought,[7] is filled with paradoxes and unstable tensions, not the least of which is revealed in her reflections on revolution. From what we have outlined thus far about the emergence and engulfing character of the social realm in the modern age, one might be tempted to think that Arendt relentlessly attacks the disaster of modernity. But this is *not* the turn that her thinking takes. On the contrary, she argues that it is only in the modern age that authentic revolutions (as distinguished from rebellions) have occurred. It is the "revolutionary spirit" that occurs spontaneously, and which has never been anticipated by "professional revolutionaries," that manifests those brief and fragile moments of the glimmerings of public freedom and participatory *action*. This spontaneous – almost miraculous – breaking out of the "revolutionary spirit" has erupted in such radically different historical contexts as the American Revolution, the Paris Commune, the original Russian soviets, and the citizens councils that have sprung up (and have been quickly crushed) in the wake of almost every modern revolution. It is from the perspective of this revolutionary spirit that she approaches "the Social Question."

What is *the* Social Question? It is the existence and attempts to confront and solve the question of poverty. More precisely – since poverty in one form or another has always existed – the Social Question is the growing public recognition of the ignominy of mass poverty and the need to eliminate it. "Poverty," she tells us "is more than deprivation, it is a state of constant want and acute misery whose ignominy consists in its dehumanizing force; poverty is abject because it puts men under the absolute dictate of their bodies, that is, under the absolute dictate of necessity. . . . It was under the rule of this necessity that the multitude rushed to the assistance of the French Revolution, inspired it, drove it onward, and eventually sent it to its doom, for this was the multitude of the poor" (*OR*, p. 54). We find here the essential clue for explaining why Arendt is so laudatory about the American Revolution and so damning of the French Revolution, which she claims has unfortunately been taken as the model of revolution for most Europeans since its occurrence. The American Revolution was essentially a *political* revolution dedicated primarily to the founding and constitution of political freedom. It was not primarily concerned with *liberation* from biological necessity, or even with *liberation* from oppressive rulers. It was the good fortune of the American Founding Fathers not to be overwhelmed by the Social Question. But the French Revolution was overwhelmed by the Social Question – and this is why, according to Arendt, it culminated in violence and terror. No revolution has or can solve the Social Question. Indeed, Arendt goes further and declares "the whole record of past revolutions demonstrates beyond doubt that every attempt to solve the social question with political means leads to terror, and that it is terror which sends revolutions to their doom" (*OR*, p. 108).[8] There is something chilling in this linkage of the Social Question of mass poverty, violence, and terror, but for Arendt this is what an unprejudiced and unsentimental tough-minded realism demands. And she is relentless in pursuing this theme. When the "masses of the poor" enter the public realm, they carry with themselves necessity and violence (See *OR*, p. 110). Where courage and joy are the virtue and passion most relevant to politics and action, the "passion of compassion" is what is evoked by the Social Question. "Because compassion abolishes the distance, the worldly space between men where political matters, the whole realm of human affairs are located, it remains, politically speaking, irrelevant and without consequence" (*OR*, p. 81). When compassion "which is directed solely, and with passionate intensity, toward suffering man himself" makes its voice heard in the public sphere, "it makes the claim for swift and direct action, that is for action with the means of violence" (*OR*, p. 82).[9]

Arendt's shocking analysis of the Social Question dovetails with her narrative of the emergence of modern society where we have become a society of job holders and consumers. In the modern age the "ideals borne out of poverty" have become dominant and all pervasive. "For abundance and endless consumption are the ideals of the poor; they are the mirage in the desert of misery. In this sense affluence and wretchedness are only two sides of the same coin; The bonds of necessity need not be of iron, they can be made of silk. . . . The hidden wish of poor men is not 'To each according to his needs,' but 'To each according to his desires'" (*OR*, p. 136).

II

It is difficult to imagine anyone having a neutral reaction to this analysis. Some will be outraged by Arendt's *apparent* insensitivity to the misery of the poor (insofar as she rules out "poverty" as a proper *political* issue), and will condemn her for what seems to be an arrogant elitism. Others (perhaps secretly) may admire her for her courage and honesty in telling it "as it is," particularly in showing how and why modern revolutionary movements link necessity, violence, and terror. I think that both of these judgments – put in this blatant form – are misguided. (This is not to deny that there is some "truth" implicit in them.) What is required, however, is thinking through her claims; for what may initially seem straightforward and sharp is much more ambiguous, ambivalent, and even internally contradictory than is *prima facie* apparent. But before scrutinizing what I take to be the tensions, difficulties, and contradictions in what she is saying, I want to clarify the dialectical context of her thinking, which at least helps to make sense of her emphases.

Even if, as I hope to show, her categorical distinction of the social and the political is untenable and will not stand up to critical scrutiny, there is something extremely important about what she stresses. What cannot be denied is that Arendt has provided us with one of the most subtle and appealing analyses of what participatory politics means. Her sensitive description stands as a shining exemplar of what politics once might have been, and even more important, what it may yet become. She is one of the rare thinkers of our time who has shown concretely that participatory democracy (at least for those who engage in it) is not a cliché. She integrates into her analysis the concepts of debate, plurality, isonomy, tangible public freedom, public happiness, and communal power.[10] She is acute in uncovering the distinctive passions and virtues that are manifest in politics. And her vision of politics stands as a critical standard in judging what today goes by the name of politics. Against those who claim that her conception of politics is "romantic" and has no relevance to our contemporary situation, I think just the opposite is true. It is not surprising that *The Human Condition* was a book that inspired many of those who participated in the early stages of the civil rights movement in America. For despite Arendt's skepticism about the modern age, the book was read not as a dispairing lament, but rather as a beacon of hope. The human condition is such that as long as we still remain human it is always a real possibility for individuals to come together, to debate, and to act collectively in deciding public matters. Even her analysis of the way in which power can spring up among participants and can grow has been borne out by events. For every revolutionary movement (or attempt to achieve radical reform) occurs "against all odds" and may initially seem to be completely futile. No one knew better than Arendt how fragile such communal action is and how much in the modern age conspires to distort and destroy the public spaces in which *praxis* can be manifested. But Arendt also persistently and brilliantly attacked and exposed the variety of arguments from "historical necessity" that drew the conclusion that such action and politics – even in the modern age – is no longer a real possibility. I also think that *Solidarity* – especially in the early stages of its development – beautifully exemplified many of Arendt's insights – especially in the spontaneous formation of citizens councils. She knew all too well that the council system "has perished everytime and everywhere, destroyed either directly by the bureaucracy of nation-states or by party machines" (*CR*, p. 231). But consider what Arendt tells us is the voice of the councils, and how this was heard again in Poland: "The councils say: We want to participate, we want to debate, we want to make our voices heard in public, and we want to have a possibility to determine the political course of our country" (*CR*, p. 232). And for those who go on to say, "Yes, but one must also not forget how easily *Solidarity* was crushed" should recall that one of Arendt's favorite and most frequent quotations was taken from Cato: "*Victrix causa deis placuit, sed victa Catoni*" ("The victorious cause pleased the gods, but the defeated one pleases Cato"). This, she said is "a curious phrase, which aptly sums up the political principle implied in the enterprise of reclamation" (–, I, p. 216).

The importance of Arendt's analysis of "participatory politics" (an expression which is redundant, because for her all authentic politics *is* participatory) goes further than what has been said thus far. Many political thinkers who identify themselves with the liberal tradition have been deeply suspicious of the concept of positive freedom, fearing that it must inevitably end in a glorification of a totalitarian general will. But Arendt has shown us that we can distinguish between liberation and public tangible freedom (where liberation is always liberation *from* something, whether it be liberation from the misery of poverty or liberation from oppressive rulers). And she has explicated the concept of public freedom in a manner that is radically anti-dogmatic and anti-totalitarian. There is no public freedom unless it is based on a genuine recognition of plurality – where variable opinions, judgment, and persuasion are manifest – a politics which excludes any violence and coercion.

There are other lessons to be learned from Arendt. Even if one thinks, as I do, that her reading and interpretation of Marx is mistaken and a gross distortion, nevertheless she highlights crucial problems that must be confronted by anyone who wants to take Marx and Marxism seriously. What kind of politics is appropriate for revolutionary *praxis*? What is to be the character of the political institutions in a post-capitalist society? We all know, or should know, the theoretical and practical disasters that result when these issues are not honestly faced.[11] But to say all this, and seek to preserve what is so relevant, vital, and true in her analysis of politics is not yet to endorse her categorical distinction between the social and the political. Indeed, I now want to argue that if we are to preserve the "truth" implicit in what she is saying we must reject this distinction as untenable.

III

Sometimes the informal remarks that an author makes about her work can be among the most revealing. I suspect that all of us have had the experience of wanting to ask certain simple and direct questions which never seem to be adequately answered in the published works. There are two occasions where something like this did occur that bear directly on the question of the social and the political. The first text is based on an interview that Arendt gave in the summer of 1970. She was asked about her notion of the "council system" which she had adumbrated in the final chapter of *On Revolution*.[12] In the interview she outlined what she meant by the council system and concluded with the following comment:

> By no means every resident of a country needs to be a member in such councils. Not everyone wants to or has to concern himself with public affairs. In this fashion a self-selective process is possible that would draw together a true political elite in a country. Anyone who is not interested in public affairs will simply have to be satisfied with their being decided without him. *But each person must be given the opportunity.* (*CR*, p. 233, emphasis added)

It is this last (almost casual statement) that I take to be so decisive. For if Arendt had really thought out what she is saying here, then it would have required a major rethinking of her distinction of the social and the political. Why? Because this claim indicates that there is a much more intimate connection between the social and the political than she frequently suggests. Arendt consistently maintained that politics can only arise when – at least for those who engage in politics – they have been liberated. Liberation from the constant pressing demands of biological necessity *and* from oppressive rulers is a necessary (although not a sufficient) condition for action, politics, and public freedom. But liberation can be achieved in a variety of ways – including the use of slaves and women to take care of the needs of the household. Let us not forget (as Arendt herself does not forget) that the two exemplars of politics which are so important for her – the Greek *polis* and the American Revolution – occurred at a time when slavery was acceptable and justified, and when women (and many others) were not considered fit to be citizens. But to claim as she does in the above passage, that *every person* must be given the opportunity to participate in politics transforms the question of society. For it means that we must honestly face the issue of how we can achieve or strive to realize a society where every person has the opportunity to engage in politics. This becomes (on her own account) a primary *political* question. And it is also clear that Arendt is not talking about a formal legal right, for to be able to participate in politics means that one has also attained a level of education and liberation from poverty where one can debate, where one can engage in the activity of mutual persuasion that is the distinctive characteristic of politics. If we do not squarely face this issue – or rather the complex of issues involved – there is always the danger that politics will degenerate into hypocrisy, self-deception, and even oppression.

But still it may be objected, that although this is a weak link in Arendt's analysis, it does not seriously call into question the conceptual distinction between the social and the political; rather it shows that in the modern age the linkage of the social and the political is far more intimate and complex than Arendt acknowledges. So let me turn to my second text. In November, 1972, a conference on "The Work of Hannah Arendt" was organized by the Toronto Society for the Study of Social and Political Thought. Arendt attended this conference and engaged in active discussion with the participants. In 1979, an edited transcript of the discussion was prepared and published by Melvyn Hill.[13] Since the question that concerns us was put to Arendt so sharply, I want to quote extensively from this transcript. Mary McCarthy, one of Hannah Arendt's closest friends and most sympathetic critics asked:

> I would like to ask a question that I have had in my mind a long, long time. It is about the very sharp distinction that Hannah Arendt makes between the political and the social. It is particularly noticeable in her book *On Revolution*, where she demonstrates, or seeks to demonstrate, that the failure of the Russian and the French Revolutions was based on the fact that these revolutions were concerned with the social, and concerned with suffering – in which the sentiment of compassion played a large role. Whereas, the American Revolution was political and ended in the foundation of something.
>
> Now I have always asked myself: "What is somebody supposed to do on the public stage, in the public space, if he does not concern himself with the social? That is, what's left?"
>
> It seems to me that if you once have a constitution, and you've had the foundation, and you have a framework of laws, the scene is there for political action. And the only thing that is left for the political man to do is what the Greeks did: make war! Now this cannot be right! On the other hand, if all questions of economics, human welfare, busing, anything that touches the social sphere, are to be excluded from the political scene, then I am mystified. I am left with war and speeches. But the speeches can't be just speeches. They have to be speeches about something.[14]

Listen carefully to Arendt's reply:

> You are absolutely right, and I may admit that I ask myself this question. Number one, the Greeks did not only make war and Athens existed prior to the Peloponnesian War, and the real flower of Athens came between the Persian Wars and the Peloponnesian War. Now what did they do them?

Life changes constantly, and things are constantly there that want to be talked about. At all times people living together will have affairs that belong in the realm of the public – "are worthy to be talked about in public." What these matters *are* at any historical *moment* is probably *utterly* different. For instance, the great cathedrals were the public spaces of the Middle Ages. The town halls came later. And *there* perhaps they had to talk about a matter which is not without interest either: the question of God. So what becomes public at every given period seems to me utterly different. It would be quite interesting to follow it through as a historical study, and I think one could do it. There will always be conflicts. And you don't need war.[15]

No one who attended that conference was satisfied with this response. (I know because I was there.) And the issue was pressed by Albrecht Wellmer.

Albrecht Wellmer: I would ask you to give one example in our time of a social problem which is not at the same time a political problem. Take anything: like education, or health, or urban problems, even the simple problem of living standards. It seems to me that even the social problems in our society are unavoidably political problems. But if this is true, then, of course, it would also be true that a distinction between the social and the political in our society is impossible to draw.

Arendt: Let's take the housing problem. The social problem is certainly adequate housing. But the question of whether this adequate housing means integration or not is *certainly* a political question. With every one of these questions there is a double face. And one of these faces should not be subject to debate. There shouldn't be any debate about the question that everybody should have decent housing.[16]

Now it strikes me that Arendt's responses to this line of questioning are evasive and feeble – what is worse, they tend to obfuscate the issues. There are several points that I want to make about these interchanges – especially in regard to what she concedes. Let us ask: What is it that properly belongs to the public political sphere? Arendt's answer here – and it is consistent with the answer that she gives throughout her writings – is only those matters that can properly be *debated*; about which we can form and test our *opinions*; matters that require *judgment*; and about which it is correct to say that we seek to persuade each other through public *argumentation*. These are the affairs that "are worthy to be talked about in public." Each of the under-scored expressions has a distinctive meaning for her. We do not, for example, *debate* about matters where there are clear decision procedures for determining whether they are true or false, e.g., mathematical truths or even empirical claims which can be settled by the appeal to facts.[17] But even if this is accepted, it still does not tell us precisely what falls into the domain of debatable political issues. We might say that the criterion of what constitutes public affairs for debate is a "formal" or procedural one, not a substantive one. In her response to McCarthy, she herself indicates just how wide the range of matters which are worthy to be talked about in public may be, and how this changes in different historical circumstances. Issues or problems do not simply come labeled "social," "political," or even "private." Indeed, the question whether a problem is itself properly social (and therefore not worthy of public debate) or political is itself frequently the central *political* issue. I am not suggesting that "everything is political," a dangerous doctrine, especially in the context of totalitarian regimes, but I am claiming that – and Arendt herself at times suggests this – that any problem may become or be transformed into a political issue (in her distinctive sense of "politics").[18] The practical significance of this must not be underestimated. One of the strongest claims of many feminists is that issues and problems which have been taken to be private matters or even social concerns (even in Arendt's sense of these terms), and which have consequently been judged not to be public political issues, are (or should be) considered to be vital public matters worthy of debate. So insofar as Arendt talks as if there is a relatively clear distinction for separating the social from the political, her claims are not only misleading but already reflect a hidden political judgment – which like all political judgments should be brought out into the open daylight and debated. But the basic issue here is even more complex and tangled than this.

Let us analyze carefully her response to Wellmer. When she says "Let's take the housing problem," she categorically asserts: "The social problem is certainly adequate housing." But is this really so clear and distinct – even on the basis of her own distinction of the social and the political? What constitutes *adequate* housing? Is not the question of *adequate* housing – as we know from experience – a debatable issue, about which there can be varying opinions and judgments? She goes on to say "With every one of these questions there is a double face. And one of these should not be subject to debate." But the hard question is – one which Arendt never satisfactorily answers – Who decides this? Who is to determine what is and what is not to be debatable in the public arena? This is not an issue to be resolved by the philosopher or the political theorist, but rather by the *participants* in a political community. When Arendt adds, "There shouldn't be any debate about the question that everybody should have decent housing" she trivializes and clouds the entire issue. It is difficult to imagine anyone today, in any political situation and regardless of their "political" persuasion who would not endorse the abstract proposition "everybody should have decent housing." But this is not the locus of any real and serious conflict. Rather, only when we come down to concrete details of what is decent housing, how it is to be financed, how this is to affect the "allocation of resources," what priority this is to have, how this relates to "property rights," do we face genuine issues of social and political conflict.

The problems and *aporias* involved in the way in which Arendt draws the distinction of the social and the political can be approached from another damaging perspective. Arendt has been one of the sharpest critics of the false pretentions of the social sciences and the so-called policy sciences. Theoretically, and at the level of concrete analysis, she has exposed the disastrous consequences for politics when social experts "rule." But there is a deep irony in her attack on the social disciplines and their practitioners. For the main brunt of her critique is that a social mentality concerned with the "administration of things" is blind to, excludes, and even destroys *action* and genuine politics. To live in a world where human beings are "normalized" and only *behave*, is to live in a world that is dead to speech and action.[19] But if social scientists would only realize that their knowledge and expertise is *limited* to what belongs to the social realm, where men behave and do not act, then they would be doing their proper business. Ironically, following out the logic of Arendt's dichotomy, this endorses and even vindicates the self-understanding that many social scientists have of themselves and their discipline. For ever since Weber, there have been those who have claimed that there is a proper domain of social knowledge where expert knowledge is relevant and where issues can be resolved by the use of proper suitable empirical techniques. These are not issues which are (or should be) debated but where social experts and engineers should be consulted. Presumably, on Arendt's analysis we can and should turn to social experts and engineers to settle social issues (or the social "face" of issues of education, health, economics, human welfare, etc.).

Think for a moment how specious and dangerous such a neat division really is. I certainly do not want to deny that there are legitimate questions where expert knowledge is important and relevant for making intelligent political decisions. If, for example, we do not know something about the effects of radiation, or whether it makes sense to talk about "clean bombs," or whether and how one can dispose of nuclear waste in safe and effective ways, one cannot make intelligent political decisions about nuclear policies. But the example that I have chosen is not simply accidental. For what the history of debates about nuclear policies during the past few decades has taught us (or should have taught us) is that it is a dangerous illusion to believe that there is antiseptic neutral expert knowledge in this field. So-called "expert knowledge" of social phenomena has been tainted with ideological biases and/or unquestioned prejudices. If there is one well established "truth" that has been borne out by the history and critiques of the social disciplines for the past one hundred years, it is this one. Paradoxically then, the very way in which Arendt draws the distinction between the social and political lends support and credence to the politically dangerous myth that there is a proper domain of social issues where social knowledge is appropriate – a domain that is better left to experts and social engineers, and which is to be excluded from the political sphere where we should be concerned only with affairs that "are worthy to be talked about in public."

There is one further deeply problematic aspect of Arendt's distinction of the social and the political that I want to explore. I have already indicated that one of Arendt's major concerns is the character and fate of revolutions in the modern age. One of her most important and enduring contributions has been the reclamation, and subtle description of the "revolutionary spirit" – the treasure that we are in danger of losing through forgetfulness. This even helps to explain why she places so much emphasis on storytelling, and the judgment of the spectator who witnesses and reclaims the fragility and futility of human action. But there is something curious about the way in which she tells the story of those historical episodes which she takes to be exemplars of the revolutionary spirit. For she acknowledges a *fact* that at times she also seems to suppress or repress. Every revolution in the modern age, including the American Revolution, emerged out of the struggles for *social* liberation. Individuals do not simply come together and mutually decide to create a public space within which freedom becomes tangible. The dynamics are quite different. Although Arendt knows this, she does not do justice to the fact that every revolutionary movement in the modern age has begun with a growing sense of some grave *social* injustice, with the demand for what she calls liberation.[20] Without a collective sense of the injustice in a concrete situation, there never would be the "motive force" for any revolution. Every instance of the spontaneous emergence of councils that Arendt cites had its origins in the demand for liberation and the overthrow of those institutions that individuals take to be oppressive. Arendt is right in seeing that the demand for social liberation is not to be identified with the demand for political freedom; and that social liberation does not automatically lead to positive political freedom. But it is just as true to assert that any attempt to found political freedom in the modern age that neglects or forgets its origins in fighting and eliminating social injustice is in danger of betraying itself. If we continue to use Arendt's categories, then we must realize that social liberation is not simply a necessary condition for the possibility of political freedom, but the fate of both are inextricably related to each other. This last point is especially important today, because if we scan the horizon and ask ourselves where there is still the possibility for the emergence of the type of politics that she envisions, then I believe the answer is that it can only arise out of the womb of the new social movements.

IV

If this critique is sound, then the question may be legitimately asked, What, if anything, is "salvageable" from her analysis – What still can be appropriated from what she says that is still relevant to our social and political situation?

First, she helps us to overcome being mesmerized into thinking that politics only occurs in what is conventionally called "politics"; in party bureaucracies, elections, the "power" of ruling cliques and interest groups. For the real hope for the type of politics that she describes may arise where it is least expected – in the dynamics of those social movements which spring up outside of the traditional political arena. This point needs to be emphasized. There is an unfortunate tendency exhibited both by those who analyze new social movements, as well as by those who participate in these movements to think of them as essentially non-political. But when this claim is made, "politics" is being conceived of in conventional terms as the domain of the modern state. Arendt opens the space for thinking of politics in a radically different manner. The issue is not merely a verbal or semantic one, for it can have the utmost significance in the *practice* of social movements.

Secondly, Arendt has elaborated a conception of positive freedom which is radically anti-dogmatic and anti-totalitarian – which takes seriously the nonreducible plurality and variability of opinion formation and judgment.

Thirdly, she incisively exposes the speciousness of the seductive theories of "historical necessity" – whether they are used to "justify" that political freedom is the *telos* of history or to support the thesis that public political freedom is no longer a real possibility in our age.

Fourthly, she alerts us to be wary and skeptical of all forms of "totalizing critique" which have become so fashionable in our time and lead to a growing sense of impotence and dispair – where we are told that "only a god can save us now" or that there is no escape from "the panoptic society" or "the carceral archipelago."

Fifthly, her analysis can direct us to a heightened consciousness that it is only in the context of the new social movements – whether it be the women's movement, the peace movement, ecological movements, the movements for social liberation – that there is a chance for politics and public freedom to become tangible. What is even more important, for the participants in these movements, she provides a critical standard of what might be achieved.

But in saying this, we must not neglect the serious problems that still confront us – many of which she struggled with but did not resolve. There is a danger of becoming sentimental about new social movements, of failing to realize how many of them not only aspire to create public spaces where freedom becomes concrete, but also seek to put an end to what Arendt takes to be politics. She herself highlighted not only the "beginning" that is characteristic of action, but its essential unpredictability. And we should not forget that the threat of totalitarianism which is also something "new" in history is an ever present danger. Arendt too, knows full well how sovereignty and the nation-state are anathema to politics, but she never provided any theoretical or practical solution to this threat. Whatever critical function her sketch of the "council system" may serve, it is not in its underdeveloped form a viable "new concept of the State" (*CR*, p. 233).

There may be no solution to these problems, and it certainly is not at all clear what would even count as a solution. But I do think that there are many different currents in contemporary thinking that keep leading us back to the problems and insights that became so central for Arendt. For whether one seeks to rehabilitate a concept of civil society which is not formed in the image of classical liberalism, or one speaks of a reintegration of the life world, or one seeks to understand those tendencies in new social movements that aspire to the realization of new forms of participatory politics, they can be understood in part as attempts to reclaim the type of politics that was at the center of Arendt's vision.

Let me conclude by returning to Arendt herself. In the final analysis, her *judgment* of "the modern age" can best be characterized as tragic – but it is tragic in a very specific sense. A central theme in Arendt's work is the recovery and reclamation of the revolutionary spirit, "the lost treasure" which we are always in danger of forgetting. In the revolutionary spirit she detected the manifestation of action, a new beginning, which seeks to create a public space where freedom can appear in the modern age. This aspiration is ultimately rooted in human natality. She claimed that her sketch of the council system corresponded to the springs of "the very experience of political action" (*CR*, p. 232). With all her skepticism about the modern age, with all the devious ways in which modern society seeks to "normalize" human beings, she did not think that we had yet become so completely "socialized" that action was no longer a human possibility. She concluded her complex study of totalitarianism by telling us:

> But there remains also the truth that every end in history necessarily contains a new beginning; this beginning is the promise, the only "message" which the end can ever produce. Beginning, before it becomes a historical event, is the supreme capacity of man; politically, it is identical with man's freedom. *Inititium ut esset homo creatus est* – "that a beginning be made man was created" said Augustine. This beginning is guaranteed by each new birth; it is indeed every man (*OT*, p. 478).

"Promise" and "hope" are ultimately grounded in the human condition. But for Arendt it is this grounding of promise and hope that gives such poignancy to her tragic vision. For she saw and recorded for us how over and over again human action is distorted, destroyed, undermined, and how easily it falls prey to violence. She did not believe that there is any historical necessity or inevitability in this destruction of politics and freedom. The most ominous threat of the modern age is that we may well become beings for whom *praxis* itself may simply wither away. Arendt leaves us with a radical ambiguity, but an ambiguity which itself seems to define our contemporary situation in which we must think and act. We can recognize with her how deeply rooted is the passion and movement toward political freedom and participatory politics, and how much in our time conspires toward its defeat and deformation. Yet it is precisely in this "gap" that we must still try to think and to act; a "gap" which frequently seems to be becoming smaller and smaller, and yet is still filled with promise, hope, and the ever present danger of defeat.

10

John Dewey on Democracy:
The Task Before Us

In 1939, at a conference celebrating the eightieth birthday of
John Dewey, he gave a talk entitled "Creative Democracy
– The Task Before Us." The title and the occasion are significant for several reasons. As Dewey pointed out, his own life
had already spanned a period of more than half the national life
of the country in which "events of the utmost significance for
the destiny" of democracy had occurred. (Dewey continued to
be active until his death in 1952.) It was characteristic of Dewey
to return once again to the theme – democracy – that had been
his life-long preoccupation, and to emphasize that it was still a
task before us. For democracy was not simply one topic among
others that he explored. It stood at the center of his being·and
his intellectual endeavors. His words and deeds always ema-
nated from his concern with the process and precarious fate of
democracy. His articulation of his vision of democracy in 1939
has a special poignancy, not only because of the ominous rise of
fascism and the growing attacks on the very idea of democracy,
but for another less well known reason.

Two years earlier Dewey had agreed to serve as chairman of
the Commission of Inquiry which was formed to hear and
evaluate the charges made against Trotsky at the Moscow
trials. Although attacked and vilified by communists and lib-
erals sympathetic with the Soviet Union, and despite threats of
violence and pleas by family and friends, Dewey made the ardu-
ous trip to Mexico City where the inquiry was held in April,
1937, and Trotsky testified. It was an opportunity to investigate
the charges made against Trotsky and his son, and publicly to
expose the terrors and horrors of the Moscow purges. Dewey's

willingness to set aside his intellectual work and serve as chairman of the Commission was thoroughly consistent with his basic convictions, for he not only wrote about the unity of thought and action, he practiced it throughout his life. When Dewey had visited the Soviet Union in 1928, he was enthusiastic and optimistic about the prospects of freedom and education, but he now expressed his "bitter disillusionment." Reflecting on what he had learned from the inquiry and his encounter with Trotsky, he wrote, "the great lesson for all American radicals and for all sympathizers with the U.S.S.R. is that they must go back and reconsider the whole question of the means of bringing about social changes and of truly democratic methods of approach to social progress. . . . The dictatorship of the proletariat had led and, I am convinced, always must lead to a dictatorship over the proletariat and over the party. I see no reason to believe that something similar would not happen in every country in which an attempt is made to establish a Communist government."[1] Democracy was threatened not only by the rise of fascism and Stalinism, but, as we shall see, Dewey came to believe that the most serious danger for democracy was an internal one – that there was an erosion and distortion of the very conditions required for the flourishing of democracy. What then did Dewey mean by democracy and what was central to his vision of democracy?

His 1939 talk provides a clue, for he focused on democracy as a *moral ideal*, a personal way of life to be concretely embodied in everyday practices. Democracy for Dewey was not primarily a set of institutions, formal procedures, or even legal guarantees. It is the culture and practice of democracy in day-to-day life that Dewey stresses. Democracy is a reflective faith in the capacity of all human beings for intelligent judgment, deliberation, and action if the proper conditions are furnished.

> Democracy as compared with other ways of life is the sole way of living which believes wholeheartedly in the process of experience as end and as means; as that which is capable of generating the science which is the sole dependable authority for the direction of further experience and which releases emotions, needs,

and desires so as to call into being the things that have not existed
in the past. For every way of life that fails in its democracy
limits the contacts, the exchanges, the communications, the
interactions by which experience is steadied while it is enlarged
and enriched. The task of this release and enrichment is one
that has to be carried on day by day. Since it is one that can
have no end till experience itself comes to an end, the task of
democracy is forever that of creation of a freer and more
humane experience in which all share and to which all contribute.[2]

If we are to grasp what Dewey is saying here – his linkage of
democracy and science, his distinctive meaning of experience
and the process of experience as end and as means, his emphasis
on communication, interaction and sharing, then we need to
explore how his understanding of democracy is related to his
larger vision.

Dewey's interests span the entire range of human affairs and
culture including education, psychology, the natural and social
disciplines, art, religious experience, as well as the political and
economic events of his time, but he was trained and primarily
thought of himself as a philosopher. Dewey strongly advocated
and sought to bring about a reconstruction of philosophy where
philosophy would no longer be thought of as a rarified discipline
exclusively concerned with the technical problems of philosophy. He was deeply skeptical and critical of what he took to be
outmoded and misguided conceptions of philosophy – as some
sort of super science, as *the* foundational discipline of culture,
or as a discipline that has access to some special realm of transcendental truth. He sought to uncover, expose, and exorcize
what he believed to be a central impulse of much of traditional
philosophy – the quest for certainty. He thought of philosophy
as having more to do with vision, imagination, and meaning
(rather than Truth), with gaining a critical perspective on the
deepest problems and conflicts in society and culture, and with
projecting ideals for achieving a more desirable future. He
characterized philosophy as the "criticism of criticisms," and
criticism is "discriminating judgment and careful appraisal."
He believed that much of modern philosophy had gotten itself

into a rut, that in its obsession with epistemology, philosophy had even lost touch with the ways in which inquiry, especially scientific inquiry, is actually practiced. He attacked what he called the "spectator theory of knowledge," and the "idea of an invidiously real reality." He was suspicious of the dualisms, dichotomies, and binary oppositions that loomed so large in modern philosophy – whether they be mind/body; subject/object; reason/experience; fact/value; individual/social; or nature/culture. Distinctions and differences are important for all philosophic thinking, but Dewey sought to unmask the tendency of philosophers to reify and hypostatize changing, fluid, functional distinctions into metaphysical and epistemological dichotomies. Dewey's critics have frequently criticized him for his alleged anti-intellectualism – and his irreverent treatment of the history of philosophy certainly offended many of his professional colleagues. But the charge of anti-intellectualism is a gross slander. Dewey was steeped in the history of philosophy and typically he would approach almost every problem by reviewing and evaluating differing philosophic approaches. But he was always seeking critically to appropriate what was still viable in the traditions that have shaped us. Viewed as a quest for certainty, or as the search for some final and definitive Truth, the history of philosophy had to be judged a failure, but understood as imaginative attempts to gain critical perspective, to locate, specify, and clarify human problems, as attempts to provide orientation and guidance, philosophy takes on a much more vital significance. What Dewey feared – and to a great extent he was prophetic – is that as philosophy becomes more academic and professional, and as philosophers become more nervous and defensive about protecting their turf, the entire discipline would become more marginal and irrelevant to the "problems of men." In *opposition* to what he took to be the strong anti-intellectual tendencies in American life, Dewey wrote:[3]

As far as any plea is implicit in what has been said, it is, then, a plea for casting off of that intellectual timidity which hampers the wings of imagination, a plea for speculative audacity, for more faith in ideas, sloughing off a cowardly reliance upon those partial ideas to which we are wont to give the name facts. I have given to philosophy a more humble function than that which is often assigned to it. But modesty as to its final place is not incompatible with boldness in the maintenance of that function, humble as it may be. A combination of such modesty and courage affords the only way I know of in which the philosopher can look his fellowmen in the face with frankness and humanity.

If philosophy is the "criticism of criticisms," if the "distinctive office, problems, and subject matter of philosophy grow out of stresses and strains . . . in community life," what did Dewey take to be the most urgent problem of his (and our time)? Although he gave a variety of formulations, the key problem is the character of our moral and political lives. It is the problem of human practice, in the sense of "practice" characterized by Aristotle when he spoke of *praxis* as the distinctive form of human activity. The question that Dewey took to be most central is the question of the moral character of "community life" itself. And democracy "is the idea of community life itself." More specifically, Dewey was concerned with the split and divorce between science and *praxis*. Despite the enormous success of the natural sciences, Dewey argued that the "spirit of scientific inquiry" had not yet adequately informed our moral and social practices. He was well aware of the growth of scientism, subjectivism, relativism, narcissism, and of the ever increasing power of science and technology to shape our lives. Dewey was not an innocent champion of the Enlightenment tradition. He was relentlessly critical of all philosophies of history that claimed that there is an ineluctable logic working itself out behind the backs of human beings leading inevitably to the realization of freedom – or to barbarism and global disaster. He wrote that "it is no longer possible to hold the simple faith of the Enlightenment that assured advance of science will produce free institutions by dispelling ignorance and superstition: – the sources of human servitude and the pillars of oppressive government."[4]

It is certainly true that at times "science" and "scientific method" seem to serve as Dewey's "god terms." But it is crucial to look and see what he meant by "scientific method" and what he sought to appropriate from his understanding of experimental science. He did not mean a set of formal decision procedures or rules for advancing and justifying scientific hypotheses and theories. He was not advocating what Sheldon Wolin has characterized as the *vita methodi* – a shaping of the human mind which under the guise of objectivity and value neutrality avoids fundamental criticism and commitment. He conceived of science as a set of interlocking practices in the sense of "practice," recently characterized by Alasdair MacIntyre – social practices which have their own internal standards of excellence which require and presuppose characteristic *virtues*.[5] It is the openness of scientific inquiry, the imagination required for its successful practice, the willingness to submit hypotheses to public test and criticism, the intrinsic communal and cooperative character of scientific inquiry that Dewey highlighted when he spoke of "scientific method." If we are to dedicate ourselves to the task of the concrete realization of "creative democracy," then, it is these virtues that must be cultivated and nurtured in our everyday moral and political lives.

If the philosopher has the responsibility of not only projecting and rationally defending ideals for the achievement of a more desirable future, but must also clarify the means by which they are to be embodied, then we can ask how did Dewey think such an end-in-view could be achieved? From this perspective we can best understand Dewey's life-long involvement in the theory and practice of education in a democratic society. The way in which Dewey conceives of the educative process contributes to and is affected by his understanding of human experience.

Dewey sought to appropriate the spirit of experimental science as a self-corrective activity, but he was also profoundly influenced by the lessons of the new biology. (Dewey was born in 1859, the year when Darwin's *Origin of Species* appeared.) Dewey's early infatuation with Hegelianism predisposed him to the influence of Darwin. In a revealing autobiographical sketch written in 1930, Dewey spoke of the "subjective reasons" for the appeal of Hegel's thought:[6]

It supplied a demand for unification that was doubtless an intense emotional craving, and yet was a hunger that only an intellectualized subject matter could satisfy. It is more than difficult, it is impossible, to recover that early mood. But the sense of divisions and separations that were, I suppose, borne in upon me as a consequence of a heritage of New England culture, divisions by way of isolation of self from the world, of soul from body, of nature from God, brought a painful oppression – or, rather, they were an inward laceration . . . Hegel's synthesis of subject and object, matter and spirit, the divine and the human, was, however, no mere intellectual formula; it operated as an immense release, a liberation. Hegel's treatment of human culture, of institutions and the arts, involved the same dissolution of hard-and-fast dividing walls, and had a special attraction for me.

The same "subjective" considerations that attracted the young Dewey to Hegel were the reasons why he "drifted away from Hegelianism," even though Dewey confessed that "acquaintance with Hegel has left a permanent deposit in my thinking." Dewey came to believe that Darwin and the new biology supplied a more concrete and richer perspective on human experience. It was not the popular Social Darwinianism of the day that appealed to Dewey. He saw through this as pseudo-science and ideology. Nor was he interested in the battles between science and religion provoked by Darwin's work. It is the understanding of life and experience as process, as change, as organic interaction that Dewey emphasized. We are neither beings with a fixed human nature which unfolds in the course of time nor are we infinitely plastic and perfectible. Human beings are continuous with the rest of nature but have the capacity to develop those habits, dispositions, sensitivities and virtues that Dewey called "reflective intelligence." Experience itself involves undergoing, suffering, activity, and consummations. In sharp contrast to the thin, emasculated, subjectivistically tinged conceptions of experience that had become entrenched in modern epistemology, he elaborated a thicker, richer, situational notion of experience, whereby experience is capable of being funded with meaning and emotion and is given direction. We are always *in media res*, there are no absolute beginnings or finalities. We are always in the process of being shaped by and shaping our history and our traditions. We are eminently fallible. We never escape from the precariousness and contingency of existence. We become fools of history if we believe that we can achieve total control by expert knowledge, or if we think we can collectively impose our wills and completely determine our destinies. Dewey had little patience with those who succumb to a nostalgia or longing for a "golden era" that never really existed, or with the type of utopian thinking that seeks to make a total break with existing realities. Both of these modes of thinking all too easily lead to despair. It was not adjustment to the status quo that Dewey advocated, but the constant challenging task of reconstruction. He was scornful of what he called "moralism" – the belief that social change can be effected by calls for moral reform. In this respect, he was close in spirit to the tradition of practical philosophy that has its roots in Aristotle's *Ethics* where leading the good life and becoming virtuous requires that we constantly seek to develop the habits, dispositions, judgment (*phronesis*), and character that can only be cultivated in a proper communal life. But the Greek *polis*, for all its glory, could no longer serve as an adequate model for communal life in advanced industrial societies.

Dewey did have enormous faith in what education and schooling could achieve in a democratic society. In all his writings on education and from his practical involvement with the founding of the Laboratory School at the University of Chicago, he stressed the role of the school as a social institution and as providing a model of community life. There is still a popular myth that Dewey, the so-called father of progressive education, advocated a child-centered conception of education that sentimentalizes and idealizes the child's development. This is one of the extremes that he opposes. "Doing as one pleases signifies a release from truly *intellectual* initiative and independence." When unlimited free expression is allowed, children "gradually tend to become listless and finally bored, while there is an absence of cumulative, progressive development of power and actual achievement in results."[7] But Dewey objected just as strongly to the theory of education that presupposes that the child is naturally recalcitrant and must have discipline forced upon him or her. It is directed, cumulative, ordered reconstruction of experience that is central to Dewey's understanding of the educative process. And in "My Pedagogic Creed" published in 1887, Dewey returns over and over again to the theme of the school as a form of community life: "Much of present education fails because it neglects this fundamental principle of the school as a form of community life."[8] But what precisely does Dewey mean by community life?

Recently, Michael J. Sandel has suggested a classification of three conceptions of community that is helpful for pinpointing the strong sense of community that Dewey has in mind. Sandel distinguishes an instrumental, sentimental, and constitutive conception of community. The first conceives of community as a social union "where individuals regard social arrangements as a necessary burden and cooperate only for the sake of pursuing their private ends." The second – the sentimental conception – assumes "the antecedent individuation of the subjects of cooperation, whose actual motivations may include benevolent aims as well as selfish ones." To the extent that there are shared values and sentiments, these are shared in the sense that each individual distributively has these values and sentiments. But the third – the constitutive or strong sense of community – questions the presupposition of the antecedent individuation of the subject; it claims on the contrary that what an individual is and the type of individuality manifested is not something that comes temporally or logically prior to community life, but is in part constituted by the type of community within which one participates. "On this strong view, to say that the members of a society are bound by a sense of community is not to say that a great many of them profess communitarian sentiments and pursue communitarian aims, but rather that they conceive their identity – the subject and not just the object of their feelings and aspirations – as defined to some extent by the community of which they are a part."[9]

All of Dewey's intellectual pathways lead to a defense of this strong sense of community. This is why he was so suspicious of the dichotomy of the individual and the social, and why he

thought that individualism versus collectivism was such a misleading contrast. It is also the reason why he was so critical of
classical forms of liberalism and individualism (what he called
the "old liberalism" and the "old individualism"). For whether
classical forms of liberalism take benign or malign forms, they
implicitly or explicitly assume that it makes sense to speak of
human individuals existing apart or independently of their social
relationships. Genuine individualism is not a given or a starting point, it is only an *achievement* – an achievement that Dewey
claimed could be realized in and through democratic communal life. Dewey stressed this strong sense of community for
both philosophical and practical reasons. Our task now is "to
re-create by deliberate and determined endeavor the kind of
democracy which in its origin . . . was largely the product of
a fortunate combination of men and circumstances."

Jefferson was always one of Dewey's heroes because his own
formulation of democracy "is moral through and through: in
its foundations, its methods, and its ends." Dewey did think
that Jefferson was right in discerning a serious threat to the
moral character of democracy in the coming industrialization
of America. But it was not "industrialization" that Dewey took
to be the main problem, but rather the resulting "dislocation
and unsettlement of local communities." Dewey was sharply
critical of a laissez-faire ideology, which under the pretense of
an appeal to an older liberalism and individualism "legitimized"
practices that undermined and manipulated communal life.
The "tragedy" of what Dewey called the "lost individual" is
due to the fact that while individuals are now caught up into a
vast complex of associations, "there is no harmonious and
coherent reflection of the import of these connections into the
imaginative and emotional outlook on life." But increasingly
Dewey came to see that the most poignant problem in the
United States, and the most serious threat to democracy, was
to be found in the rise and spread of the "corporate mentality."

> The business mind, having its own conversation and language,
> its own interests, its own intimate groupings in which men of
> this mind, in their collective capacity, determine the tone of

society at large as well as the government of industrial society . . .
we now have, although without formal or legal status, a mental
and moral corporateness for which history affords no parallel.[10]

This growing corporateness and the mentality that it fosters is
the most serious threat to the type of communal life that Dewey
took to be the life-blood of a creative democracy.

In the *Public and Its Problems*, which was written in part as a
response to the beginnings of elitist conceptions of democracy,
Dewey called for a radicalization of democracy, for a reconstruction of local communities, for a revitalization of public
life. In Arendt's phrase, he called for the cultivation of those
"public spaces" where "debate, discussion and persuasion"
would become manifest. Dewey spoke of the search for the
Great Community, but he did not mean a single undifferen-
tiated Community in which all individuality is submerged.
Rather his vision was that of a community of communities, but
he realized that this makes no sense unless we begin with local,
face-to-face communal life.

> Unless local communal life can be restored, the public cannot
> adequately solve its most urgent problem; to find and identify
> itself. But if it be reestablished, it will manifest a fullness, variety
> and freedom of possession and enjoyment of meanings and
> goods unknown in the contiguous associations of the past. For it
> will be alive and flexible as well as stable, responsive to the com-
> plex and world-wide scene in which it is enmeshed. While local,
> it will not be isolated.[11]

It has become fashionable and all too facile to attack Dewey
from a variety of perspectives. The sad truth is that many professional philosophers barely take him seriously today. The
reconstruction of philosophy that Dewey sought to bring about
has not only failed to occur, but many professional philosophers
have become more and more obsessed with the "problems of
philosophy." It is true that Dewey, for all his talk about being
concrete and specific, could be incredibly vague. In his desire
to soften all dichotomies, distinctions, and dualisms, at times
he seems to deprive us of the analytic tools needed for advanc-

ing our understanding. Social theorists who are sympathetic with Dewey tend at times to take a patronizing attitude toward him. His vision of democracy which did inspire many of his contemporaries can now strike us as flat. Even if we credit him with being sensitive to the problems that continue to plague us – the eclipse of public life, the breakdown of local communities, the distortions of social life effected by the growth of corporateness – Dewey provides little guidance about how to meet and solve these problems. Dewey did call for a radical transformation of economic and political institutions, but does not seem to address the issues of what this concretely means or how it is to be achieved. We may also feel that even after a sympathetic reading of Dewey's understanding of "scientific method," he does not sufficiently help us to understand the crucial differences between scientific and democratic communities, or how instrumental rationality and scientism can deform the deliberation and judgment required for the practice of democracy. Witnessing the way in which our educational institutions, from elementary schools to institutions of higher learning, are deformed by the imperatives of a corporate society, it is difficult to see how they might become the beacons for democratic communal life that Dewey saw as their primary function. There is a genuine need to engage in the type of criticism of his own philosophy that Dewey took to be the mark of all philosophy.

But there is a danger of "overkill" – of forgetting how much in Dewey endures and has special relevance for us. Once again there is a growing uneasiness in philosophy. It is not accidental that a philosopher such as Richard Rorty who has brilliantly criticized much of the sterility and irrelevance of recent philosophy cites Dewey as one of the most important philosophers of the twentieth century and calls for a return to the spirit of Dewey's pragmatism.[12] It is instructive, that despite recent attempts to articulate and defend a variety of classical versions of liberalism, many of these doctrines founder because they do not do justice to the strong constitutive sense of community that defines our moral and political identities. Sometimes it seems as if we are living through a rage against modernity, a total disenchantment with the hopes and aspirations of what is best in our own democratic heritage, and with the type of fallibilistic humanism that Dewey advocated. But perhaps, after the dialectic of fashionable forms of relativism and domesticated nihilism work themselves out, we may return to the spirit of Dewey. For what is most enduring in Dewey is his sanity and his courage, his refusal to submit to dispair. Dewey did emphasize the projective and future-oriented dimension of all thinking, and he was aware of the ways in which history and tradition are always effectively shaping what we are in the process of becoming. But his central focus was with the living present, with facing our present conflicts and problems with honesty and imagination, and with finding the concrete ways in which we can reconstruct experience where free communication, public debate, rational persuasion and genuine sharing are integrated into our everyday practices. Creative – radical – democracy is still "the task before us."

Notes

INTRODUCTION

1. William James, "A World of Pure Experience," *Journal of Philosophy, Psychology, and Scientific Methods*, I (1904), p. 533.
2. John Dewey, "The Need for a Recovery of Philosophy," reprinted in *The Philosophy of John Dewey*, ed. John J. McDermott (Chicago: University of Chicago Press, 1973), I, p. 96.
3. John Dewey, Introduction to the 198 reprint of *Reconstruction in Philosophy*, in *John Dewey: The Middle Works, 1899–1924*, ed. Jo Ann Boydston (Carbondale: Southern Illinois University Press, 1982), 12, p. 256.
4. Bruce Kuklick tells the story of "The Triumph of Professionalism," (this is the title of his conclusion) in his illuminating study, *The Rise of American Philosophy* (New Haven: Yale University Press, 1977).
5. Richard Rorty, "Philosophy in America Today" in his *Consequences of Pragmatism* (Minneapolis: University of Minnesota Press; Brighton, Sussex: Harvester Press, 1982), p. 215.
6. Ibid., pp. 215–16.
7. Michael Dummett, "Can Analytical Philosophy be Systematic, and Ought It To Be?" in his *Truth and Other Enigmas* (London: Gerald Duckworth, 1978), p. 458.
8. Richard Rorty, *The Linguistic Turn* (Chicago: University of Chicago Press, 1967).
9. Thomas Kuhn, *The Structure of Scientific Revolutions*, 2nd enl. ed. (Chicago: University of Chicago Press, 1970), p. 91.
10. See my discussion of the Cartesian Anxiety in *Beyond Objectivism and Relativism* (Philadelphia: University of Pennsylvania Press, 1983), pp. 16–20.

11. See *Praxis and Action* (Philadelphia: University of Pennsylvania Press, 1971); *The Restructuring of Social and Political Theory* (Philadelphia: University of Pennsylvania Press, 1976); and, *Beyond Objectivism and Relativism* (Philadelphia: University of Pennsylvania, 1983).

12. William James, "A World of Pure Experience," p. 533.

13. For a careful review of the development and breakdown of the "Received View," see the foreword and afterword of Frederick Suppe, *The Structure of Scientific Theories*, 2nd ed. (Urbana: University of Illinois Press, 1977).

14. See Mary Hesse, "In Defence of Objectivity," in her *Revolutions and Reconstructions in Philosophy of Science* (Brighton: Harvester Press, 1980). See my discussion of the philosophy of science in part 1 and part 2 of *Beyond Objectivism and Relativism*.

15. Thomas Kuhn, *The Essential Tension* (Chicago: University of Chicago Press, 1977), pp. xiii, xv.

16. Charles Taylor, "Interpretation and the Sciences of Man," reprinted in *Interpretive Social Science: A Reader*, ed. P. Rabinow and W. Sullivan (Berkeley: University of California Press, 1979).

17. Anthony Giddens, *Studies in Social and Political Theory* (London: Hutchinson/New York: Basic Books, 1977), p. 12.

18. Dewey, "The Need for a Recovery of Philosophy," p. 95.

19. Alasdair MacIntyre, *After Virtue* (Notre Dame: University of Notre Dame Press, 1981; London: Duckworth, 1982), p. 245.

20. Rorty, "Pragmatism, Relativism, Irrationalism," in his *Consequences of Pragmatism*, p. 166.

21. Jürgen Habermas, "A Reply to My Critics" in *Habermas: Critical Debates*, ed. John B. Thompson and David Held (London: The Macmillan Press, 1982), p. 227.

22. John Dewey, "What I Believe," reprinted in *John Dewey: The Later Works, 1925–1953*, ed. Jo Ann Boydston (Carbondale: Southern Illinois Press, 1984), 5, pp. 276–8.

23. Dewey, "The Need for a Recovery of Philosophy," p. 96.

1 PHILOSOPHY IN THE CONVERSATION OF MANKIND

1. Richard Rorty, *Philosophy and the Mirror of Nature* (Princeton: Princeton University Press, 1979; Oxford: Basil Blackwell, 1981). All page numbers in brackets refer to this volume.

2. "Sensations and Brain Processes," reprinted in *The Philosophy of Mind*, ed. V. C. Chapell (Englewood Cliffs, N.J.: Prentice Hall, 1962), p. 161.

3. In his essay, "Can Analytical Philosophy be Systematic, and Ought It to Be?" Dummett says, "Only with Frege was the proper object of philosophy finally established; namely, first that the goal of philosophy is the analysis of *thought*, secondly that the study of *thought* is to be sharply distinguished from the study of the psychological process of *thinking*; and finally, that the only proper method for analyzing thought consists in the analysis of *language* . . . it has taken nearly a half century since his death for us to apprehend clearly what the real task of philosophy, as conceived by him involves." *Truth and Other Enigmas* (London: Duckworth, 1978), p. 458.

4. See Richard Rorty, "Dewey's Metaphysics," in *New Studies in the Philosophy of John Dewey*, ed. Steven M. Cahn (Hanover, N.H.: University of New England Press, 1977).

5. Wilfrid Sellars, "Philosophy and the Scientific Image of Man," *Science, Perception, and Reality* (New York: Humanities Press; London, Routledge [International Library of Philosophy], 1963).

2 WHAT IS THE DIFFERENCE THAT MAKES A DIFFERENCE? GADAMER, HABERMAS, AND RORTY

1. This essay was presented at a symposium sponsored by the Philosophy of Science Association. There were incisive critical responses by Charles B. Guignon and Thomas McCarthy. See Charles B. Guignon, "Saving the Differences: Gadamer and Rorty," and Thomas McCarthy, "The Differences that Make a Difference," *PSA 1982*, vol. 2, ed. Peter D. Asquith and Thomas Nickles (East Lansing, Michigan: Philosophy of Science Association, 1983), pp. 360–73. I sent this essay and "From Hermenutics to Praxis," to Hans-Georg Gadamer. For his response, see the Appendix to *Beyond Objectivism and Relativism* (Philadelphia: University of Pennsylvania Press, 1983; Oxford: Basil Blackwell, 1984), pp. 261–5.

2. William James, *A Pluralistic Universe* (London: Longmans, Green, and Co., 1909), pp. 20–1.

3. Michael Dummett, "Can Analytical Philosophy Be Systematic, and Should It Be?" in *Ist Systematische Philosophie Möglich?*, ed. D. Henrich (Bonn: Bouvier Verlag Herbert Grundmann, 1977),

pp. 305–26. Reprinted as "Can Analytical Philosophy Be Systematic, and Ought It to Be?" in *Truth and Other Enigmas* (London: Duckworth, 1978), pp. 437–58).

4. Richard Rorty, *Philosophy and the Mirror of Nature* (Princeton: Princeton University Press, 1979; Oxford: Basil Blackwell, 1981), p. 315.

5. Hans-Georg Gadamer, *Le Problème de la conscience historique* (Louvain: Institut Supérieur de Philosophie, Université Catholique de Louvain, 1963). Reprinted as "The Problem of Historical Consciousness," in *Interpretive Social Science: A Reader*, ed. P. Rabinow and W. M. Sullivan, trans. J. L. Close (Berkeley: University of California Press, 1979), p. 113.

6. Hans-Georg Gadamer, *Wahrheit und Methode*, 2nd ed. (Tübingen: J. C. B. Mohr, 1965). Reprinted as *Truth and Method*, trans. G. Barden and J. Cumming (New York: Seabury Press, 1975; London: Sheed & Ward, 1981), pp. 274 ff.

7. Gadamer, *Le Problème de la conscience historique*, p. 107.

8. Gadamer, *Wahrheit und Methode*, p. 289.

9. Ibid., p. 289.

10. Hans-Georg Gadamer, "Practical Philosophy as a Model of the Human Sciences," *Research in Phenomenology*, 9 (1980), p. 83.

11. Hans-Georg Gadamer, "Hermeneutics and Social Science," *Cultural Hermeneutics*, 2 (1975) p. 316.

12. Ibid., p. 316.

13. Hans-Georg Gadamer, "Was ist Praxis? Die Bedingungen gesellschaftlicher Vernunft," *Universitas*, 11 (1974). Reprinted as "What is Practice? The Conditions of Social Reason," in *Reason in the Age of Science*, trans. F. G. Lawrence (Cambridge, Mass.: MIT Press, 1981), p. 80.

14. Ibid., p. 87.

15. Hans-Georg Gadamer, "Hegels Philosophie und ihre Nachwirkungen bis heute," *Akademiker Information*, 3 (1972). Reprinted as "Hegel's Philosophy and Its Aftereffects until Today," in *Reason in the Age of Science*, p. 37.

16. Gadamer, "Hermeneutics and Social Science," p. 316.

17. Gadamer, *Wahrheit und Methode*, p. 319.

18. Ibid., p. xxv.

19. Gadamer, *Le Problème de la conscience historique*, p. 108.

20. For a more detailed development of these criticisms of Gadamer, see chapter 3 of this volume, "From Hermeneutics to *Praxis*".

21. Jürgen Habermas, "Die Hermeneutische Ansatz," in *Zur Logik*

der Sozialwissenschaften (Frankfurt: Suhrkamp, 1970), pp. 251–90. Reprinted as "A Review of Gadamer's Truth and Method," in *Understanding and Social Inquiry*, ed. Fred R. Dallmayr and Thomas A. McCarthy (Notre Dame: University of Notre Dame Press, 1977), p. 351.

22. For one of the clearest statements of this point about the internal relation between understanding *meaning* and *assessing* validity claims, and its significance for a theory of rationality, see Jürgen Habermas, *Theorie des kommunikativen Handelns*, 2 vols. (Frankfurt: Suhrkamp, 1981), I, pp. 152 ff.

23. Charles Taylor, *Hegel* (Cambridge: Cambridge University Press, 1975), p. 218.

24. Jürgen Habermas, "Was heisst Universalpragmatik," in *Sprachpragmatik und Philosophie*, ed. Karl-Otto Apel (Frankfurt: Suhrkamp, 1976), pp. 174–273. Reprinted as "What is Universal Pragmatics?" in *Communiction and the Evolution of Society*, trans. Thomas A. McCarthy (Boston: Beacon Press; London: Heinemann, 1979), p. 24.

25. Ibid., p. 24.

26. See Rorty, *Philosophy and the Mirror of Nature*, chapters 5 and 6.

27. Thomas McCarthy, *The Critical Theory of Jürgen Habermas* (Cambridge, Mass.: MIT Press, 1978; Cambridge, UK: Polity Press, 1984), p. ix.

28. Jürgen Habermas, "Einleitung: Historischer Materialismus und die Entwicklung normativer Strukturen," in *Zur Rekonstruktion des Historischen Materialismus* (Frankfurt: Suhrkamp, 1976), pp. 9–49. Reprinted as "Historical Materialism and the Development of Normative Structures," in his *Communication and the Evolution of Society*, p. 97.

29. For a discussion of the complexities involved in evaluating conflicting and competing interpretations, see Charles Taylor, "Interpretation and the Sciences of Man," *The Review of Metaphysics*, 25 (1971), pp. 3–51, and Paul Ricoeur, "The Model of the Text: Meaningful Action Considered as a Text," *Social Research*, 38 (1971), pp. 529–62. One of the primary reasons why critics of hermeneutics have been suspicious of its claim to "cognitive legitimacy" is that the decision or choice among competing interpretations has been contrasted with science where there are presumably clear determinate rules or criteria for choosing among rival theories or paradigms. But despite internal disputes among postempiricist philosophers and historians of

science, there has been a growing rational consensus that this is a *myth*. Kuhn, Lakatos, Feyerabend, Toulmin (and many others) have emphasized the essential openness and indeterminacy of the criteria in choosing among rival theories, paradigms, or research programs. All of the above would agree with Kuhn's famous claim that "there is no neutral algorithm for theory-choice, no systematic decision procedure which, properly applied, must lead each individual in the group to the same decision" (Thomas Kuhn, *The Structure of Scientific Revolution*, 2nd ed. [Chicago: University of Chicago Press, 1970], p. 200). Kuhn himself realizes how the claims that he has been making bear a close affinity with those which have been central to contemporary hermeneutics. See the preface and essay, "Objectivity, Value Judgment, and Theory Choice," in *The Essential Tension* (Chicago: University of Chicago Press, 1977).

30. Hans-Georg Gadamer and Leo Strauss, "Correspondence Concerning *Wahrheit und Methode*," *The Independent Journal of Philosophy*, 2 (1978), p. 10.

31. Karl Popper, "Normal Science and Its Dangers," in *Criticism and the Growth of Knowledge*, ed. I. Lakatos and A. Musgrave (Cambridge: Cambridge University Press, 1970), p. 56.

32. Richard Rorty, "Pragmatism, Relativism, and Irrationalism," *Proceedings and Addresses of the American Philosophical Association*, 53 (1980), p. 736.

33. Rorty, *Philosophy and the Mirror of Nature*, p. 316.

34. Rorty, "Pragmatism, Relativism, and Irrationalism," p. 736.

35. Ibid., p. 734.

36. Ibid., p. 733.

37. Ibid., pp. 734–5.

38. Ibid., p. 737.

39. Ibid., p. 737.

40. Richard Rorty, "Nineteenth Century Idealism and Twentieth Century Textualism," *The Monist*, 64 (1981), p. 165.

41. Ibid., p. 167.

42. Paul K. Feyerabend, *Science in a Free Society* (London: New Left Books, 1978), pp. 8–9.

43. Rorty, "Nineteenth Century Idealism," pp. 167–8.

44. See my discussion of "epistemological behaviorism" and "holism" in chapter 1 of this volume, "Philosophy in the Conversation of Mankind."

45. Rorty, "Nineteenth Century Idealism," p. 159.

46. See Rorty's discussion of the "end of philosophy" in the Introduction to *Consequences of Pragmatism* (Minneapolis: University of Minnesota Press; Brighton, Sussex: Harvester Press, 1982).

47. Rorty, *Philosophy and the Mirror of Nature*, p. 354.

48. Rorty, "Nineteenth Century Idealism," p. 162.

49. Rorty, "Pragmatism, Relativism, and Irrationalism," p. 724.

50. Ibid., p. 727.

51. Ibid., p. 738.

52. Rorty, "Nineteenth Century Idealism," p. 173.

53. Richard Rorty, "Pragmatism, Categories, and Language," *The Philosophical Review*, 70 (1961), pp. 197–223.

54. Rorty, "Pragmatism, Relativism, and Irrationalism," p. 719.

55. John Dewey, "Creative Democracy – The Task Before Us, in *The Philosopher of the Common Man* (New York: G. P. Putman's Sons, 1940), pp. 220–8. As reprinted in *Classic American Philosophers*, ed. Max Fisch (New York: Appleton-Century-Crofts, 1951), pp. 389–94.

56. Jacques Derrida, "La pharmacie de Platon," *Tel Quel*, 32, 33 (1968), pp. 3–48, 18–59. Reprinted as "Plato's Pharmacy," in *Dissemination*, trans. Barbara Johnson (Chicago: University of Chicago Press, 1981), pp. 61–171.

3 FROM HERMENEUTICS TO *PRAXIS*

1. See Gadamer's discussion of application in the section entitled, "The Rediscovery of the Fundamental Hermeneutic Problem," *Truth and Method* (New York: The Seabury Press, 1975; London: Sheed and Ward, 1981), pp. 274 ff. The expression "application" (*Anwendung*) is used to translate the corresponding Latin term. This translation can be misleading. For example, when we speak of "applied physics" or "applied mathematics" we normally want to distinguish between the pure or theoretical disciplines and their applications. We do not think of the applications as integral or internally related to the corresponding pure disciplines. We can call this the "technical" sense of application. But, as we shall see, for Gadamer this is *not* what is distinctive about application as it pertains to understanding. Such application is integral to all understanding. The English expression "appropriation" better conveys what Gadamer means – especially when we think of appropriation as transforming and becoming constitutive of the individual who understands.

2. Unless otherwise noted, all page references in the text are to *Truth and Method*. I have also given references to the German text, *Wahrheit und Methode*, 4, *Auflage* (Tübingen: J. C. B. Mohr, 1975).

3. Gadamer also discusses the Hermeneutical Problem and Aristotle's *Ethics* in "The Problem of Historical Consciousness," which is reprinted in *Interpretive Social Science: A Reader*, ed. P. Rabinow and W. M. Sullivan (Berkeley: University of California Press, 1979), pp. 135 ff.

4. "Hermeneutics and Social Science," *Cultural Hermeneutics*, 2 (1975), p. 316.

5. See the essay "Hermeneutics and Historicism," included in *Truth and Method*, p. 489. See also "Heidegger and Marburg Theology," *Philosophical Hermeneutics*, ed. D. E. Linge (Berkeley: University of California Press, 1976), p. 201.

6. Cf. "The Problem of Historical Consciousness" where Gadamer says, "it is useless to restrict the elucidation of the nature of the human sciences to a purely methodological question: it is a question not simply of defining a specific method, but rather, of recognizing an entirely different notion of knowledge and truth" (p. 113).

7. There is a parallel between Wittgenstein's critique of the attempt to reduce understanding to "psychological processes" in *The Philosophical Investigations*, and Gadamer's critique of this type of psychological reductionism in the context of hermeneutics. Both stress the essential linguistic character of understanding. See Gadamer's discussion of Wittgenstein in his essay, "The Phenomenological Tradition," *Philosophical Hermeneutics*, pp. 173 ff.

8. Gadamer tells us, "The best definition for hermeneutics is: to let what is alienated by the character of the written word or by the character of being distantiated by cultural or historical distances speak again. This is hermeneutics: to let what seems to be far and alienated speak again" ("Practical Philosophy as a Model of the Human Sciences," *Research in Phenomenology*, 9, p. 83).

9. "The Universality of the Hermeneutical Problem," *Philosophical Hermeneutics*, p. 9. See also the analysis of prejudices in *Truth and Method*, pp. 235 ff.; *WM*, pp. 250 ff. The German word which is translated as "prejudice" is *Vorurteil*. This can be translated as "prejudgment" in order to avoid the exclusively pejorative meaning that "prejudice" conveys in English. Gadamer's main point is to emphasize that *pre*-judices or *pre*-judgments are *pre*-

conditions for all understanding. But for Gadamer, *both* negative or unfounded prejudices and positive or justified prejudices are constitutive of our being. He tells us, "This recognition that all understanding inevitably involves some prejudice gives the hermeneutical problem its real thrust" (*TM*, p. 239; *WM*, p. 254).

10. Gadamer cites Heidegger's description of the hermeneutical circle from *Being and Time* which stresses the anticipatory dimension of all forestructures. See *TM*, pp. 235 ff.; *WM*, pp. 250 ff. See also "The Problem of Historical Consciousness," pp. 148 ff.

11. "The Problem of Historical Consciousness," p. 107.

12. Ibid., p. 140.

13. Ibid.

14. According to Gadamer, *phronesis* involves a knowledge of both ends and means. See his discussion of this point in "The Problem of Historical Consciousness," p. 143; and *Truth and Method*, pp. 286 ff.; *WM*, pp. 304 ff.

15. See "Hermeneutics and Social Science."

16. Ibid., p. 312.

17. Ibid., p. 313.

18. Ibid., p. 316.

19. There is a problem that arises in Gadamer's frequent appeals to a "different kind of knowledge and truth." Gadamer never provides a detailed analysis of the type of knowledge and truth that is appropriate to the natural sciences. Consequently, it is never quite clear what is *common* to these *different* kinds of knowledge and truth. Furthermore, there are conflicting tendencies in what he does say. At times, Gadamer suggests that these two types of truth are compatible as long as we are aware of the limits and proper domain of scientific method. But there is also a strain in Gadamer's thinking that suggests that Method is never sufficient to achieve and guarantee truth. Although Gadamer, in some of the papers that he has published since *Truth and Method*, acknowledges the recovery of the hermeneutical dimension of the natural sciences, he does not fully appreciate the extent to which the very idea of Method (as an adequate way of characterizing the natural sciences) has been called into question by developments in the post-empiricist philosophy of science. The issue here is not denying that there are important differences between the *Naturwissenschaften* and *Geisteswissenschaften*, but rather questioning whether the contrast between Method and Truth is helpful in

illuminating these differences. For a discussion of the hermen-
eutical dimensions of the natural sciences, see Mary Hesse, "In
Defence of Objectivity," *Revolutions & Reconstructions in the
Philosophy of Science* (Brighton, Sussex: Harvester Press, 1980).

20. For a discussion of the concept of truth, see also "Wahrheit in
den Geisteswissenschaften," and "Was ist Wahrheit?," *Kleine
Schriften*, vol. I (Tübingen: J. C. B. Mohr [Paul Siebeck], 1967).

21. Concerning Hegel, Gadamer writes:

> For Hegel, it is necessary, of course, that the movement of con-
> sciousness, experience should lead to a self-knowledge that no
> longer has anything different or alien to itself. For him the perfec-
> tion of experience is "science," the certainty of itself is knowledge.
> Hence his criterion of experience is that of self-knowledge. That is
> why the dialectic of experience must end with the overcoming of
> all experience, which is attained in absolute knowledge, i.e., in the
> complete identity of consciousness and object. We can now under-
> stand why Hegel's application to history, insofar as he saw it as
> part of the absolute self-consciousness of philosophy, does not do
> justice to the hermeneutical consciousness. The nature of ex-
> perience is conceived in terms of that which goes beyond it; for
> experience itself can never be science. It is the absolute antithesis
> to knowledge and to that kind of instruction that follows from
> general theoretical or technical knowledge. The truth of experi-
> ence always contains an orientation towards new experience. . . .
> The dialectic of experience has its own fulfillment not in definitive
> knowledge, but in that openness to experience that is encouraged
> by experience itself. (*TM*, p. 318; *WM*, p. 337)

22. "The Problem of Historical Consciousness," p. 107. Gadamer
typically links truth (*Wahrheit*) with the thing (*die Sache*) itself. He
tells us, "I repeat again what I have often insisted upon: every
hermeneutical understanding begins and ends with the 'thing
itself'" ("The Problem of Historical Consciousness," p. 159). In
appealing to the thing itself, Gadamer does *not* mean Kant's
Ding-an-sich. Rather he *plays* on the associations of what is suggested by Aristotle in the *Ethics* when he tells us that the appropriate form of knowledge and reasoning is conditioned by the
subject matter that it treats; the way in which Hegel in the *Phenomenology of Spirit* is always directing us to *die Sache* in order to
reveal the dialectical movement of consciousness (*Bewusstsein*):
the significance of the call for the "return to the things themselves" in Husserl; and the way in which this demand is radically
transformed in Heidegger's "hermeneutics of facticity." But this

appeal to *die Sache* is not sufficient to clarify the concept (*Begriff*) of truth. For the question can always be asked, when do we have a *true* understanding of the thing (*die Sache*) itself? Gadamer implicitly recognizes that this is always a proper question when he emphasizes that our anticipatory interpretations "may not conform to what the thing is" ("The Problem of Historical Consciousness," p. 149). The crucial point as it pertains to truth is that however prominent the thing itself may be in testing our prejudices, a *true* (although not a final) understanding of the thing itself must be *warranted by the appropriate forms of argumentation* which are intended to show that we have properly grasped what the thing itself says.

23. See Gadamer's discussion of the concept of tradition in *Truth and Method*, pp. 245 ff.; *WM*, pp. 261 ff. It is instructive to compare Gadamer's understanding of tradition with that of Alasdair MacIntyre when he says,

> A tradition then not only embodies the narrative of an argument, but is only to be recovered by an argumentative retelling of that narrative which will itself be in conflict with other argumentative retellings. Every tradition therefore is always in danger of lapsing into incoherence and when a tradition does so lapse it sometimes can only be recovered by a revolutionary reconstitution. ("Epistemological Crises, Dramatic Narrative and the Philosophy of Science," *The Monist*, 60 [1977], p. 461)

24. "The Problem of Historical Consciousness," p. 108.
25. "Hermeneutics and Social Science," p. 312; p. 316.
26. "The Problem of Historical Consciousness," p. 141.
27. Ibid., p. 142.
28. Gadamer approaches this problem of corruption indirectly. This can be seen in his perceptive interpretations of Plato's *Dialogues*, especially the *Republic*. For the central "political" problem that Plato confronts is the *corruption* of the polis. Gadamer says the following about the *Republic*:

> Thus the exposition of this ideal state in the *Republic* serves in educating the political human being, but the *Republic* is not meant as a manual on educational methods and materials, and it does not point out the goal of the educational process to the educator. In the background of this work on the state is a real educational state, the community of Plato's academy. The *Republic* exemplifies the purpose of the academy. The community of students applying

themselves rigorously to mathematics and dialectic is no apolitical society of scholars. Instead, the work done here is intended to lead to the result which remained unattainable for the current sophistic paideia, with its encyclopedic instruction and arbitrary moralistic reformulations of the educational content of ancient poetry. It is intended to lead to a new discovery of justice in one's own soul and thus to *the shaping of the political human being. This* education, however, the actual education to participation in the state, is anything but a total manipulation of the soul, a rigorous leading of it to a predetermined goal. Instead, precisely in extending its questioning behind the supposedly valid traditional moral ideas, it is in itself the new experience of justice. Thus this education is not authoritative instruction based on an ideal organization at all: rather it lives from questioning alone. "Plato and the Poets." (*Dialogue and Dialectic* [New Haven: Yale University Press, 1980], p. 52. See also "Plato's Educational State" in *Dialogue and Dialectic*.)

The "moral" that can be drawn from this for *our* hermeneutical situation is that the *political* task of the philosopher is to help revive that deep sense of questioning which can lead to a discovery "of justice in one's own soul and thus to *the shaping of the political human being*." My quarrel with Gadamer is not to suggest that he is wrong about this; on the contrary, I think he is essentially right. But rather, I want to emphasize the Hegelian point that the "discovery of justice in one's own soul" is only the *beginning* of "the shaping of the political human being." This discovery is in danger of becoming merely "abstract" and "false" unless one confronts the concrete practical tasks of shaping or reshaping one's actual community in order to cultivate genuine dialogue among participants.

29. "Man and Language," *Philosophical Hermeneutics*, p. 66.
30. Gadamer's acknowledgment of the difference between a living dialogue where the other person can literally answer questions, and the hermeneutical dialogue where "the text is expressed only through the other partner, the interpreter" opens a pandora's box of problems for philosophical hermeneutics. It is fundamental for Gadamer's understanding of philosophical hermeneutics that although we always understand and interpret *differently*, nevertheless we are interpreting the *same* text, the same "universal thing." "To understand a text always means to apply it to ourselves and to know that, even if it must always be understood in different ways, it is still the same text presenting itself to

us in these different ways" (*TM*, p. 359; *WM*, p. 375). But if the interpreter must not only open himself or herself to what the text "says to us" and the "claim to truth" that it makes upon us, but is also the linguistic medium for answering for the text, then this raises questions concerning what sense if any, we can speak of the *same* text, the same "universal thing." For it is not the text *an sich* that answers the interpreter, but only the text as understood, and all understanding is conditioned by our prejudices and pre-judgments. This is a point that was already pressed by Nietzsche and which has become so central for post-structuralist thinking. And as Nietzsche showed, this can lead to a questioning of the very idea of truth, and the "claim to truth" that texts and tradition make upon us. This also raises problems in an ethical and political context concerning what sense, if any, we can speak of the *same* universal principles, laws, or norms that are mediated by *phronesis*.

31. Many critics (and defenders) of Gadamer stress the conservative implications of his philosophical hermeneutics. Certainly, Gadamer seeks to *conserve* the "truth" that speaks to us through tradition, although he strongly denies that the emphasis on the essential factor of tradition in all understanding implies an un-critical acceptance of tradition or a "socio-political conser-vatism." But what has been neglected is the *latent* radical strain implicit in Gadamer's understanding of hermeneutics as a prac-tical philosophy. This is reflected in his emphasis in recent years on freedom and solidarity that embraces *all of humanity*. He tells us "for there is no higher principle of reason than that of free-dom. Thus the opinion of Hegel and thus our own opinion as well. No higher principle is thinkable than that of the freedom of all, and we understand actual history from the perspective of this principle; as the ever-to-be renewed and the never-ending strug-gle for this freedom" (*Reason in the Age of Science* [Cambridge, Mass: MIT Press, 1982,), p. 9). And in a passage that echoes The Frankfurt School's radical interpretation of Hegel, Gadamer writes: "The principle that all are free never again can be shaken. But does this mean that on account of this, history has come to an end? Are all human beings actually free? Has not history since then been a matter of just this, that the historical conduct of man has to translate the principle of freedom into reality? Obviously this points to the unending march of world history into the open-ness of its future tasks and gives no becalming assurance that everything is already in order" (ibid., p. 37).

Concerning the principle of solidarity, Gadamer tells us "genuine solidarity, authentic community, should be realized" (ibid., p. 80). In summarizing his answer to the question, "What is practice?" he writes: "practice is conducting oneself and acting in solidarity. Solidarity, however, is the decisive condition and basis of all social reason. There is a saying of Heraclitus, the 'weeping' philosopher: The *logos* is common to all, but people behave as if each had a private reason. Does this have to remain this way?" (ibid., p. 87).

4 NIETZSCHE OR ARISTOTLE? REFLECTIONS ON ALASDAIR MacINTYRE'S *AFTER VIRTUE*

1. This essay was presented at a conference on Practical Philosophy held at Dusquene University. Paul Santilli was the commentator. Alasdair MacIntyre has written a spirited rejoinder. See "Bernstein's Distorting Mirrors: A Rejoinder," *Soundings*, 47 (Spring, 1984), pp. 30–41.
2. Alasdair MacIntyre, *After Virtue* (Notre Dame: University of Notre Dame Press, 1981; London; Duckworth, 1982). All page numbers in brackets refer to this volume.
3. By the "strong" sense of tragedy, I am referring to MacIntyre's interpretation of Sophoclean tragedy where choosing between rival and incompatible claims upon me "does not exempt me from the authority of the claim which I choose to go against" (p. 134). MacIntyre contrasts this understanding of tragedy with Aristotle's understanding of tragedy as due to a tragic human flaw. Aristotle's understanding of tragedy (unlike that of Sophocles) is compatible with the claim that "the virtues are all in harmony with each other and the harmony of individual character is reproduced in the harmony of the state" (p. 147).
4. MacIntyre's narrative does not end with "the rational case" for the Aristotelian tradition of the virtues. To complete his story he explores the "kinds of degeneration [to which] it has proved liable" (p. 209). This requires following the narrative from the *virtues to virtue* and *after virtue* (Chapters 16–18).
5. MacIntyre also claims that "the progress in the development of the concept is closely related to, although it does not recapitulate in any straightforward way, the history of the tradition of which it forms the core" (p. 174). Roughly speaking, the first stage corresponds to the dimension of the virtues that is prominent in

Homer, the second to what Aristotle emphasizes, and the third to the contribution of medieval thinkers.

6. See Nancy Fraser, "Foucault: Empirical Insights and Normative Confusions" *Praxis International* 1 (October, 1981) where she explores the meaning of "practices" in Foucault.

7. MacIntyre himself underscores this point when he writes: "Human beings, like the members of all other species, have a specific nature, and that nature is such that they have certain aims and goals, such that they move by nature towards a specific *telos*. The good is defined in terms of their specific characteristics. Hence, Aristotle's ethics, expounded as he expounds it, presupposes his metaphysical biology" (p. 139).

8. This line of defense was suggested to me by David Burrell.

9. MacIntyre is always calling for a careful concrete historical analysis of the social and cultural context of moral philosophies if they are to become intelligible. A healthy antidote to his interpretation of the Enlightenment can be found in Peter Gay's *The Enlightenment: An Interpretation*, 2 vols. (New York: Alfred A. Knopf, 1966); and Hans Blumenberg, *The Legitimacy of the Modern Age*, trans. Robert M. Wallace (Cambridge, Mass.: MIT Press, 1983).

10. Charles Taylor, *Hegel* (Cambridge: Cambridge University Press, 1975), pp. 414, 416.

5 WHY HEGEL NOW?

1. This essay was written as a critical study of Charles Taylor, *Hegel* (Cambridge: Cambridge University Press, 1975) All page numbers in brackets refer to this volume. Writing this essay was an occasion to reflect on the resurgence of interest in Hegel among Anglo-American philosophers.

2. John Dewey, "From Absolutism to Experimentalism," in *John Dewey, On Experience, Nature, and Freedom*, ed. Richard J. Bernstein (New York: Liberal Arts Press, 1960), p. 10.

3. See Chapter 2, "From Hegel to Darwin" in my book, *John Dewey* (New York: Washington Square Press, 1966).

4. Charles Sanders Peirce, *Collected Papers*, eds. Charles Hartshorne and Paul Weiss (Cambridge, Mass.: Harvard University Press, 1931–35), 5.436. See Max H. Fisch, "Hegel and Peirce," in *Hegel and the History of Philosophy*, Proceedings of the 1972 Hegel Society of America Conference, eds. J. T. O'Malley, K. W. Algozin, and F. G. Weiss (The Hague: Nijhoff, 1974).

5. William James, *A Pluralistic Universe* (New York: E. P. Dutton & Co., 1971), p. 123.

6. Ibid., p. 163.

7. Ibid., p. 165.

8. Ibid., p. 169.

9. Ibid. For a fuller discussion of James's critique of Hegel and the Idealists, see my introduction to the new edition of *A Pluralistic Universe* (Cambridge, Mass.: Harvard University Press, 1977).

10. "From Absolutism to Experimentalism," p. 9.

11. See, for example, Chapter IV of Russell's *The Problems of Philosophy* (London: Home University Library, 1912).

12. G. E. Moore, "The Refutation of Idealism," *Mind*, NS, XII (1903), pp. 433–53. For a lucid account of the rise and fall of Absolute Idealism in English Philosophy, see A. M. Quinton, "Absolute Idealism," Dawes Hicks' Lecture on Philosophy: British Academy, 1971. From the *Proceedings of the British Academy*, Vol. LVII (London: Oxford University Press).

13. Walter Kaufmann, "Coming to Terms with Hegel," *Times Literary Supplement*, (2 January 1976), p. 13.

14. Wilfrid Sellars, "The Double-Knowledge Approach to the Mind-Body Problem," *The New Scholasticism*, 45 (1971), p. 270.

15. Mary Hesse, "In Defence of Objectivity," *Proceedings of the British Academy*, Vol. 58 (London: Oxford University Press, 1972).

16. Paul Feyerabend, *Against Method* (London: New Left Books, 1975).

17. Richard Rorty, "The World Well Lost," *Journal of Philosophy*, 69 (1972), pp. 649–65.

18. See also Charles Taylor, "The Opening Arguments of the Phenomenology," in *Hegel*, ed. Alasdair MacIntyre (New York: Doubleday Anchor, 1972).

19. See Part IV, "The Concept of Action," in my *Praxis and Action* (Philadelphia: University of Pennsylvania Press, 1971).

20. Georg H. von Wright, *Explanation and Understanding* (Ithaca, N.Y.: Cornell University Press, 1971), p. 8.

21. See Shlomo Avineri, *Hegel's Theory of the Modern State* (Cambridge: Cambridge University Press, 1972). Avineri concludes his study by declaring: "Nothing in what has been said until now should be construed to imply that the answers Hegel gave to the other questions raised by him should always be regarded as satisfactory or adequate. But the ability to ask the right kind of questions about the nature of post-1789 society and to incorporate them into a general

philosophical system, as well as the realization that consequently classical political theory stands in need of rectification and renaissance – all this makes Hegel into more than a mere chapter in the history of ideas. His questions – if not always his answers – point to the direction of understanding that which is, today as much as in his own time" (p. 241).

6 NEGATIVITY: THEME AND VARIATIONS

1. This essay was prepared for a "Symposium on the Thought of Herbert Marcuse," sponsored by the Philosophy Department of the University of California at San Diego. The symposium was held during the Spring of 1980 to commemorate Herbert Marcuse who had been a professor of philosophy at the University of California at San Diego.
2. See my earlier paper, "Herbert Marcuse: An Immanent Critique," *Social Theory and Practice*, (Fall, 1971) 1, no. 4.
3. *Reason and Revolution: Hegel and the Rise of Social Theory* (New York: Humanities Press, 1955), p. vii.
4. Ibid., pp. 26–7.
5. Hegel's *Phenomenology of Spirit*, trans. A.V. Miller (Oxford: Oxford University Press, 1977), p. 19.
6. *Reason and Revolution*, p. 26.
7. Ibid., p. 147.
8. Ibid., p. 66.
9. Ibid., p. 148.
10. Ibid., p. 261.
11. Ibid., p. 258.
12. "Philosophy and Critical Theory," *Negations: Essays in Critical Theory* (Boston: Beacon Press, 1968), p. 143.
13. Ibid., p. 142.
14. Ibid., p. 148.
15. See "The Concept of Essence" in *Negations*, pp. 55 ff.
16. *Eros and Civilization* (Boston: Beacon Press, 1955), p. 35.
17. Ibid., p. 93.
18. Ibid., p. 121.
19. Ibid., p. 19.
20. Ibid., p. 118.
21. Ibid., p. 122.
22. "The Foundations of Historical Materialism," *Studies in Critical Philosophy* (London: New Left Books, 1972), p. 3.

23. *Eros and Civilization*, p. 172.
24. Ibid., p. 140.
25. Ibid., p. 149.
26. *Soviet Marxism* (New York: Colombia University Press, 1958), p. 132.
27. *One-Dimensional Man* (Boston: Beacon Press, 1964), p. xv.
28. Ibid., p. 257.
29. "Industrialization and Capitalism in the Work of Max Weber," *Negations*, pp. 225–6.
30. Hegel's *Phenomenology of Spirit*, p. 49.
31. *Eros and Civilization*, p. 224.
32. *Five Lectures* (Boston: Beacon Press, 1970), p. 68.
33. See my discussion of Peirce and Dewey in *Praxis and Action* (Philadelphia: University of Pennsylvania Press, 1971).
34. *Reason and Revolution*, p. 42.
35. Hegel's *Phenomenology of Spirit*, p. 111.
36. *Eros and Civilization*, p. 89.

7 HEIDEGGER ON HUMANISM

1. This essay was written for a Conference on American Pragmatism and Phenomenology which was held during the Summer of 1984 at Pennsylvania State University. I also read a version of this essay at the 1984 annual meeting of the Society for Phenomenology and Existential Philosophy.

2. G. W. F. Hegel, *Phenomenology of Spirit*, trans. A.V. Miller (Oxford: Oxford University Press, 1977), p. 6. I am not suggesting that we can or ought to "return" to the mood of the nineteenth century.

3. Martin Heidegger, *The End of Philosophy*, trans. Joan Stambaugh (New York: Harper & Row, 1973), p. 86. This passage is cited from Heidegger's text, *Überwindung Metaphysics*. The difference in mood that I am speaking about is reflected in the difference between Nietzsche's and Heidegger's use of *Überwindung*. For Heidegger's use of this term, see Joan Stambaugh's note on p. 84. Joseph J. Kockelmans has pointed out that this passage was written during the late 1930s, and reflects the events leading up to the Second World War and what many people felt at the time. But there were others, including Heidegger's teacher, Husserl, who gave expression to very different sentiments. Compare Heidegger's lament with Husserl's passionate plea (written at approximately the same time) for

a philosophy with the deepest and most universal self-understanding of the philosophic ego as the bearer of absolute reason coming to
itself . . . that reason is precisely that which man *qua* man, in his
innermost being, is aiming for, that which alone can satisfy him,
make him "blessed"; that reason allows for no differentiation into
"theoretical," "practical," "aesthetic," or whatever. That being
human is teleological being and an ought-to-be, and that this
teleology holds way in each and every activity and project of an
ego (Edmund Husserl, *The Crisis of European Sciences and
Transcendental Phenomenology*, trans. David Carr [Evanston Il.:
Northwestern University Press, 1970], pp. 340–1.)

I do not think that what Heidegger says in the cited passage can
be "localized" to a pre-Second World War context. For similar
thoughts are expressed in his later essays on technology and his
Der Spiegel interview.

4. Throughout this essay, I speak of Heidegger's "later writings" to
distinguish them from *Sein und Zeit*. I do not, however, agree with
those who think there is a total break or reversal between *Sein und
Zeit* and Heidegger's subsequent writings. Fred Dallmayr presents
a more subtle and discriminating periodization of Heidegger's
writings, distinguishing an early, middle, and late period. See
Fred R. Dallmayr, "Ontology of Freedom: Heidegger and
Political Philosophy," *Political Theory*, 12 (May, 1984). See also
Reiner Schürmann, "Political Thinking in Heidegger," *Social
Research*, 45 (1978).

5. See Pierce's papers, "Questions Concerning Certain Faculties
Claimed for Man," "Some Consequences of Four Incapacities,"
and "Grounds of Validity of the Laws of Logic." These papers
are included in vol. 5 of Charles S. Peirce's *Collected Papers*, ed.
Charles Hartshorne and Paul Weiss (Cambridge, Mass: Harvard University Press, 1932–35).

6. "*Letter on Humanism*" in Martin Heidegger, *Basic Writings*, ed.
David F. Krell (New York: Harper & Row, 1977; London: Routledge, 1978). Page references to the *Letter* cited in this paper are
from this translation. Heidegger typically speaks of "man" when
referring to man and woman. For stylistic reasons, I have followed
his use of the masculine term.

7. In *Beyond Objectivism and Relativism* (Philadelphia: University of
Pennsylvania Press, 1983; Oxford: Basil Blackwell, 1984), I
have discussed the significance and appropriation of Aristotle's
conception of *praxis* and *phronesis* by Gadamer. See also
Gadamer's "Letter" included as an Appendix to this book.

8. Hans-Georg Gadamer, *Truth and Method*, trans. G. Barden and J. Cumming (New York: Seabury Press, 1975; London: Sheed and Ward, 1981), p. 289.

9. Hans-Georg Gadamer, "Hermeneutics and Social Science," *Cultural Hermeneutics* 2 (1975), p. 316.

10. "Only a God Can Save Us Now," trans. D. Schendler, *Graduate Faculty Philosophy Journal*, New School for Social Research, 6 (1977), p. 16.

The German original reads:

Wenn ich kurz und vielleicht etwas massiv, aber aus langer Besinnung antworten darf: Die Philosophie wird keine unmittelbare Veränderung des jetzigen Weltzustandes bewirken können. Dies gilt nicht nur von der Philosophie, sondern von allem blossmenschlichen Sinnen und Trachten. Nur noch ein Gott kann uns retten. Uns bleibt die einzige Möglichkeit, im Denken und im Dichten eine Bereitschaft vorzubereiten für die Erscheinung des Gottes oder für die Abwesenheit des Gottes im Untergang: dass wir im Angesicht des abwesenden Gottes untergehen.

See also William J. Richardson's translation of this interview in *Heidegger: The Man and the Thinker*, ed. Thomas Sceehan (Chicago, Precendent Publishing, 1981) pp. 45–73.

Many scholars of Heidegger object to relying on this interview for understanding his "serious" thinking. While nothing in my own argument depends on the use of this text (Heidegger expresses similar thoughts in many other places), I fail to see the rationale for not taking the interview seriously. Heidegger fully understood the importance of the interview, agreed to it on the condition that it would be published posthumously, and even had the opportunity to edit his remarks.

11. *Truth and Method*, p. xxv.

12. See "A Letter by Professor Hans-Georg Gadamer" in *Beyond Objectivism and Relativism*, p. 264.

13. The English translation of the *Letter* by Frank A. Capuzzi translates the second sentence as follows: "We view action as causing an effect." But this translation fails to capture the difference between the first and second sentence, between "*Wir bedenken . . .*" and "*Man kennt . . .*"

14. See the discussion of the issues raised by these distinctions in *Beyond Objectivism and Relativism*.

15. Jürgen Habermas, "Dogmatism, Reason, and Decision: On

Theory and Praxis in Our Scientific Culture" in *Theory and Practice*, trans. John Viertel (Boston: Beacon Press, 1973), p. 255.

16. In the *Letter on Humanism*, Heidegger writes: "we must free ourselves from the technical interpretation of thinking. The beginnings of that interpretation reach back to Plato and Aristotle. They take thinking itself to be a *techne*, a process of reflection in the service of doing and making. But here reflection is already seen from the perspective of *praxis* and *poiesis* (p. 194). For an excellent review and critique of Heidegger's interpretation of Plato, see Robert Dostal, "Beyond Being: Heidegger's Plato," *Journal of the History of Philosophy*, 23 (January, 1985).

17. "Overcoming Metaphysics," in *The End of Philosophy*, p. 106.

18. Ibid., p. 96.

19. "The Question Concerning Technology," in *Basic Writings*, pp. 309–10.

20. Ibid., p. 317. The tendency to pass over the distinctions between *poiesis* and *praxis, techne* and *phronesis* is even more striking in this text given as a lecture in 1949 and revised in 1953. For Heidegger explicitly mentions the chapter from Aristotle's *Nicomachean Ethics* in which these distinctions are drawn (and which was the basis of his seminar given in the early 1920s). But although Heidegger explicitly discusses the meanings of *poiesis* and *techne* and their relation to *aletheia*, he does not mention either *praxis* and *phronesis*. When this lecture reaches its climax, when Heidegger speaks of the extreme or supreme danger of *Gestell* and the growth of the "saving power," Heidegger turns to *poiesis* and *techne*, not *praxis* and *phronesis*. What he says and does not say is at once revealing and concealing.

21. *An Introduction to Metaphysics*, trans. Ralph Manheim (New Haven: Yale University Press, 1959), p. 38.

22. "The Age of the World Picture" in *The Question Concerning Technology and Other Essays*, trans. William Lovitt (New York: Harper Books, 1977), p. 133.

23. Richard Rorty, "A Discussion" by Dreyfus, Taylor, and Rorty, *The Review of Metaphysics*, 34 (1980), p. 52. I have not explicitly raised the tangled issue of "Heidegger and the Nazis" in this paper. I think that one of the most balanced summaries of the facts is presented by George Steiner in his sympathetic and perceptive book on Heidegger in the Penguin Modern Masters series. I fully endorse his own judgment when he writes: "But nauseating as they are, Heidegger's gestures and pronouncements

during 1933–34 are tractable. It is his complete silence on Hitlerism and the holocaust after 1945 which is very nearly intolerable." *Martin Heidegger* (Harmondsworth and New York: Penguin Books, 1978), p. 123. See also Fred Dallmayr's discussion in "Ontology of Freedom: Heidegger and Political Philosophy."

24. "Overcoming Metaphysics," p. 93.

25. *An Introduction to Metaphysics*, p. 37.

26. In the *Letter*, Heidegger writes: "With regard to this more essential *humanitas* of *homo humanus* there arises the possibility of restoring to the word 'humanism' a historical sense that is older than its oldest meaning chronologically reckoned. . . . To restore a sense to it can only mean to redefine the meaning of the word. That requires that we first experience the essence of man more primordially, but it also demands that we show to what extent this essence in its own way becomes fateful. The essence of man lies in ek-sistence" (p. 224).

27. See Dallmayr's discussion of Heidegger in *Twilight of Subjectivity: Contributions to a Post-Individualist Theory of Politics* (Amherst: University of Mass. Press, 1981); *Language and Politics* (Notre Dame: University of Notre Dame Press, 1983); and in "Ontology of Freedom: Heidegger and Political Philosophy," *Political Theory*, 12 (May, 1984).

28. See especially Chapter 2 "Intersubjectivity and Political Community" in *Twilight of Subjectivity*.

29. *Twilight of Subjectivity*, p. 31.

30. Ibid., p. 68–9.

31. Ibid., p. 70.

32. See especially the discussion of the meaning of "freedom" in Dallmayr's "Ontology of Freedom." Dallmayr is extremely perceptive in revealing what Heidegger means by "freedom." But here, too, I have critical reservations when he claims: "Instead of vouchsafing individual isolation and selfishness, freedom in this view is not merely an accidental ingredient, but the essential grounding of human solidarity (or socialism) – just as solidarity properly construed denotes a reciprocal effort of liberation or mutual 'letting-be'" (p. 228). Dallmayr, at this point in his paper, does not elaborate further on such implications, but turns to a discussion of Hannah Arendt. For all Arendt's indebtedness to Heidegger, I do not think her own original interpretation of freedom as coterminus with the open space of disclosure in the

public realm of action (*praxis*) represents "tentative steps in the direction sketched by Heidegger." Rather it is an attempt to bring into a clearing, just what Heidegger obscures. Arendt tells us: "Men *are* free – as distinguished from their possessing the gift of freedom – as long as they act, neither before nor after; for to *be* free and to act are the same" ("What is Freedom?" *Between Past and Future* [New York: 1968], p. 153). See my discussion of Arendt in *Beyond Objectivism and Relativism*.

Just as Heidegger leads us to a misleading dichotomy between man as the lord of Being *or* the shepherd of Being, there is a similar misleading dichotomy in his treatment of freedom. For Heidegger writes as if all modern treatments of freedom ultimately reduce themselves to conceiving of freedom as the (causal) property of autonomous subjects. It is against this subjective understanding of freedom that Heidegger elaborates his "alternative." But posing the issue in this manner obscures the various "modern" approaches to freedom that stress its intrinsically communal character and which do not assimilate freedom to a type of spontaneous causality by a self-sufficient subject. In addition to Arendt, see, for example, John Dewey, "Philosophies of Freedom," in *John Dewey: On Experience, Nature, and Freedom*, ed. R. J. Bernstein (New York: Liberal Arts Press, 1960).

33. Dallmayr shows that a close reading of Heidegger's texts reveals that already in the late 1930s he was extremely critical of the abuses of "nationalism." This is frequently emphasized by those who claim one should not judge Heidegger *solely* on the basis of his writings between 1933 and 1935. My point, however, is to highlight the *gap* between the ontological and the ontic level of analysis; to point out the lack of mediation or determinate negation. So while I reject the claim of those who argue that there is an intrinsic or logical connection between Heidegger's philosophy and his misjudgments about the *Führer* and the Nazis, it is philosophically more troubling to see the compatibility of widely divergent ontic judgments with Heidegger's "fundamental ontology."

34. The essays by John Caputo that are especially relevant to the question of Heidegger and Humanism are: "Hermeneutics as the Recovery of Man," *Man and World*, 15 (1982); and "The Thought of Being and the Conversation of Mankind: The Case of Heidegger and Rorty," *The Review of Metaphysics*, 36 (1983).

35. "Hermeneutics as the Recovery of Man," p. 343.

36. Ibid., p. 344.
37. Ibid., p. 354.
38. Ibid., p. 360.
39. "The Thought of Being and the Conversation of Mankind," p. 662.
40. Ibid., p. 682.
41. *An Introduction to Metaphysics*, pp. 38–9.
42. Reiner Schürmann has offered a very different reading of Heidegger's "political thinking" – one which seems to be opposed to, and flatly contradicts the interpretations of Dallmayr and Caputo. Schürmann speaks of "the symbolic difference as subversion."

> The symbolic difference, at the middle term that carries the phenomenological destruction into practical subversion, translates the "turn" in thinking into an "overturn" in action. The categories for understanding such action, as I see them, are at least five: (1) the abolition of the primacy of teleology in action; (2) the abolition of the primacy of responsibility in the legitimation of action; (3) action as a protest against the administered world; (4) a certain disinterest in the future of mankind, due to a shift in understanding of destiny; (5) anarchy as the essence of the "memorable" requiring thought as well as of the "do-able" requiring action. (Reiner Schürmann, "Political Thinking in Heidegger," *Social Research*, 45, [1978], p. 201.)

   If one accepts this interpretation, then it would make good sense that the late Heidegger "abandons" *praxis*. But each of Schürmann's "categories" for understanding action is negative. Indeed his analysis of action is not only reminiscent of "negative theology" but entangles us in similar *aporias*. I do not see how the symbolic difference is "a middle term," how it enables us to understand what is the *determinate* character of political thinking and action. What kind of political action satisfies these five categories? I find it troubling that "symbolic gratuitous terrorism" seems to satisfy Schürmann's five categories for "political" action. For a critique of Schürmann, see Bernard P. Dauenhauer, "Does Anarchy Make Political Sense? A Response to Schürmann," *Human Studies*, 1 (1978), pp. 369–75.

43. Martin Heidegger, *Discourse on Thinking*. A translation of *Gelassenheit* by John M. Anderson and E. Hans Freud (New York: Harper & Row, 1966), p. 46.

8 JUDGING - THE ACTOR AND THE SPECTATOR

1. This essay was written for a conference based on the work of Hannah Arendt: History, Ethics, Politics. The conference was held in October, 1981, and sponsored by Empire State College.

2. Arendt insisted on using masculine pronouns and nouns when referring to human beings. For stylistic reasons, I have followed her practice. References to Arendt's works are abbreviated as follows:

   HC - *The Human Condition* (Chicago: University of Chicago Press, 1958)

   BPF - *Between Past and Future* (New York: The Viking Press, 1961)

   OR - *On Revolution* (New York: The Viking Press, 1962; Harmondsworth: Penguin, 1973).

   CR - *Crises of the Republic* (New York: Harcourt Brace Jovanovich, 1969)

   LM - *The Life of the Mind* (New York: Harcourt Brace Jovanovich; London: Secker & Ward, 1978)

3. Arendt's analysis of action and politics also influences her interpretation of power, which she carefully distinguishes from strength, force, and violence. "In distinction to strength, which is the gift and the possession of every man in his isolation against all other men, power comes into being only if and when men join themselves together for the purpose of action, and it will disappear when for whatever reason they disperse and desert one another. Hence binding and promising, combining, and conventing are the means by which power is kept in existence, where and when men succeed in keeping intact the power which sprang up between them during the course of any particular act or deed, they are already in the process of foundation, of constituting a stable worldy structure to house, as it were, their combined power of action" (*OR*, p. 174).

4. Opinion must not only be sharply distinguished from *truth*, it must also be distinguished from *interest*. "Interest and opinion are entirely different political phenomena. Politically, interests are relevant only as group interests, and for the purification of such group interests it seems to suffice that they are represented in such a way that their partial character is a safeguard under all conditions, even under the condition that the interest of one group happens to be the interest of the majority. Opinions, on the contrary, never belong to groups but exclusively to

individuals, who 'exert their reason cooly and freely,' and no multitude, be it the multitude of a part of the whole of society, will ever be capable of forming an opinion. Opinions will arise whenever men communicate freely with one another and have the right to make their views public; but these views in their endless variety seem to stand also in need of purification and representation . . ." (*OR*, p. 229).

5. For a judicious and sensitive analysis of *phronesis*, and the ways in which it differs from *episteme* and *techne*, see Hans-Georg Gadamer, *Truth and Method* (New York: Seabury Press, 1975), pp. 278 ff. It is instructive to compare the differing ways in which Arendt and Gadamer bring out the differences between *phronesis*, Kant's analysis of reflective judgment, and taste. For Gadamer's discussion of taste, judgment, and the *sensus communis*, see *Truth and Method*, pp. 19 ff.

6. There is a deep irony that lies at the heart of Arendt's struggle to show how judging is the by-product of "the liberating effect of thinking." It is clear for Arendt that the type of thinking that she has in mind is *not* that of "professional thinkers" but rather a capacity that *can* be exercised by *every* human being. Nevertheless, Martin Heidegger was the concrete exemplar of the authentic thinker in the twentieth century. The rumor that attracted so many students to Marburg and later Freiburg (including Arendt) was that "Thinking has come to life again. . . . There exists a teacher; one can perhaps learn to think" ("Martin Heidegger at Eighty," *The New York Review of Books* [October, 1971]). It is also clear that Arendt's analysis of thinking in *The Life of the Mind* is indebted to Heidegger's own meditations on *Denken*. I am skeptical about Arendt's thesis concerning the delicate relation between thinking and judging. The most generous claim that one can make about Heidegger – the *thinker* par excellence – is that when the "stakes were on the table," he exercised such poor *judgment*. His thinking did not prevent him from catastrophe, not even "for the self."

7. One might want to say that *all* judging is political in the sense that it always anticipates "communication with others with whom I know I must finally come to some agreement." But to say this does not yet help us to understand what differentiates the judging exemplified when one says this is right, this is beautiful, or this is what is to be done. This essay was written before the publication of Hannah Arendt, *Lectures on Kant's Political Philosophy*

(Chicago: University of Chicago Press, 1982). For a different interpretation of her analysis of judging, see Ronald Beiner's interpretive essay included in this volume.

8. *Hannah Arendt: The Recovery of the Public World*, ed. M. A. Hill (New York: St. Martin's Press, 1979), p. 303.

9   RETHINKING THE SOCIAL AND THE POLITICAL

1. This essay was written for the Hannah Arendt Memorial Symposium in Political Philosophy held at the Graduate Faculty of the New School for Social Research in May, 1984. The theme of the symposium was "Labor, Work, Action."

2. As in "Judging – the Actor and the Spectator," I use abbreviations for all Hannah Arendt's works as follows:

   HC – *The Human Condition* (Chicago: University of Chicago Press, 1958)

   OT – *The Origins of Totalitarianism* (New York: Meridian Books, 1958)

   BPF – *Between Past and Future* (New York: The Viking Press, 1961)

   OR – *On Revolution* (New York: The Viking Press, 1962; Harmondsworth: Penguin, 1973)

   CR – *Crises of the Republic* (New York: Harcourt Brace Jovanovich, 1969)

   LM – *The Life of the Mind* (New York: Harcourt Brace Jovanovich; London: Secker & Ward, 1978).

3. As in Chapter 7 I have, for stylistic reasons, followed Arendt's practice of using masculine nouns and pronouns when referring to human beings. But this linguistic practice tends to obscure the fact that traditionally labor and work are activities characteristic of men and women, while action has been limited to men. To speak of "the basic conditions under which life on earth has been given to man" obscures this crucial difference.

4. Martin Heidegger, "The Question Concerning Technology," in *Martin Heidegger, Basic Writings*, ed. David F. Krell (New York: Harper and Row, 1977; London: Routledge, 1978).

5. The expressions "man-kind," "mankind," and "men" have distinctive meanings for Arendt. "I use here and in the following the word 'man-kind' to designate the human species, as distinguished from 'mankind' which indicates the sum total of human beings" (*HC*, p. 24, n. 4). She reserves the term "men"

for calling attention to human beings in their *plurality*. "Action, the only activity that goes on directly between men without the intermediary of things or matter corresponds to the human condition of plurality" (*HC*, p. 7).

6. Arendt sharply distinguishes between "no rule" where we confront each other as peers and equals, and the "rule of nobody," which is the form of government exemplified by modern bureaucracies.

7. For a poetic statement of what she means by exercises in political thought, see the preface of *Between Past and Future* (*BPF*).

8. A close reading of Arendt's analysis of the social question reveals a counter tendency. She recognizes that social issues – including the question of poverty – can be *transformed* into political issues. Writing about Marx, she says: "His most explosive and indeed most original contribution to the cause of revolution was that he interpreted the compelling needs of mass poverty in political terms as an uprising, not for the sake of bread or wealth, but for the sake of freedom as well. What he learned from the French Revolution was that poverty can be a political force of the first order" (*OR*, p. 56). Reading Arendt from this perspective opens the possibility of seeing that any social issue can be transformed into a political question, but she never fully develops this theme. And indeed she claims that Marx "finally strengthened more than anybody else the politically most pernicious doctrine of the modern age, namely that life is the highest good, and that the life process of society is the very center of human endeavor. Thus the role of revolution was no longer to liberate men from the oppression of their fellow men, let alone to found freedom, but to liberate the life process of society from the fetters of scarcity so that it could swell into a stream of abundance. Not freedom but abundance became now the aim of revolution" (*OR*, p. 58).

9. Arendt draws a strong contrast between pity, "the perversion of compassion" and solidarity. "Solidary is a principle that can inspire and guide action, compassion is one of the passions, and pity is a sentiment. Solidarity though it may be aroused by suffering, is not guided by it . . . it remains comitted to 'ideas' – to greatness, or honor, or dignity – rather than to any 'love' of men" (*OR*, p. 84).

10. For a discussion of how she weaves these themes together, see Chapter 8 in this volume.

11. For an illuminating discussion of this issue in the context of Marxism and Critical Theory, see Albrecht Wellmer, "Reason,

Utopia, and the Dialectic of Enlightment," in *Habermas and Modernity*, ed. Richard J. Bernstein (Cambridge, Mass.: MIT Press, 1985/Cambridge: Polity Press, 1985), pp. 35–66.

12. If one compares the analysis of politics and action in *On Revolution* and in *The Human Condition*, one is struck by a subtle but consequential change of emphasis. In *The Human Condition* she approaches the question of action primarily from the perspective of the Greek experience. Her emphasis is on the way in which the *polis* transformed the traditional heroic Greek virtues. The *polis* is the locus of the heroic *agon*, where men seek glory. It is the arena in which men seek to prove themselves, and to achieve "immortal fame." But in *On Revolution* and in subsequent writings she places much greater emphasis on the participatory character of action and politics, the type of isonomy it requires, the role of mutual persuasion, and testing of opinions that takes place through public debate. In part this difference of emphasis can be accounted for by the change of context from the classical Greek *polis* to modern revolutionary movements, but one should not underestimate the influence of Arendt's growing awareness – especially during the 1960s – of the many signs of spontaneous emergence of the type of politics she was describing. There is a radicalization of her vision of politics – a radicalization that became apparent when she adumbrated the "council system" and declared every person must be given the opportunity to participate in such councils.

13. See *Hannah Arendt: The Recovery of the Public World* ed. Melvyn A. Hill (New York: St. Martin's Press, 1979), pp. 301–39.

14. Ibid., pp. 315–16.

15. Ibid., p. 316.

16. Ibid., p. 317.

17. In order to defend the integrity of political life Arendt emphasizes the prominent role of variable opinion (*doxa*), judgment, and debate. She sharply contrasts the coerciveness of "truth," and the disciplines which are primarily concerned with "truth seeking" with the variable domain of political opinion and persuasion. She believes that philosophers, when they have turned their attention to politics, have explicitly or implicitly judged politics by the alien standards of truth. But Arendt ignores the extent to which debate, argumentation, and persuasion are central for scientific inquiry. In *Beyond Objectivism and Relativism* I have argued that recent philosophy of science shows that scientific inquiry

exemplifies many of the characteristics of practical argumentation that Arendt takes to be distinctive traits of political debate.

18. At times Arendt interprets the distinction of the social and the
political in a different manner. The difference concerns *how* an
issue is articulated – as a social problem requiring management
and administration or as a political problem requiring debate and
judgment. This interpretation has been suggested by my colleague
Sara Shumer. But even if we read Arendt in this way, there is
still the primary question of *who* decides how an issue with a
"double face" is to be articulated.

19. Michel Foucault's incisive study of micropractices and the spread
of the disciplinary society can be read as providing concrete
detailed support for Arendt's claims about the drive toward
"normalization" in modern society. Unlike Foucault, Arendt
contrasts the normalization of modern society with the possibility
of the spontaneous eruption of action and politics. Foucault,
however, is much more ambiguous and ambivalent about
whether such politics is still a genuine possibility.

20. It is curious how little Arendt has to say about justice and its relation to politics. This is perhaps the most glaring difference between
Arendt and Aristotle from whom she draws so much inspiration.
Typically, when she speaks of "political passions" she includes
"courage, the pursuit of public happiness, the taste of public
freedom, an ambition that strives for excellence" (*OR*, p. 280),
but *not* the passion for justice. It is not even clear whether justice
is a social or a political virtue (or whether justice too has a social
and political "face").

But thinking through the role of justice in society and politics
also calls into question Arendt's sharp dichotomy. See Hanna F.
Pitkin's perceptive discussion, "Justice: On Relating Private and
Public," *Political Theory*, 9 (1981), pp. 327–52.

10 JOHN DEWEY ON DEMOCRACY: THE TASK BEFORE US

1. *Washington Post*, 19 December 1937.
2. "Creative Democracy – The Task Before Us," reprinted in
M. Fisch (ed.), *Classic American Philosophers* (New York: Apple-
ton–Century–Crofts, 1951), p. 394.
3. "Philosophy and Civilization," in *Philosophy and Civilization* (New
York: Minton, Balch, 1931), p. 12.

4. *Freedom and Culture* (New York: G. P. Putnam's Sons, 1939), p. 131.

5. See Alasdair MacIntyre, *After Virtue* (Notre Dame: University of Notre Dame Press; London: Duckworth, 1982), pp. 175 ff.

6. "From Absolutism to Experimentalism," reprinted in R. J. Bernstein (ed.) *John Dewey: On Experience, Nature, and Freedom* (New York: Liberal Arts Press, 1960), p. 10.

7. *Construction and Criticism* (New York: Columbia University Press, 1930), p. 11; "Individuality and Experience," *Journal of the Barnes Foundation*, 2 (1926), p. 1.

8. "My Pedagogic Creed," reprinted in J. McDermott, *The Philosophy of John Dewey* (Chicago: University of Chicago Press, 1981), p. 446.

9. Michael J. Sandel, *Liberalism and the Limits of Justice* (Cambridge: Cambridge University Press, 1982), pp. 147 ff.

10. *Individualism: Old and New* (New York: Minton, Balch, 1930), p. 41.

11. *The Public and Its Problems* (New York: Henry Holt, 1927), p. 216.

12. See *The Consequence of Pragmatism* (Minneapolis: University of Minnesota Press, 1982).

Index

absolute idealism 143, 145–6
abstract negativity 177
action
  in Arendt 206, 207, 221–3,
    236–7, 238–9
  communicative 16, 69, 70, 72–6,
    79
  in Heidegger 205–8
  theory of 154–6, 159
  see also praxis
Adorno, Theodor W. 135, 149, 186
aesthetic, the
  in Marcuse 184–5
After Virtue (MacIntyre) 6–7, 8, 102,
  115–40
alienation 173–4
America *see* United States
analytic epistemology 152–4
analytic philosophy xi, 3–9, 16
  and epistemology 37–8
  and ethics 15
  and Hegel 150–9
  and the natural sciences 11–12
  in Rorty 3–4, 5, 7–9, 22–4, 26–7,
    39
Apel, Karl-Otto 39, 191
Arendt, Hannah 15, 16, 17, 18–19,
  102, 270
  and action 206, 207, 221–31,
    236–7, 238–9
  and classical Greece 223–4,
    230–1, 241–2
  and debate 222, 226, 231, 250–3
  and equality 223–4
  and freedom 224–6, 247,
    294–5 n32
  and judging 221–37
  and Kant 228–9, 231, 232–3, 236
  Life of the Mind 231–2
  and opinions 226–8, 297–8n4

  and power 297n3
  and *praxis* 219
  and revolution 225, 243–5, 246,
    255, 258
  the social and the political 238–59
  and thinking 231–4, 235–7, 298n6
  and truth 226–7
  see also politics
Aristotle 30, 61, 107, 108
  and action 206
  and *episteme* 99–100, 101
  and hermeneutics 94–5
  and Hegel 155
  and human life 164
  and MacIntyre 7, 115, 118, 127–8,
    136–7
  and Marcuse 182, 191
  and natural law 110
  and potentiality 191
  and *praxis* 103–4, 126, 165, 201,
    202, 206, 264
  and *telos* 99
  and virtue 115, 119, 120, 134,
    135, 165, 267
  see also phronesis
art
  in Marcuse 184, 185–6
Austin, J. L. 4
authentic community
  in Heidegger 214, 220
Avineri, Shlomo 288–9
Ayer, A. J. 2

Beaufret, Jean 204
Being
  in Heidegger 199, 202, 204–5,
    207, 208, 209–10, 211, 213
Benjamin, Walter 187–8
Bradley, F. C. 143, 145

Caputo, John 211, 215–18
Carnap, Rudolf 2, 4
Cartesian Anxiety 10–11, 42, 47
Cartesianism 200
Chomsky, Noam 73, 74
commensuration 43–4
communication 18–19
communicative action 16, 69, 70,
    72–6, 79
communism
    in Dewey 261
community
    in Dewey 264, 268–70
    in Hegel 173–5
    in MacIntyre 18, 132, 138
    and *phronesis* 110, 111–12
    and pragmatism 219
    in Rorty 18, 86
    see also authentic community
consciousness 30–3
conversation 89–90
    in Gadamer 112–14
    in Rorty 45–6, 56
corporate mentality
    in Dewey 269–70
cosmic order
    in Hegel 161
cosmic spirit (*Geist*)
    in Hegel 163, 166, 172
Critical Theory 194, 195
    and Marcuse 179–81, 185, 187,
    191
criticism
    in Gadamer 68, 71, 105, 108–9

Dallmayr, Fred
    and Heidegger 211–15, 216, 218,
    294–5
Darwin, Charles 142, 265, 266
Davidson, Donald 4, 38
debate
    in Arendt 222, 226, 231
    and social issues 250–3
democracy
    in Arendt 246
    in Dewey 89, 260–72
    in Hegel 139, 174–5

Derrida, Jacques 16, 26, 39, 59, 84,
    85, 88, 90
    and Heidegger 215, 216
Descartes, René 9, 24, 25, 30, 98,
    164
determinate negation 177, 191, 195
Dewey, John
    and community 17, 264, 268–70
    and democracy 89, 260–72
    and education 267–8
    and epistemological
        behaviorism 36
    and Gadamer 92
    and Habermas 91
    influence of Hegel on 142, 145
    and practical rationality 191
    and pragmatism 218
    and Rorty 21, 22, 44, 47–8, 80,
        88, 271
    and scientific method 17, 264–5,
        271
dialectics
    in Hegel 72, 168, 170, 171
dialogue
    in Gadamer 112–14
Diderot, Denis 139
Dilthey, Wilhelm 13
Dummett, Michael 6, 38, 58–9,
    275n3

edifying philosophers 44–6
education
    in Dewey 267–8
embodiment
    in Hegel 171–3
emotivism
    in MacIntyre 116–17, 138
empiricism
    in James 143
    and Marcuse 191
    and science 151
    see also logical empiricism
Enlightenment
    in Arendt 224
    in Hegel 139
    in MacIntyre 135–6, 137, 138,
    139–40

episteme
   in Aristotle 99–100, 101
epistemological behaviorism 36, 41, 85
epistemology 27, 33–8, 48, 76, 85
   analytic 152–4
   in Gadamer 81
   in Rorty 33–8, 76, 153, 154
equality
   in Arendt 223–4
Eros and Civilization (Marcuse) 181, 182–6
ethos
   in Heidegger 214
experience
   in Dewey 266
expressivism 162, 163, 164–5

Feyerabend, Paul 12, 26, 39, 59, 83, 152
Foucault, Michel 16, 26, 39, 85, 88, 89, 123, 135, 302n19
   and humanism 92
freedom 194
   in Arendt 224–6, 247, 294–5n32
   in Hegel 193
   in Heidegger 294–5
   in Marcuse 189, 192
Frege, Gottlob 4, 38, 275n3
Freud, Sigmund 85, 176, 181, 182–3, 191, 193
Gadamer, Hans-Georg ix, x, 18, 39, 61–72, 77–9
   and action 206, 207
   and criticism 68, 71, 105, 108–9
   and dialogue 112–14
   and Habermas 64, 65, 66, 69–72, 78–9
   and Hegel 282n21
   and Heidegger 67, 91, 106–7, 112
   and hermeneutics 13, 17, 61–9, 81–2, 94–105, 111–14, 202, 280–5
   and humanism 92–3
   and play 96, 112
   and prejudices 97–9
   and pragmatism 91–2

and Rorty 81–4, 87, 89
   and *techne* 100, 101, 103
   and truth 67–8, 71, 82, 105–8, 281n19
   Truth and Method 94–114, 202
   see also phronesis; praxis
Galileo 50–1
Geist see cosmic spirit
Giddens, Anthony 14–15
Greece, classical
   in Arendt 223–4, 230–1, 241–2
   see also Aristotle; Plato; Sophocles

Habermas, Jürgen 14, 15, 16, 17, 18, 39, 72–81, 90
   and action 206, 207
   and communicative action 16, 72–6
   and Gadamer 64, 65, 66, 69–72, 78–9
   and humanism 93
   and *phronesis* 71, 72, 102
   and *praxis* 219
   and rationality 60, 69, 191
   and Rorty 79–81, 82–4, 87, 89
Happiness 194
   in Marcuse 189, 192
Harris, W. T. 141
Hegel, G. W. F. x, 10, 59, 141–75
   and action theory 154–6
   and analytic epistemology 152–4
   and analytic philosophy 150–9
   Anglo-American attitudes to 141–7
   and Aristotle 155
   and community 173–5
   and cosmic order 161
   and cosmic spirit 163, 166, 172
   and democracy 139, 174–5
   and Dewey 265–6
   and dialectics 72, 168, 170, 171
   and embodiment 171–3
   and Gadamer 65, 282n21
   and idealism 172–3
   and Kant 85, 138
   Logic 167, 169, 171, 172, 178
   and logical positivism 146

Hegel (*cont.*)
  and MacIntyre 137, 138–9
  and Marcuse 176–9, 189, 190,
    191
  and Marxism 147–50
  and necessity 165–7, 170
  Phenomenology of Spirit 167–9, 171,
    172, 177–8, 193
  and pragmatism 143, 147
  and science 151–2
  and the self 161–5
  and Spirit 165–6, 167, 177–8, 197
  and truth 67, 106
  and Understanding 153, 158
Heidegger, Martin 16, 21, 22, 26,
  39, 47, 85, 90
  and action 205–8
  and authentic community 214,
220
  and Being 199, 202, 204–5, 207,
    208, 209–10, 211, 213
  and *ethos* 214
  and freedom 294–5
  and Gadamer 67, 91, 106–7, 112
  and hermeneutics 13, 96, 97, 98,
    216
  and humanism 17, 92, 197–220
  Letter on Humanism 203–11, 214,
    215
  and MacIntyre 135
  and metaphysical humanism
    199–200, 202, 208, 209–11
  and metaphysics 60, 198, 201,
    207, 209–10
  and Nietzsche 201, 204
  and *phronesis* 203
  and pragmatism 200–1, 218–19
  and *praxis* 201–2, 203, 206, 220
  and Rorty 24, 44, 215, 216
  and technology 207, 209, 240
  and truth 106
Hempel, Carl G. xi, 2
Hendel, Charles W. xi
Herder, Johann Gottfried 162
hermeneutical (interpretative)
    dialectics
  in Hegel 72, 168, 170, 171

hermeneutics 12, 13, 14, 16, 17,
  277n29
  in Gadamer 13, 17, 61–9, 81–2,
    94–105, 111–14, 202, 280–5
  in Heidegger 13, 96, 97, 216
  in Rorty 43, 60–1, 80
Hesse, Mary 12, 151
historicism
  in Rorty 40–1, 42, 49, 54
history of philosophy
  in Dewey 263
  in Rorty 24–7, 43
Hölderlin, J. C. F. 199, 204
holism 36, 85
homo faber
  in Arendt 239–40
Horkheimer, Max 135, 149
human life, unity of
  in MacIntyre 127–31
human potentiality *see* potentiality,
  human
humanism 17, 92–3
  in Heidegger 17, 92, 197–220
  in Rorty 92–3
Hume, David 3, 9, 164
  and logical positivism 150–1
Husserl, Edmund G. A. 9, 38, 39,
  182, 212, 215

idealism
  absolute 143, 145–6
  in Hegel 172–3
individualism
  in Dewey 269
interpretative dialectics *see* hermeneutical dialectics

James, William 1, 2, 4, 21, 46, 76,
  80, 84, 88, 90, 91
  and Hegel 142, 143–4, 145, 146
Jefferson, Thomas 269
judging
  in Arendt 221–37
    and action 221–31, 236–7
    and thinking 231–2, 235–7
  in Kant 228–9, 231, 232–3, 236

justice
  in MacIntyre 124

Kant, Immanuel x, 3, 9, 24, 54, 73,
    151
  and Hegel 85, 138
  and humanity 136, 237
  and judging 228-9, 231, 232-3,
    236
  and Marcuse 182
  and the self 163
Kaufmann, Walter 147, 148
Kierkegaard, S. A. 85, 164, 217
knowledge, theory of *see* epistemology
Kohlberg, Lawrence 73, 74
Kuhn, Thomas 9, 11, 12-13, 26,
    39, 43, 50

Leibniz, Gottfried Wilhelm 3
liberation
  and politics 224-5, 249
Lichtheim, George 150
Locke, John 24, 25, 164
logical empiricism 2, 4
  and the natural sciences 12, 13, 14
  and the social sciences 15
logical positivism 2, 4
  and Hegel 146
  and hermeneutics 13
  and Hume 150-1
  and the natural sciences 11-12, 151
Lukács, Georg 149, 240

McCarthy, Mary 250
McCarthy, Thomas 76
McIntyre, Alasdair x, 16-17
  After Virtue 6-7, 8, 102, 115-40
  and analytic philosophy 7-9
  and Aristotle 7, 115, 118, 127-8,
    136-7
  and community 18, 132, 138
  and emotivism 116-17, 138
  and the Enlightenment 135-6,
    137, 138, 139-40
  and Hegel 137, 138-9
  and moral philosophy 7, 17, 115-
    16

and *telos* 119, 126, 127-31, 132-3
and universalization 137-8
see also virtue
McTaggart, J. M. E. 145
Marcuse, Herbert 15, 16, 17, 149
  and the aesthetic 184-5
  and Aristotle 182, 191
  and art 184, 185-6
  and Critical Theory 179-81, 185,
    187, 191
  Eros and Civilization 181, 182-6
  and freedom 189, 192
  and Happiness 189, 192
  and Marx 180, 184-5, 191
  and negativity 176-96
  and Nietzsche 183-4
  One-Dimensional Man 186-8
  and phantasy 184, 185
  and Reason 178-9, 183, 189-91,
    194
  and revolution 194
  and social life 192-3
Marx, Karl 85, 148, 149, 176, 182,
    197, 198
  and Arendt 300n8
  and Marcuse 180, 184-5, 191
Marxism 149-50
  and Arendt 247-8
  and Marcuse 185
Mead, G. H. 2, 16, 80, 90, 91
  and practical rationality 191
metaethics 15
metaphysical humanism
  in Heidegger 199-200, 202, 208,
    209-11
metaphysics
  in Heidegger 60, 198, 201, 207,
    209-10
mind-body problem
  in Rorty 27-33
modernity 16, 58, 84, 90, 240, 271
  in Hegel 139
  in MacIntyre 135
Moore, G. E. 145-6, 147
moral choice
  in Rorty 54-5
moral philosophy
  in Arendt 233

moral philosophy (*cont.*)
  and logical empiricism 15
  in MacIntyre 7, 17, 115–16
moral tradition
  in MacIntyre 131–4

natural sciences, philosophy of 11–13, 16
  and the social sciences 13–15
necessity
  in Hegel 165–7, 170
negativity
  in Marcuse 176–96
neo-pragmatism 80, 88
Nietzsche, Friedrich 16, 80, 84, 85, 106, 198
  and Heidegger 201, 204
  and MacIntyre 134, 135
  and Marcuse 183–4
  and morality 117–18, 120, 128, 133
  and practice 126
  and the self 164
nihilism 40, 41–2, 198
non-foundational pragmatic humanism 90

objective spirit
  in Hegel 173–4, 175
objectivity 52, 53
opinions
  in Arendt 226–8, 297–8n4

Pierce, Charles Sanders ix, 2, 4, 16, 90, 91, 191
  and Cartesianism 200
  influence of Hegel on 142–3, 145
  and Rorty 80, 88
phantasy
  in Marcuse 184, 185
Phenomenology of Spirit (Hegel) 167–9, 171, 172, 177–8, 193
Philosophy and the Mirror of Nature (Rorty) 6, 7–8, 21–57, 88, 102,
phronesis
  in Aristotle 55, 62, 66, 68, 94, 99, 100, 101, 103–4, 111, 202, 219, 231, 234
  and community 110, 111–12
  in Gadamer 61–2, 63, 66, 68, 71–2, 93, 99–104, 105, 110–12, 113, 202, 203
  in Habermas 71, 72, 102
  in Heidegger 203
  and judgment 231, 234
  in MacIntyre 133
  and pragmatism 91, 219
  in Rorty 55–6, 86
Piaget, Jean 73, 74
Plato 24, 30, 90, 112, 136, 182
  and action 206
  Republic 283–4
  and virtue 119, 120, 134
play
  in Gadamer 96, 112
pluralism 18
poesis
  and the virtues 126
political philosophy
  and logical empiricism 15
politics
  in Arendt 221–37
    and judging 221–37
    and society 238–59
Popper, Karl 40, 78, 146–7
positivism 85–6
  and Marcuse 191
  see also logical positivism
positivity 177
postmodernity 58, 59, 84, 90
potentiality, human
  in Marcuse 191–2
poverty
  in Arendt 243–5
power
  in Arendt 297n3
practical rationality 190–1
practice
  in MacIntyre 121–27, 129, 265
pragmatism x, 16, 17–18, 19, 90–2
  and action 206, 207
  in Gadamer 91–2
  in Habermas 91

and Hegel 143, 147
in Heidegger 200–1, 218–19
and practical rationality 191
and *praxis* 219
in Rorty 85, 86–9
praxis 93, 217
in Aristotle 103–4, 126, 165, 201, 202, 206, 264
in Dewey 264
in Gadamer 17, 61, 63–4, 66, 72, 99, 102, 103, 104–5, 109, 110, 111, 114, 219
in Heidegger 201–2, 203, 206, 220
in Marx 149
and pragmatism 219
prejudices
in Gadamer 97–9
Putnam, Hilary 4, 38, 102

Quine, W. Van Orman 3, 4, 12, 34–6, 37, 46, 47, 90

rationality 55–6
in Habermas 60, 69, 191
practical 190–1
in Rorty 50–6, 60
and science 152
reason
in Marcuse 178–9, 183, 189–91, 194
Recognition
in Hegel 193
Reichenbach, Hans 2
relativism 40, 41, 42, 83
revolution
in Arendt 225, 243–5, 246, 255, 258
in Marcuse 194
Rorty, Richard 17, 59
and analytic philosophy 3–4, 5, 7–9, 22–4, 26–7, 39
and commensuration 43–4
and community 18, 86
and Dewey 21, 22, 47–8, 80, 88, 271
and edifying philosophers 44–6

and epistemology 33–8, 76, 153, 154
and Gadamer 81–4, 87, 89
and Habermas 79–81, 82–4
and Heidegger 215, 216
and hermeneutics 43, 60–1, 80
and historicism 40–1, 42, 49, 54
and the history of philosophy 24–7, 43
and humanism 92–3
and moral choice 54–5
and the mind-body problem 27–33
and nihilism 40, 41–2
Philosophy and the Mirror of Nature 6, 7–8, 21–57, 88, 102
and *phronesis* 55–6, 86
and pragmatism 85, 86–9
and rationality 50–6, 60
and relativism 40, 41
and skepticism 40, 41
Rousseau, Jean-Jacques 242
Royce, Josiah 2
influence of Hegel on 142, 143, 144, 145
Russell, Bertrand 4, 39, 145, 146, 147
Ryle, Gilbert 4

Sandel, Michael J. 268
Santayana, George 2
Sartre, Jean-Paul 39, 59, 164, 204
Schiller, F. von 182
Schleiermacher, F. E. D. 13
Schürmann, Reiner 296n42
science, philosophy of 151–2
in Dewey 264–6
see also natural sciences; social sciences
scientific method
in Dewey 264–5, 271
self, conception of 161–5
Self-Consciousness
in Hegel 193
Sellars, Wilfrid 34–5, 37, 47, 90, 151, 157–8
skepticism 40, 41, 42
Smith, John E. xi

social identity
  in MacIntyre 132
social liberation
  in Arendt 255-6
social life
  in Marcuse 192-3
social and the political
  in Arendt 238-59
Social Question
  in Arendt 243-5
social sciences
  in Arendt 253-5
  philosophy of 13-15
society, modern
  in Arendt 242-5
Socrates 81
Sophocles
  and *ethos* 214
  and morality 119-20, 135, 138
Soviet Union
  and Dewey 260-1
spectators
  and judging 221, 231, 234, 235,
    236
speech and action
  in Arendt 222-3, 226
Spirit
  in Hegel 165-6, 167, 177-8, 197
  see also cosmic spirit; objective
    spirit
Strauss, Leo 108
Strawson, Peter 151
strict dialectics
  in Hegel 72, 168, 171
subjectivity 52
  human 163-5

Tarski, Alfred 2, 4
Taylor, Charles 14, 72, 139
  and action theory 155
  and Hegel 159-75
techne
  in Gadamer 100, 101, 103
technology
  in Heidegger 207, 209
telos
  in Aristotle 99
  in Habermas 77

  in MacIntyre 119, 126, 127-31,
    132-3
thinking
  in Arendt 231-4, 235-7, 298n6
totalitarianism 194, 195, 257, 258
tradition
  in Gadamer 283n23
  see also moral tradition
Trotsky, Leon 260
truth
  in Arendt 226-7
  in Gadamer 67-8, 71, 82, 105-8,
    281n19
  in Heidegger 106
  and morality 120
Truth and Method (Gadamer) 94-114,
    202

Understanding
  in Hegel 153, 158
United States 2
  analytic philosophy 3, 4
  influence of Hegel 141-5
  see also pragmatism
universalization
  in MacIntyre 137-8
U.S.S.R. *see* Soviet Union

validity claims 69-70, 73, 75, 79, 80
Vienna Circle 2, 11, 146
virtue
  in Aristotle 119, 120, 134, 135,
    165
  in MacIntyre 118-34
    and human life 127-31
    and moral tradition 131-4
    and practice 121-7
vita activa 238-9
  see also action
vita comtemplativa 231, 235, 239
  see also thinking
Von Wright, George H. 155

Weber, Max 189, 240
Weiss, Paul xi
Wellmer, Albrecht 251
Whitehead, A. N. 2, 3
Winch, Peter 14

Wittgenstein, Ludwig 4, 14, 21, 22, 44, 47, 85, 90
  and epistemological

behaviorism 36
  and Peirce 88
Wolin, Sheldon 265